EDUCATIONAL
INEQUALITY
AND
SCHOOL
FINANCE

EDUCATIONAL INEQUALITY AND SCHOOL FINANCE

Why Money Matters for America's Students

BRUCE D. BAKER

HARVARD EDUCATION PRESS
Cambridge, Massachusetts

Paperback ISBN 978-1-68253-242-3
Library Edition ISBN 978-1-68253-243-0

Library of Congress Cataloging-in-Publication Data

Names: Baker, Bruce D., author.
Title: Educational inequality and school finance : why money matters for America's students / Bruce D. Baker.
Description: Cambridge, Massachusetts : Harvard Education Press, 2018. | Includes bibliographical references and index.
Identifiers: LCCN 2018028242| ISBN 9781682532423 (pbk.) | ISBN 9781682532430 (library edition)
Subjects: LCSH: Education—United States—Finance. | Education—United States—States—Finance. | Public schools—United States—Finance. | Education—Economic aspects—United States. | Education and state—United States—Finance.
Classification: LCC LB2825 .B325 2018 | DDC 379.1210973—dc23 LC record available at https://lccn.loc.gov/2018028242

Published by Harvard Education Press,
an imprint of the Harvard Education Publishing Group

Harvard Education Press
8 Story Street
Cambridge, MA 02138

Cover Design: Endpaper Studio
Cover Image: Endpaper Studio
The typefaces used in this book are Adobe Garamond Pro, Calibri, Gotham, Helvetica Neue, and MillerDisplay

This book is dedicated to the memory of William Duncombe of the Maxwell School at Syracuse University. Bill was exceedingly generous in providing me (and many others) support, data (and code), and conceptual and technical guidance throughout the early stages of my career in school finance. His vast body of scholarship is foundational to nearly every chapter in this book (especially chapter 10).

CONTENTS

CHAPTER 1

WHY MONEY MATTERS

Education funding makes up the largest single component of state budgets and state and local expenditures. Federal funds make up about 10 percent of education spending. Combined, it's a lot of money. Separately, it's still a lot of money. And that should matter to all of us, as taxpayers and as beneficiaries (both directly and indirectly) of those investments.

Too often, though, knowledge of the inner workings of state school finance, state budgets, and federal formulas is held by only a select few powerbrokers in state and federal government, and by an even more select few who advise them. That knowledge is power—power over the distribution of large sums of money intended as an investment in the public good.

With this in mind, I aim to encourage broader public empowerment and engagement. The more people who are deeply knowledgeable about the historical underpinnings and conceptual and technical issues related to school funding, the more people who can actively and productively engage in public debate on these topics. This broader distribution of knowledge can help shape future education finance policies across states, inform the media on those policies, guide policy makers, and enable advocates to challenge rhetoric and policies that do not always comport with the best available empirical evidence or conceptual frameworks.

In this book I draw on my twenty-plus years of experience and research in state school finance policy, from my graduate training at Columbia University to my tenure at the University of Kansas and then, most recently, at Rutgers University. To understand the financing of education, I have conducted numerous academic studies of state school finance systems, consulted for state legislatures, and participated in legal challenges to state school finance systems across the country. Here I draw heavily on my work with the Education Law Center of New Jersey, which involved the preparation of a national data archive of state indicators of the equity and adequacy of school funding, the *School Funding Fairness Data System*.[1] Based on this research, I contend that the most productive path forward starts with recognizing the realities of education financing in the United States and is guided by sufficient understanding of history, conceptions, and values and necessarily involves application of appropriate and rigorous methods and data.

Educational Inequality and School Finance is about school finance, the school and classroom resources derived from school funding, and how and why those resources matter. It examines how money matters in determining the quality of public schooling and how the availability and distribution of money determines the equity and adequacy of our public schools, as well as any other schools we choose to subsidize with public resources. The persistent denial by pundits across the political spectrum of the importance of money for determining school quality and for achieving equity has contributed in recent decades to diminished funding, thus compromising the equity and adequacy of US schools. And that denial has often been coupled with false promises of cost-free solutions and claims that equity can be achieved without equitable funding or that adequate schooling can be achieved regardless of money, by simply doing more with less. However, we have the tools, methods, and data to better understand the equity and adequacy of our school systems and to set targets for and reinvigorate state school finance systems. These tools are derived from long-established conceptions, values, and historical understanding. The most productive path forward starts with understanding these conditions and is guided by sufficient understanding of history, conceptions, and values, and necessarily involves application of appropriate and rigorous methods and data.

THE PERSISTENT DENIAL THAT MONEY MATTERS

US public schools have faced a great deal of criticism over the past few decades. The modern bipartisan refrain holds the following truths to be self-evident: US schools are bloated bureaucracies, spending more than double what they did in past decades yet showing no improvement on national assessments; US schools are among the worst in the world, falling behind most developed nations on international assessments while at the same time costing more than any other nation's schools.

While exaggerated, these declarations fall within the mainstream of political punditry on school spending and quality in the United States, espoused by business leaders and state and national political leaders. For example, in 2011 Microsoft cofounder Bill Gates laid out both claims. He argued in a *Washington Post* op-ed that "over the past four decades, the per-student cost of running our K–12 schools has more than doubled, while our student achievement has remained virtually flat. Meanwhile, other countries have raced ahead."[2] And in the *Huffington Post* he claimed that "compared to other countries, America has spent more and achieved less."[3] Others have gone so far as to make the bombastic statement that "the United States spends more on schools than any society in human history."[4] To be clear, these claims are not original to the likes of Bill Gates. They are prevalent in school finance policy debates.

Some critics of US public schools assert that the primary reason for our skyrocketing spending, lack of improved outcomes, and relative inefficiency is public schools' overdependence on underproductive human resources (teachers, administrators, and support staff). The increased dependence on human resources has been described by some as a staffing surge, with public schools employing more and more staff despite flat or declining enrollments over the past few decades.[5] Others have asserted that our public education system suffers from Baumol's cost disease, an affliction of human resource-intensive industries wherein personnel costs continue to rise while yielding no gains in productivity.[6] The claim is that spending has skyrocketed primarily because staffing costs have skyrocketed, yet those increases in staffing, and/or compensation (salaries and benefits) for staff, have been largely inefficient. Public schools have faced little or no pressure to seek more efficient technological substitutions, whether by replacing staff with emerging technologies or using emerging technologies to select and retain fewer, less costly, more productive teachers.

Another, related claim is that US schools have not changed for over a century, while the world around them has, largely due to technological innovations. Human resources are deployed now much in the same way they were a century ago—teachers lecturing in front of rows of children in desks—except that there are more of them. It is argued that our failure to change with the times is seen as a main reason for our international noncompetitiveness, and our failure to adapt to emerging technologies contributes to our high spending and resulting inefficiency. The failures of our schools relative to a time in the distant past and relative to other nations are seen as a function of the stagnant model on which we rely: kids in rows, sitting at desks, listening to a teacher at the front of the class. So according to this view, it would be foolish to continue investing more money into such a costly and outdated stagnant practice, especially given the proclamations of dreadful and declining performance.

While it may be true that our schools must adapt to a changing world, claims that they have not been doing so, that they are trapped in a distant past, are greatly exaggerated. These arguments obscure a far simpler explanation: many schools and districts simply do not have sufficient resources to provide an adequate and equitable, much less evolving, education for their students.

The sharp economic downturn following the collapse of the housing market in 2007–08, and persisting through about 2011, provided state and federal elected officials a pulpit from which to argue that our public school systems must learn how to do more with less.[7] It was the "new normal," Secretary of Education Arne Duncan declared. This idea was embraced by pundits like David Brooks and by conservative organizations like the American Enterprise Institute (AEI).[8] As part of the US Department of Education's campaign, it unveiled on its website a series of supporting documents explaining how public school districts can live within that new normal, stretching their dwindling dollars by becoming more productive and efficient.[9]

Meanwhile, governors on both sides of the aisle, facing tight budgets and the end of federal aid that had been distributed to temporarily plug state budget holes, ramped up their rhetoric for even deeper cuts to education spending. Florida governor Rick Scott, for example, in justifying his cuts to the state's education budget, remarked, "We're spending a lot of money on education, and when you look at the results, it's not great." In his 2011 "State of the State" address, New York governor Andrew Cuomo declared, "Not only do we spend too much, but we get too little in return. We spend more money on education than any state in the nation, and we are number 34 in terms of results." More recently, in reference to a legal challenge brought against New York State by small city school districts, Cuomo opined: "We spend more than any other state in the country. It ain't about the money. It's about how you spend it—and the results." Similarly, New Jersey governor Chris Christie told the *Wall Street Journal* that "New Jersey taxpayers are spending $22,000 per student in the Newark school system, yet less than a third of these students graduate, proving that more money isn't the answer to better performance."[10]

Notably, the attack on public school funding was driven largely by preferences for conservative tax policies at a time when state budgets experienced unprecedented drops in income and sales tax revenue. But the rhetoric has persisted, and perhaps even escalated, despite modest but steady economic recovery.

CONSEQUENCES FOR PUBLIC SCHOOLS

The slow but steady economic recovery has not yet yielded a turnaround in funding for public schools, and the damage that was done to state school finance systems beginning in 2008 has not been rectified. According to a 2016 report from the Center on Budget and Policy Priorities (CBPP):

- Thirty-five states provided less *overall* state funding per student in the 2014 school year (the most recent year available) than in the 2008 school year, before the recession took hold.
- In 27 states, local government funding per student fell over the same period, adding to the damage from state funding cuts. In states where local funding rose, those increases rarely made up for cuts in state support.[11]

In addition, using data from the *School Funding Fairness Data System*, which builds on prior recurring reports on school funding equity ("Is School Funding Fair?"), and applying an adjustment for maintenance of competitive employee wages over time, I've found that only ten states had increases in current expenditures (on average) from 2008 to 2015: Washington, Iowa, Minnesota, Nebraska, Pennsylvania, New York, New Hampshire, North Dakota, Connecticut, District of Columbia, Illinois, Alaska.[12] The vast majority of states still spend less than they did, on average, across districts at the onset of the economic crisis.

The Kansas saga is particularly illustrative of the connection between widely held tax policy preferences and school funding. Sam Brownback was elected governor of Kansas in 2010 and took office in 2011 with the promise of introducing dramatic tax cuts that would be like a "shot of adrenaline into the heart of the Kansas economy."[13] Instead, Brownback's tax cuts were more like an overdose of Propofol for the state's economy and public schools. In May 2012, as the economy was beginning to slowly rebound nationally, Governor Brownback signed major tax cuts that went into effect in January 2013. The state budget, already in tenuous territory, soon after suffered a $700 million shortfall, leading to bond rating downgrades and substantial cuts to school funding in subsequent years. In March 2015, state legislators, with encouragement from the governor, abandoned the school finance formula altogether.

School years ended early in some districts due to funding shortfalls, and the state faced additional bond rating downgrades, having spent down operating savings and dealing with further budget shortfalls.[14]

As of 2017, state general aid for schools in Kansas was down 13 percent from 2008. Only Kentucky, Alabama, and Oklahoma have cut more.[15] The tax cuts did not, as Governor Brownback asserted, pay for themselves through economic stimulus. Rather, Kansas job growth has been an anemic 3.3 percent compared to the fall 2016 national average of 8.4 percent.[16] In 2016 Kansans elected new legislators who promptly reversed the tax cuts and then overrode the governor's veto of that reversal. But for too long ideology trumped reality. The Kansas tax policy "experiment" went horribly wrong, and the victims of that experiment are a generation of Kansas schoolchildren.

Some might declare Kansas as a particularly bad outlier. As a caricature of conservative social and economic ideology, Kansas is a convenient punching bag.[17] Certainly, the damage inflicted by the Brownback tax experiment does warrant criticism. But, by the numbers, Kansas remains among the most average of average states in our nation on many metrics, with many other states spending far less on their schools and performing much more poorly on available measures of school quality and student outcomes.

Perhaps the most important truth regarding US public schools is that our education system is actually fifty-one separate educational systems providing vastly different resources, on average, and with vastly different outcomes. Some of those fifty-one systems have invested in equitable and adequate school systems, have shown great improvement in student outcomes, and compare favorably with even the highest-performing nations. Other states, however, have not made that investment, and their outcomes show it. Nonetheless, US schools on average have shown significant improvement on national assessments during periods when average spending has increased across states but have declined in more recent years as average spending declined.[18]

FALSE PROMISES OF COST-FREE SOLUTIONS

The response of the education reform community to the narrative that US public schools are inefficient and noncompetitive, a narrative they themselves largely crafted and promoted, has been to propose quick-fix remedies and magic elixirs, which fall more broadly into the category of "cost-free solutions." The theory of action guiding these remedies and elixirs is that public, government-run schooling can be forced to operate more productively and efficiently if it can be reshaped and reformed to operate more like privately run, profit-driven corporations/businesses. If the public system is failing and inefficient, and investing more doesn't solve the problem, then we must look to more efficient enterprises and sectors for solutions. Broadly, popular reforms have been built on the beliefs that the private sector is necessarily more efficient; that competition spurs innovation (and that there may be technological solutions to human capital costs); that data-driven human capital policies can increase efficiency/productivity by improving the overall quality of the teacher workforce.

One core element of such reform posits that US schools need market competition to spur innovation and that market competition should include government-operated schools, government-sanctioned (charter) privately operated schools, and private schools. In the extreme case, some have argued that the government-run schools should cease to exist and that government (or a private board appointed by mayors or governors) should merely oversee a portfolio of privately managed providers. This may include, among other things, technological substitution (e.g., replacing in-person teaching with online alternatives and "unbundling" education in order to better prepare students for future careers that don't yet exist). Another asserts that US schools need to adopt the analytics and data mining methods to reshape the teacher workforce—that is, to identify and dismiss the "bad" teachers and to pay the "good" teachers more. Effective implementation requires elimination of teacher job protections, including any preferences for seniority status as well as tenure and due process requirements, both of which serve as barriers to speedy dismissal.

Aside from the question of how well these strategies have worked in the private sector—there's plenty of evidence that they have not—there is little reason to believe that these magic elixirs will significantly change the productivity/efficiency equation or address issues of equity, adequacy, and equal opportunity.[19]

TOOLS AND DATA FOR ESTABLISHING THE BASELINE

These days, we have readily available the data, tools, and a significant body of research to enable us to fact-check the foundations of the failing schools narrative and to evaluate the efficacy of proposed quick fixes. We don't need to be so readily coerced into a panic state that requires immediate policy response. More importantly, we must avoid falling for the claim that "anything is better than the status quo," because it is always possible to make things worse, especially when acting in haste. Better understanding the status quo, and how we got there, is a first step toward determining the best path forward.

A reality check on long-term national trends in actual student outcomes and in school resources is in order. The need for disruptive reform and magic elixirs derives primarily from what critics see as our massive increases in spending coupled with our virtually flat student outcomes over time. But are those claims even remotely correct?

First, are US student outcomes really "virtually flat" over time? Richard Rothstein of the Economic Policy Institute critiqued Bill Gates's assertion of "virtually flat" student outcomes in a memo titled "Fact-Challenged Policy," showing that, in fact, "on these exams [National Assessment of Educational Progress], American students have improved substantially, in some cases phenomenally."[20] Related work by Rothstein and Martin Carnoy has confirmed that, when accounting for differences in student disadvantage, US students perform much better than what is suggested by commonly cited, unadjusted rankings that fail to account for changes in subgroup proportions when aggregating test results.[21]

In 2010, Educational Testing Service (ETS) released "The Black-White Achievement Gap: When Progress Stopped," a report in which Paul Barton and Rich Coley explored the Black-White achievement gap from the 1970s to 2008.[22] Their goal was to explore trends in Black-White achievement gaps and changing conditions that may explain those trends. Barton and Coley explained that "from the early 1970s until the late 1980s, a very large narrowing of the gap occurred in both reading and mathematics, with the size of the reduction depending on the subject and age group examined." Reductions in achievement gaps were particularly pronounced in reading among thirteen- and seventeen-year-olds, though they were still significant in mathematics. However, "during the 1990s, the gap narrowing generally halted, and actually began to increase in some cases." The authors noted some additional gap narrowing from 1999 to 2004 and mixed findings from 2004 to 2008. Even during the period from 1990 to 2008, though, achievement gains for Black fourth- and fifth-grade students have been substantial in mathematics in particular and have outpaced their White peers.[23]

Figure 1.1 displays the long-term trends for Black and White children at age thirteen on the National Assessment of Educational Progress (NAEP) long-term trend assessments. Both Black and White scores trend upward,

FIGURE 1.1   NAEP long-term trends on reading and math for thirteen-year-olds

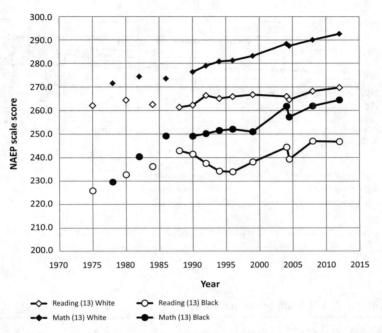

Sources: NAEP long-term trend reading assessments for 1971, 1975, 1980, 1984, 1988, 1990, 1992, 1994, 1996, 1999, 2004, 2008 (Washington, DC: National Center for Education Statistics); NAEP long-term trend math assessments for 1978, 1982, 1986, 1990, 1992, 1994, 1996, 1999, 2004, 2008, 2012 (Washington, DC: National Center for Education Statistics).

and, as noted by Barton and Coley, Black students' scores increase significantly from the 1970s through 1990. Figure 1.2 shows more recent trends for children by income status for reading, and figure 1.3 shows the trends for math at fourth grade and eighth grade. For reading, fourth-grade scores have continued to trend upward for all groups, but for eighth graders scores dipped slightly in 2015. For math, the overall upward trend was also consistent across grades, but, again, with a dip in 2015. It would be premature to assume any cause for the 2015 dip.

The second part of the question is whether spending has in fact skyrocketed while achievement has remained "virtually flat." Figure 1.4 compares nominal (not inflation adjusted) current spending per pupil to current spending per pupil adjusted for the costs of maintaining competitive wages over time. Figure 1.3 shows escalating spending accompanied by "virtually

FIGURE 1.2 NAEP reading by income status

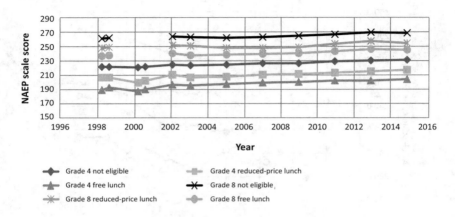

Sources: NAEP long-term trend reading assessments for 1992, 1994, 1998, 2000, 2002, 2003, 2005, 2007, 2009, 2011, 2013, 2015.

FIGURE 1.3 NAEP math by income status

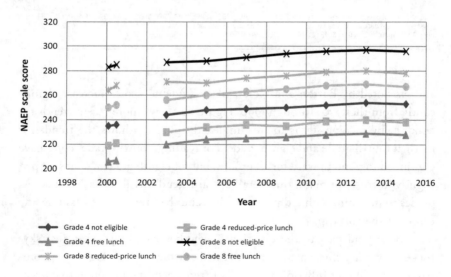

Sources: NAEP long-term trend math assessments for 1990, 1992, 1996, 2000, 2003, 2005, 2007, 2009, 2011, 2013, 2015.

FIGURE 1.4 Current operating expenditures per pupil adjusted for labor costs

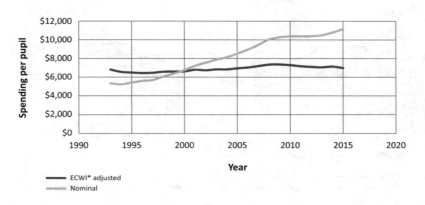

Note: *Education Comparable Wage Index (http://bush.tamu.edu/research/faculty/Taylor_CWI/)
Source: Baker et al., *School Funding Fairness Data System.*

flat" test scores; a recurring figure that my colleagues and I refer to as "The Graph" uses a consumer price index, which is less appropriate for evaluating the value of the education dollar over time. By 2015 the average school district nationally was roughly at a ten-year break-even point on per-pupil spending; that is, per-pupil spending hasn't risen for a decade and has barely risen for over two decades (2.5 percent). So no, school spending is not dramatically increasing over time and has in fact declined in real terms from 2009 to 2015 (the most recent national district-level data). Figure 1.5 shows how, across decades, direct government expenditure on elementary and secondary education as a share of gross domestic product (GDP) has oscillated but is presently about where it was both fifteen years earlier (2000) and forty years earlier (1975). In short, education spending is not outstripping our economic capacity to pay for it.

School spending is largely driven by staffing costs. The wages paid and the number of staff are substantial drivers of current operating expenses (wage x quantity = personnel spending). But have those wages and staff numbers really escalated as much as some have claimed, thus driving increasingly inefficient spending? There is some truth to the fact that teaching specialists and school-level administrative positions have increased over time, in

FIGURE 1.5 Direct education expense as a share of gross domestic product and income

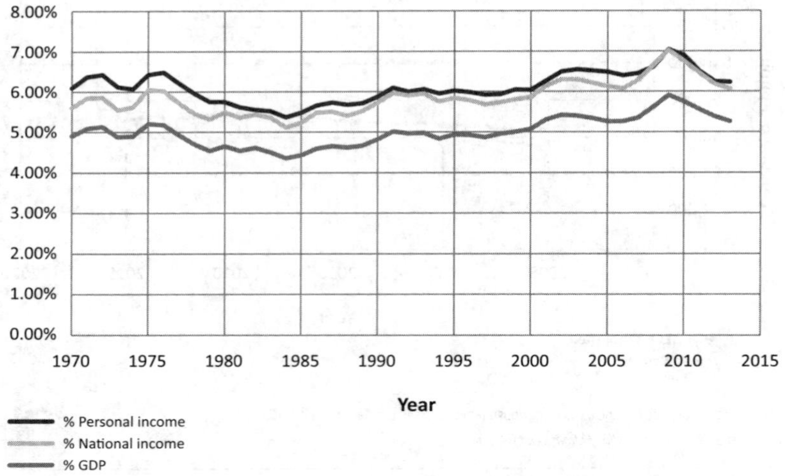

Sources: Current Population Survey: Income, US Census Bureau, http://www.census.gov/hhes/www/income/data/historical/families/; Population Estimates, US Census Bureau, http://www.census.gov/popest/data/historical/2010s/vintage_2013/national.html and http://www.census.gov/popest/data/national/asrh/2014/index.html; State and Local Government Finances, US Census Bureau, http://www.census.gov/govs/local/; National Income and Product Accounts Tables, Bureau of Economic Analysis, US Department of Commerce, http://www.bea.gov/iTable/index_nipa.cfm.

part because of additional legal protections for specialized programs and services for children with disabilities.[24] But, as figure 1.6 shows, total numbers of teachers (including specialists) per 100 pupils have been at a break-even point for the last twelve to fourteen years. That means that since the early 2000s (when NAEP progress seemed to slow down), teaching staff numbers have remained relatively flat. There was a modest bump in the mid-2000s, but that subsided during the "new normal" period and has not since rebounded. It's worth noting here that a recent comprehensive meta-analysis of interventions which improve outcomes for low-income students found that the most effective interventions were those involving increased human resources.[25]

Figure 1.7 shows a comparison of teachers' weekly wages to those of college-educated nonteachers from 1979 to 2015. For the past fifteen years, teacher wages have held constant at about 77 percent of nonteacher wages. Some assert that a teacher's healthy and growing pension benefits are a substantial offset to this gap, noting that teacher benefits have increased by about 10–20 percent of wages since the early 2000s, whereas private-sector benefits

FIGURE 1.6   Teachers (all) per 100 pupils over time

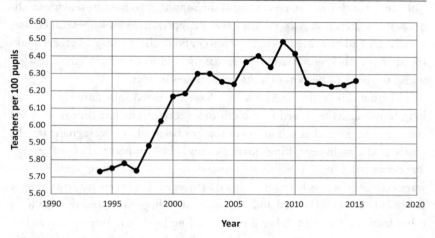

Source: Baker et al., *School Funding Fairness Data System*.

FIGURE 1.7   Ratio of teacher weekly wages to college-educated nonteacher weekly wages

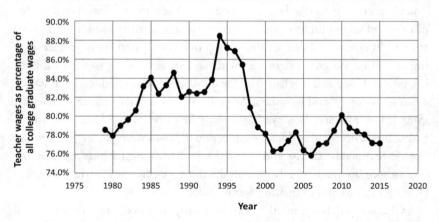

Notes: "College graduates" excludes public school teachers, and "all workers" includes everyone (including public school teachers and college graduates). Wages are adjusted to 2015 dollars using the CPI-U-RS. Data are for workers aged 18–64 with positive wages (excluding self-employed workers). Nonimputed data are not available for 1994 and 1995; data points for these years have been extrapolated and are represented by dotted lines (see appendix A for more detail).

Source: Sylvia Allegretto and Lawrence Mishel, "The Teacher Pay Gap Is Wider Than Ever: Teachers' Pay Continues to Fall Further Behind Pay of Comparable Workers" (report, Economic Policy Institute, Washington DC, August 9, 2016), http://www.epi.org/publication/the-teacher -pay-gap-is-wider-than-ever-teachers-pay-continues-to-fall-further-behind-pay-of-comparable-workers/.

have held constant at 10 percent of wages.[26] One problem with this is that the difference is expressed in percent, and the supposed 20 percent rate for teachers is over a wage that is 23 percent lower than private sector wages. Of course, it's a larger and growing percent of a lower and declining wage. Yet, even taking that percent as accurate, the increase would at best have raised teacher wages to about 84 percent of nonteacher wages in 2015.[27]

The data show that NAEP scores have increased substantively over the long term but have slowed in growth more recently, as has closure of racial achievement gaps; that school spending has been relatively stagnant for the past decade, as have staffing quantities and the competitiveness of teacher wages; and that over the shorter term, since 2008, spending, staffing, and wage competitiveness have all declined. This means that our students are not doing as badly as is claimed and we are not spending more, and there may be other factors affecting teacher quality (staffing levels and wage competitiveness) related to the decline in spending. These long-term trends are roughly the opposite of those used most often to proclaim the failures of American education. One clear implication of these trends, though, is that US public schools have in fact become more efficient over time, not less.

MOVING FORWARD BY GOING BACK TO BASICS

The chapters that follow begin by taking us back to the conceptual underpinnings of school finance and the historical origins and basis for our current system. In chapter 2 I discuss the prerequisite conceptual frames for evaluating education systems, beginning with an overview of principles of financing public goods and services, and lay out conceptions of educational *equity*, *equal opportunity*, and *adequacy*. After all, if state school finance policies are intended to advance these goals, we must first understand what they mean. I also introduce conceptions of educational *productivity* and *efficiency*. We cannot reasonably discuss and evaluate whether proposed interventions and innovations are likely to advance productivity or efficiency in the absence of clear definitions and evaluation frameworks.

Chapter 3 delves into the common misperceptions and misdirections used to deemphasize the importance of money for improving school quality and achieving greater equity and for paving the way for cost-free alternatives. In this chapter I address five common arguments used for asserting that money really doesn't matter for school quality or equity. These range from deceptive presentation of research evidence, to manipulative representation of data, to anecdotal claims of egregious spending and massive failures. I also examine two common arguments used to deflect focus from the amount of school spending, including the assertion that how money is spent is more important than how much and the argument that student background matters more than school spending.

In chapter 4 I make connections between revenue generated for education systems, spending allocated to schools, and the real resources in schools and classrooms derived from that spending. These connections are made across both states, based on vastly different state investment in public schooling, and districts within states. Where schools have more access to financial resources, schools can provide more staff, programs, and services and can compensate their staff more competitively. These connections hold for traditional public schools, charter schools, and for private schools. In each case, where schools have access to more financial resources, they tend to spend those resources on more and better-compensated people. Education remains a human resource–intensive endeavor. The quantity and talent of those human resources matter, and both cost money.

Chapter 5 dives into the research literature validating the importance of financial resources for schools and the real resources supported by those financial resources. A thorough review of major national studies shows that substantive infusions of financial resources resulting from judicial intervention have resulted in significant short-term and long-term gains for children attending schools that received the additional resources. In this chapter I also review literature on numerous studies of state-specific school finance reforms that yield findings largely consistent with recent national studies and look at studies of how that money is spent, specifically on the connections between class size and student outcomes and teacher compensation and student outcomes. Again, it all comes down to human resources.

An overview of the mechanics and design of state school finance systems makes up chapter 6, looking at how funding is calculated and how those calculations connect to principles of equity and adequacy. Here I also address those features of state school finance systems that are not necessarily connected to principles of equity and adequacy and instead are a function of political tradeoffs, some of which work in direct opposition to equity and adequacy goals.

Chapter 7 is a reality check on the state of state school finance systems. Using data from the *School Funding Fairness Data System*, I show that the decline of state school finance systems has been uneven across states and has unevenly affected districts and schools and the children they serve. I also illustrate the intersection between the equity and adequacy of resources between local public school districts and resources for schools within those districts, including the role of charter school expansion in disrupting and eroding equity within school districts.

The final three chapters move us toward policy solutions. In chapter 8 I discuss frameworks and methods for evaluating productivity and efficiency of reforms and innovations and lay out a role for the federal government and state education agencies in providing technical support to evaluate educational interventions, while in chapter 9 I detail frameworks for understanding, evaluating, and informing the reform and revitalization of state school finance systems. In the final chapter I use two national data sets—the *School Funding Fairness Data System* and the *Stanford Education Data Archive*—to generate estimates of the costs of providing all districts and states with the resources necessary to achieve the relatively modest goal of current national average outcomes.[28] These estimates can be used to evaluate just how far we have to go to achieve even that modest goal in some states, such as Tennessee, Mississippi, Arizona, and New Mexico. This final chapter proposes a new approach for federal aid distribution that focuses on raising states to this modest standard while considering whether states themselves are contributing their fair share.

CHAPTER 2

SCHOOL FINANCE 101

The central policy objective of government-financed public school systems is to provide for an equitable system of schooling that makes efficient use of public resources to achieve desired (or, at the very least, adequate) outcome goals. There's a lot to unpack in that statement. To do that work, I begin with a brief discussion of the rationale behind the provision of public goods and services, touching on pure economic theory and providing some historical background on racial and economic segregation. I then review the long-standing literature and modern conceptions of *equity*, *adequacy*, and *equal educational opportunity* and address conceptions of education *productivity*, *cost*, and *efficiency*. (I save for later chapters more detailed discussions of methods for measuring costs, productivity and efficiency, and indicators for evaluating equity and equal opportunity.) I conclude the chapter with a brief discussion of the conflation of liberty and equality by those advocating for increased choice through vouchers and charter schooling, which conveniently ignores the historical backdrop and political and economic theories behind the provision of taxpayer-financed public goods. To suggest that liberty leads to equity is to suggest we can have our cake and eat it too. Instead, as Toqueville wrote in *Democracy in America*, these two societal preferences have always existed in tension with one another.[1]

EDUCATION AS A TAXPAYER-FINANCED (QUASI) PUBLIC GOOD

Consider broadly the provision of public goods and services through a system of taxpayer support. In the United States, for elementary and secondary education in particular, that system combines federal (about 10 percent) and state and local (vary by state) tax dollars to pay for the provision of public education systems. These systems are largely state governed. Local tax dollars are generally raised from property taxes on residential, commercial, and industrial properties within geographic spaces defined in state law as local public school districts. In some states, these districts are contiguous with other municipal boundaries; in others they are not. Generally, the rules for and parameters determining local taxation are governed by states. State dollars typically come from general funds fueled by state income and sales taxes and are allocated to local districts through various aid formulas governed by state legislatures. Similarly, federal aid is allocated to states by various formulas governed by Congress from revenue derived primarily from federal income taxes.

Governments, established by the people for the people, collect and redistribute tax dollars to provide for the mix of public goods and services. Investment in public schooling is investment in human capital, and the collective returns to that investment are greater than the sum of the returns reaped by each individual who furthers her education.[2] We invest public resources into the education of the public for the benefit of the public.

The dollars provided via taxation support both infrastructure and annual operations for public goods and services. This includes schools, roads, public safety (police/fire), national security, public utilities, parks. Investment in public infrastructure serves not only immediate users but users for generations to come. Support of annual operations also does not benefit just those using the service or good today or this year. Contributors of tax dollars include those who directly and indirectly benefit (parents of school-aged children and property owners without school-aged children). One indirect benefit accrued from investment in a system of public schooling is capitalization in housing values—"better" schools increase property values.

PURE THEORIES CLASH WITH UGLY REALITIES

Since the 1950s, economists have attempted to wrap market theories around the provision of public goods and services. Specifically, Charles Tiebout argued that households choose among jurisdictions based on the prices paid (taxes) for public goods and services and their preferences for the quality and types of services provided, much like one chooses to purchase any other product or service on the market.[3] Thus, a free market with multiple jurisdictions with varied prices and services, and households with varied preferences, should lead to an optimal (efficient) distribution of households across jurisdictions. Families with children and preferences for "good schools" will concentrate in communities with high-quality schools and the taxes to support them (just as empty-nest, chain-smoking narcoleptics will settle in communities with well-funded fire departments), leading to eventual perfect equilibrium. Under a perfect free-market system, preferences for prices and services will be optimally aligned. Households will have the mix of public goods and services they desire at the price (in taxes) they are willing and able to pay.

Pure theoretical assumptions, however, are often undermined by distortions, market failures, or, in lay terms, reality. These are not flaws in the pure theory but, rather, what happens when pure theory is applied to reality. Two conditions for markets to achieve their goals are perfect information and perfect mobility. First, consumers (or "homevoters") need to have good information on the quality of services and the connection between service quality and price, which is tricky for complex public services.[4] Second, consumers need complete flexibility to choose one price/service quality alternative over another. Yet, choosing a neighborhood in which to live isn't as easy as choosing Target over Walmart or Dunkin' Donuts instead of Krispy Kreme. Many households simply can't afford to live in a neighborhood with the quality of schools they desire. The benefit of capitalization of school quality into home values is a double-edged sword, reinforcing economic disparity across neighborhoods and, in turn, reinforcing tax revenue disparity for schools—the rich get richer and the poor get poorer.

More pointedly, for decades real estate developers in collaboration with state and local policy makers engaged in formal policies and practices that codified and exacerbated racial and economic segregation of neighborhoods. Minority families, subject to restrictive covenants in property deeds, weren't permitted to buy homes in certain neighborhoods and for decades thereafter were discouraged and/or not shown homes in certain neighborhoods and faced higher interest rates for otherwise comparable purchases.[5] Policies and government-sanctioned practices prohibited free market choices among households that were already far from equitable. Manipulative real estate developers and their investors, in collaboration with elected officials, crafted our racially segregated neighborhoods and schools.

Decades of legal challenges to school and district segregation attempted to mitigate these disparities. But a handful of US Supreme Court decisions have significantly limited lower courts' and policy makers' authority to remedy segregation. The 1954 *Brown v. Board of Education* decision, as groundbreaking as it was, merely declared that publicly operated school systems could not explicitly provide separate facilities for Black and White children.[6] And the next year, *Brown II* went further to establish guidance for remedying school segregation.[7] In the period following, federal district courts were charged with overseeing the integration of previously segregated school systems.[8] At the same time, however, real estate developers were instigating and then capitalizing on the flight of White families to suburbia.

District court judges were hindered by the 1973 *Milliken v. Bradley* decision, which indicated that suburban districts could not be forced to play a role in urban desegregation if those districts did not intentionally play a role in creating the segregation.[9] Given that most racial (and economic) segregation occurs across districts and municipal boundaries, not merely across schools or neighborhoods within the same city, this constraint severely undermined future school desegregation efforts. Concurrently, the US Supreme Court declared it acceptable for Texas to permit local control and property taxation that lead to disparities in school funding across school districts. At this point, the Supreme Court withdrew itself from most further debates over school funding equity or adequacy, leaving these questions to be handled on a state-by-state basis.

In the decades that followed, the Court lowered the thresholds for deciding when lower courts should declare that segregated districts had achieved "unitary" (sufficiently integrated) status and in 2006 put constraints on the extent to which local districts could even consider student race in school assignment policies in order to achieve greater integration.[10] Disturbingly, in recent years state lawmakers have allowed district boundary reorganizations and secessions that have exacerbated racial segregation.[11] In one particularly egregious case, Tennessee merged Shelby County schools with the predominantly Black Memphis City School District and then allowed predominantly White townships in the county to leave the newly configured district. In another instance the predominantly White northeastern corner of the Kansas City, Missouri, district was permitted to secede from the predominantly Black district and merge with the Whiter neighboring Independence district.[12]

The local organization of schools in the United States, coupled with reliance (in some states more than others) on local property taxes for a large share of school funding (especially capital financing), leads to substantial disparities in educational opportunities that remain strongly associated with income, housing values, and race.

EVOLVING CONCEPTIONS OF EQUITY, EQUAL OPPORTUNITY, AND ADEQUACY

Because of the vast inequities that exist across our public school systems, legal scholars, advocates, and analysts have sought to develop conceptual frameworks and empirical measures to illustrate sources, causes, and consequences of such disparities in order to influence policy makers and guide courts in evaluating student and family rights.[13] In the post-*Brown* era it became increasingly apparent that dismantling of segregation would be a long and incomplete process. Further, even where greater integration was achieved, significant disparities persisted in the quality of schooling and available resources both across schools within states and across states. While racial integration remained a major national policy concern, resolving persistent, deep resource disparities across schools and communities gained momentum in the late 1960s and early 1970s.

In 1979 Robert Berne and Leanna Stiefel synthesized conceptual frameworks from public policy and finance and evidence drawn from early court cases challenging inequities in state school finance systems to propose a framework and series of measures for evaluating equity in state school finance systems.[14] Their important work laid the foundation for subsequent conceptual and empirical developments regarding equity measurement applied to preK–12 settings. They used two framing questions: Equity of what? Equity for who? On the "what" side, they suggested that equity could be framed in terms of financial inputs to schooling, real resource inputs (such as teachers and their qualifications), and outcomes. Their framework, however, predated both judicial application of outcome standards to evaluate school finance systems and the proliferation of state outcome standards, assessments, and accountability systems first in the 1990s and then in the 2000s under No Child Left Behind. The "who" side typically involved "students" and "taxpayers": a state school finance system should be based on fair treatment of taxpayers and yield fair treatment of students. Drawing on literature from tax policy, Berne and Stiefel adopted a definition of *fairness* that provided for both "equal treatment of equals" (horizontal equity) and "unequal treatment of unequals" (vertical equity).[15] That is, if two taxpayers are equally situated, their tax treatment should be similar; likewise, if two students have similar needs, their access to educational programs and services or financial inputs should be similar. But if two taxpayers are differently situated (homeowner versus industrial or commercial property owner), then differential taxation might be permissible; and, if two students have substantively different educational needs requiring different programs and services, then different financial inputs might be needed to achieve equity.

In recent decades, research has shown the shortcomings of horizontal and vertical equity delineations. First, horizontal equity itself does not preclude vertical equity; equal treatment of equals does not preclude the need for differentiated treatment for some (nonequals). Second, vertical equity requires value judgments that lead to categorical determinations of *who* is unequal and *how unequal* their treatment must be in order to be "equitable." Differences in individual students and population needs don't always fall into neat boxes; rather, they run along continua.

Nonetheless, laws—federal and state statutes and regulations—often try to put things into neat boxes, and conceptions of equity often intersect with legal claims that one group is not receiving equitable treatment when compared with another, thus requiring courts to consider how to remedy those inequities. Significant federal laws enacted in the 1970s operate under this model, applying categorical declarations as to who is eligible for different treatment and frequently requiring judicial intervention to determine how much differentiation is required for legal compliance.[16] But most children do not fall into the categories set forth under federal (or state) laws, even though there exist vast differences in needs across those children.

An alternative, unifying approach is to suggest that the treatment is not the inputs the child receives but the outcomes that are expected of all children under state standards and accountability systems. In this sense, all children under the umbrella of these state policies are similarly situated and similarly expected to achieve the common outcome standards. Thus, the obligation of the state is to ensure that all children, regardless of their background and where they attend school, have equal opportunity to achieve those common outcome standards.

The provision of *equal educational opportunity* requires differentiation of programs and services, including additional supports—vertical equity. This input (and process) differentiation is toward a goal of equal treatment (treatment = outcome goals) rather than unequal treatment (treatment = inputs).

Further, if differentiation of programs and services is required to provide equal opportunity to achieve common outcomes, there exists a more viable legal *equity* argument on behalf of the most disadvantaged children not separately classified under federal statutes. Whether children fit neatly into the protected boxes identified in federal statutes does not alone determine whether those children require additional resources. The conception of equal opportunity to achieve common outcome goals has thus largely replaced vertical equity in the vernacular of K–12 equity analysis.[17]

The late 1980s and early 1990s saw a shift in legal strategy regarding state school finance systems away from emphasizing achieving equal revenue across settings (neutral of property wealth) and toward identifying some benchmark for minimum educational adequacy. Some advocates for this approach saw it as politically infeasible for states to raise sufficient state aid to close the spending gap between the poorest and most affluent districts, meaning that achieving spending parity likely required leveling down affluent districts. Thus, a focus on a minimum adequacy bar for the poorest districts would alleviate this concern and potentially garner political support of affluent communities that no longer had anything to lose.[18] Bill Koski and Rob Reich explain that this approach is problematic in part because minimum adequacy standards are difficult to define; also, when some are provided merely minimally adequate education but others provided education that far exceeds minimum adequacy, the former remain at a disadvantage. Further, the adequacy of the minimum bar is diminished by increasing that gap, because education is, to a large extent, a *positional good*, whereby individuals compete based on relative position for access to higher education and economic prosperity.[19]

Others have adopted a more progressive "adequacy" view that focusing on state standards and accountability systems could hold legislators' feet to the fire to provide sufficient resources for all children to meet those standards, and state constitution education articles could be used to enforce this mandate.[20] Under this more progressive alternative, equal opportunity and adequacy goals are combined. The state must provide equal opportunity for all children to achieve "adequate" educational outcomes. Funding must be at a sufficient overall level and resources, programs, and services must be provided to ensure that children with varied needs and backgrounds have the supports they need to achieve the mandated outcomes.

It remains important, however, to be able to separate equal opportunity and adequacy objectives both for legal claims and for empirical analysis. The adequacy bar can be elusive.[21] State courts are not always willing to declare that adopted accountability measures and outcome standards determine the state's minimum constitutional obligation. The state's ability to support a specific level of adequacy may be subject to economic fluctuations.[22] Importantly, at those times when revenue falls short of supporting high outcome standards, equal opportunity should still be preserved: equal opportunity can be achieved for a standard lower than, equal to, or higher than the single adequacy standard.[23]

The practical implications of modern equity, equal opportunity, and adequacy conceptions are that state school finance systems must strive to achieve two simultaneous goals: account for differences in the costs of achieving equal educational opportunity (to achieve desired outcomes) across schools and districts and the children they serve; and account for differences in the ability of local public school districts to cover those costs. The first goal relates primarily to the sorting of students and populations by needs across local schools and districts, warranting substantial differentiation of funding to provide equal educational opportunity, as well as to geographic differences in the costs of labor and other school operations. The second goal stems from the continued reliance on local property taxation to support that system. Because local jurisdictions vary widely in the revenue they can raise when applying common tax rates or effort, states must distribute aid to offset these discrepancies, to achieve dollar parity.

DEFINING PRODUCTIVITY, COST, AND EFFICIENCY

The central problem with US public schools is often characterized as an efficiency problem. We spend a lot and don't get much for it; and over time we've spent more and more but our outcomes have remained virtually flat. Yet rarely are these claims accompanied by thorough analysis or empirical evidence of cost-effectiveness or efficiency.[24]

We must not get too caught up in the possibility of identifying the perfectly efficient school or district or the absolute minimum that might possibly be spent to achieve a given level of outcomes with x children under y conditions. Measuring such hypothetical extremes is impractical. That said, much can be learned by better understanding the average efficiency at which existing schools and districts produce certain outcome measures for their students and the deviations around those averages.

Some basic definitions are in order:

- *productivity*: The output of our system of schooling, measured in terms of quantity of output or quality of output, or both. Quantity measures often include total numbers of students served or graduated; quality measures are often reduced to measures derived from standardized tests, usually of reading and mathematics achievement between grades 3 and 8. Increasingly, the quality of outcomes produced is measured in terms of changes in assessment scores over time associated with students' time of attendance in a particular school or district (value-added estimates). Outcomes may also include longer-term outcomes, such as income or civic participation.
- *spending*: Expenses (current and deferred) associated with the provision of educational programs and services and related supports (food, transportation, overhead), regardless of outcomes
- *cost*: The minimum amount that would need to be spent to achieve a specific level of student outcomes, given the backgrounds of the students served and other potential contextual constraints (variations in the competitive wages for qualified employees, remoteness and population sparsity, economies scale, etc.). Cost necessarily connects spending with outcomes.
- *efficiency*: Given the previous two definitions it is possible to spend more than would be needed to achieve a given level of outcomes. That margin of difference is *inefficiency*.

$$spending - inefficiency = cost$$

or

$$cost + inefficiency = spending$$

The margin of spending above cost is labeled *inefficiency*; but when we discuss measurable inefficiency of schools, the term takes on broad meaning, including spending on programs and services that may be valued but not measured as primary goals/objectives. For example, institutional expenditures may include expenditures on community-based programs and events, athletics, and arts that may marginally, if at all, contribute to student test scores. This is not to suggest, however, that these expenditures are unnecessary or inappropriate. Rather, they are simply not captured by the outcomes being measured because they serve a different, but still valued, purpose.

Often, when pundits talk about "cost-cutting" measures, they are really talking about spending reductions, whether they result in declining outcomes or whether outcomes remain constant. Actual cost cutting that holds outcomes constant—doing the same with less—would, theoretically, be efficiency improvement. By contrast, less spending leading to lower outcomes is a break-even on efficiency.

EVALUATING EFFICIENCY AND PRODUCTIVITY

Education productivity has been explored through two branches of academic research. The first, *efficiency analysis*, involves studies of the production and cost efficiency of schools and school systems—that is, the study of sufficiently large numbers of institutions (schools and districts) over time striving to achieve common goals—and the second looks specifically at the cost-effectiveness of educational models, strategies, or broad-based reforms.

In efficiency analysis, researchers attempt to use statistical models that capture the complexity of the real world to identify the outcome levels that can be produced with certain students given certain levels of spending or, alternatively, to determine the spending levels needed to produce certain outcomes with certain students. Some schools and districts do better than expected, and others do worse. The goal is to figure out why this is the case. Researchers have addressed the conceptual basis and empirical methods for evaluating technical efficiency of production and cost efficiency in education or government services more generally.

In the US public education system there are approximately 100,000 traditional public schools in roughly 15,000 traditional public school districts, plus 5,000 or so charter schools. Accordingly, there are significant and important differences in the ways these schools get things done. The educational status quo thus entails considerable variation in approaches and in quality, as well as in the level and distribution of funding and in the population served.

Each organizational unit—be it a public school district, a neighborhood school, a charter school, a private school, or a virtual school—organizes its human resources, material resources, capital resources, programs, and services differently from all others. The reason to use efficiency analysis to evaluate education reform alternatives is to learn from these variations, something that has been largely ignored in recent policy making. Too often policy makers gravitate toward an idea without any empirical basis, assuming that it offers a better approach despite having never been tested. It is far more reasonable, however, to assume that we can learn how to do better by identifying those schools or districts that do excel and then evaluating how they do it. Not all schools in their current forms are woefully inefficient, and any new reform strategy will not necessarily be more efficient. So it is sensible for researchers and policy makers to make use of the variations across those 100,000 schools by studying them to see what works and what does not. These are empirical questions, and they can and should be investigated.

Efficiency analysis can be viewed from one of two perspectives: production efficiency or cost efficiency. Production efficiency (also known as technical efficiency of production) measures the outcomes of organizational units such as schools or districts given their inputs and given the circumstances under which production occurs. Which schools or districts get the most bang for the buck? Cost efficiency is essentially the flip side of production efficiency. In cost efficiency analysis, the goal is to determine the minimum cost at which a given level of outcomes can be produced under certain circumstances. What's the minimum number of bucks we need to spend to get the bang we want? In both approaches three moving parts are involved. First, there are measured outcomes, such as student assessment outcomes. Second, there are existing expenditures by those organizational units. And third, there are the conditions, such as the varied student populations, and the size and location of the school or district, including differences in competitive wages for teachers and health care, heating and cooling, and transportation costs.

It is important to understand that all efficiency analyses, whether cost efficiency or production efficiency, are relative. Efficiency analysis is about evaluating how some organizational units achieve better or worse outcomes than others do (given comparable spending), or how or why the cost of achieving specific outcomes using certain approaches and under some circumstances is more or less in some cases than in others. Comparisons can be made to the efficiency of average districts or schools or to those that appear to maximize output at a given expense or minimize the cost of a given output. Efficiency analysis in education is useful because there are significant variations in key aspects of schools: what they spend, who they serve and under what conditions, and what they accomplish.

In cost-effectiveness analysis researchers identify the various costs of implementing alternative programs, models, or strategies intended to improve the same outcome measure and then compare those cost estimates to the differences in outcomes achieved under highly controlled conditions. The ultimate goal is to determine which strategy improves the most the outcome measures in question for a given cost. Which strategy is most cost-effective?[25]

Two main types of cost analyses are cost-effectiveness analysis and cost-benefit analysis, the latter of which can focus on either short-term cost savings or longer-term economic benefits. Each of these approaches requires an initial determination of the policy alternatives to be compared. Typically, the baseline alternative is the status quo. The status quo is not a necessarily a bad choice. One embarks on cost-effectiveness or cost-benefit analysis to determine whether there is something better than the status quo; but it is not a given that anything one might do is better than what is currently being done. In fact, it is almost always possible to spend more and get less using new strategies than when maintaining the current course.

ON LIBERTY AND EQUALITY

Liberty and equality are desirable policy outcomes. Thus, it would be convenient if policies simultaneously advanced both. But it's never that simple. A large body of literature on political theory explains that liberty and equality are preferences that most often operate in tension with one another.[26] While not mutually exclusive, they are certainly not one and the same. Preferences for and expansion of liberties often leads to greater inequality and division among members of society, whereas preferences for equality moderate those divisions.[27] The only way expanded liberty can lead to greater equality is if available choices are substantively equal, conforming to a common set of societal standards. But if available choices are substantively equal, then why choose one over another? Systems of choice and competition rely on differentiation, inequality, and both winners and losers.

In applying the real-world context of America's racially and socioeconomically segregated system of public schooling, choice advocates assert that the liberty of school choice necessarily disrupts the inequitable relationship between ones' zip code and the quality of schooling available. Providing choices across jurisdictional boundaries can also disrupt the capitalization relationship that drives growing inequality. If housing isn't linked to local schools, then housing prices are less likely to respond to differences in local school quality.[28]

economy of scale

Choice advocates are divided on whether expanded school choice should include vouchers for private schools or merely subsidies for private operators of government-sanctioned charter schools, the line between the two being more blurred in legal terms than typically acknowledged.[29] Regardless, in most cases choice-based systems of schooling remain highly limited by geography and are often restricted to the same geographic boundaries that define local public school districts and municipalities. For example, in many states charter school choice is functionally limited to district schools and charter schools within the district boundaries. So charter school choice and voucher systems in cities like Milwaukee merely permit the reshuffling of urban minority children among a limited set of alternatives. But broader geographic expansion faces significant political and operational hurdles (e.g., "perfect mobility").

Further, expansion of charter schooling has largely led to yet more vastly unequal choices.[30] Some charter schools, those operated by politically connected and financially well-endowed management companies, are able to provide extended school years, longer days, smaller classes, and richer curricula.[31] Those schools are the ones with the longest waiting lists—which demonstrates that the choices are unequal and unequally accessible. A system of unequal choices is still an unequal system. As for "adequacy," a system where the most available choices are the least adequate is not adequate. We must be willing as a society to deal openly with our preferences for liberty versus equality and design systems that best balance these often-competing preferences.

The necessity of addressing the basic connections between taxation and the provision of public goods comes about partly in response to a frequent argument of school choice (voucher and charter) advocates that the public tax dollars (should) belong to the child, not the schools.[32] They see institutions, especially government institutions, as faceless bureaucracies, as "bad" (whereas children are "good"). While this claim makes for a compelling sound bite, it falsely assumes an oversimplified linear tax-collection-to-spending-distribution path and an individualistic benefit basis for public goods and services. It contends that the parents of schoolchildren are the exclusive contributors to the tax revenue pool and that their children should thus be the exclusive beneficiaries of those resources in that moment in time, according to parents' individual, not collective, preferences. Any collective, societal interests are set aside in favor of individual liberties of families with school-aged children— but financed with collective resources of the community at large. The interests

outcomes based—what is the min. needed to get to a standard outcome

of contributors/taxpayers other than parents in that moment are disregarded. With this thinking, individual parent preferences for the use of public dollars always supersede societal preferences, an ideology that runs contrary to the basic concept of public goods and services.

The "money belongs to the child" claim also falsely assumes that the only expenses associated with each individual's education choice are the current annual expenses of educating that individual and that the expenses associated with educating (equitably) the first, second, and third child are the same as the ninety-ninth child choosing any one institution. It ignores entirely marginal costs and economies of scale, foundational elements of origins of public institutions. We collect tax dollars and provide public goods and services because it allows us to do so at an efficient scale of operations. The tax dollars collected belong to (are governed or controlled by) the democratically governed community (local, state, federal) that established the policies for collecting those tax dollars, which are to be distributed according to the demands—preferred goods and services—of that community within the constraints of the law. Public spending does not matter only to those using it here and now. Those dollars don't just belong to parents of children presently attending the schools, and the assets acquired with public funding, often with long-term debt (fifteen to twenty years), do not belong exclusively to those parents. This is not to suggest that this is the perfect or even best possible system; rather, this is the system we have in place, one that provides for democratic control and taxpayer financing of public schooling and is governed and regulated by the appropriate local, state, and federal authorities and laws.

LESSONS LEARNED AND LOOKING FORWARD

This chapter lays the groundwork for better evaluating the existing conditions of our public schooling system and potential strategies, policies, and structural changes for reforming that system:

- understanding theories regarding the provision of public goods and services and the limitations of those theories when applied to reality;
- understanding the democratic structures that govern and finance the current system of public schooling in the United States;
- applying conceptions of equity, adequacy, and equal educational opportunity with clarity and rigor to evaluate the existing systems of public schooling and any and all proposed alternatives;

- applying conceptions of productivity and efficiency with clarity and rigor to evaluate the existing system of public schooling and any and all proposed alternatives; and
- rejecting feel-good sound bites that don't meet basic requirements of theoretical consistency or conceptual, definitional precision or accuracy.

Many critics of US public schools argue that traditional theories of the public good and our government structures are in fact the problem and require substantial disruption if not outright replacement. Andrew Smarick, for example, suggests replacing publicly provided schooling with portfolios of privately managed and operated schools, praising the value of "sector agnosticism."[33] Who manages and operates schools—public or private entities—really doesn't matter as long as they are "great" schools. Similarly, Neerav Kingsland, a self-proclaimed "thought leader," preaches the high moral ground of "relinquishing" control of public systems to their immediate constituents (parents and children), who can then choose among providers and provider types.[34] However, these "agnostic" fixes are far less well conceived from both accountability and public financing perspectives than the system they claim to fix.

There may in fact be a legitimate case for substantively disrupting and altering the way we conceive of and provide for public education. But we should avoid the pressures of expedience and urgency when making such consequential decisions. Undoubtedly, our current system of schooling is inequitable and imperfect. Yet tales of the general collapse of that system are greatly overblown. More than anything else, our system of public schooling requires renewed emphasis on equitable, adequate, and economically sustainable public financing at a level that will provide all children equal opportunity to achieve the outcomes we, as a society, desire for them.

CHAPTER 3

MONEY MYTHS
AND MISDIRECTIONS

There is a long-standing debate about whether increased resources actually improve student achievement. This debate emerged in the 1960s with the Coleman Report, which found that student background had a strong effect on student achievement. Its most commonly cited finding was that student backgrounds matter a lot and that resource measures studied have trivial effects by comparison. After the release of the report, numerous scholars took advantage of new and richer data sources, largely focusing on exploring in greater depth why schools didn't seem to matter—a common, and now discredited, interpretation of the Coleman Report. In 1986 economist Eric Hanushek published a paper that arguably became the most widely cited source for the claim that money simply doesn't matter when it comes to improving school quality and student outcomes.[1] A meta-analysis of the large collection of post-Coleman studies, the paper used data from a variety of contexts, small and large, in the United States and elsewhere. Hanushek analyzed the findings of those studies—some of which found a positive relationship between spending and student outcomes while others found no relationship or a negative one—and came to the conclusion (which he italicized for emphasis) that *"there appears to be no strong or systematic relationship between school expenditures and student performance."*[2]

Hanushek's paper was the first in a long series of back-and-forth analyses summarizing the studies that came before them by what I call the vote count method, by looking at how many estimated relationships within studies found (voted "yes") that money or other school resources do matter as compared to how many did not (voted "no" or abstained). The assumption is that if "yes" wins, then money matters; if "no" wins, money doesn't matter.

And if it's a close call, then we don't know if money matters and would be foolish to start spending more of it on schools. This approach presumes the mere quantity of studies landing on one side or the other to be determinative of the truth, regardless of quality.

In the years that followed, Hanushek's finding became a mantra for many politicians and advocates, echoing through the halls of state and federal courthouses where school funding is deliberated. To this day, despite being grounded in the dated and methodologically limited evidence used in meta-analyses in the 1980s and 1990s, it maintains an impressive air of credibility in many circles, and its author has evolved his original conclusion into one of even greater confidence about the unimportance of money for student outcomes.[3]

In assessing Hanushek's original conclusion, it is important to distinguish between inconsistent findings about the spending-outcomes relationship on the one hand and bold declarations that money doesn't matter on the other. Within a developed body of research on almost any topic, there is always at least some degree of inconsistency in findings. The key is to adjudicate between studies in terms of their quality and scope and to assess whether a general conclusion might be drawn from the preponderance of the high-quality evidence.

The most direct rebuttal to Hanushek's characterization of the findings of existing research came in a series of reanalyses by Rob Greenwald, Larry Hedges, and Richard Laine, who gathered the studies Hanushek cited in 1986 and conducted meta-analyses of those that met certain quality parameters.[4] They included studies that had appeared in a refereed journal or book, used US data, had outcome measures that were some form of academic achievement, used data at the district or less-aggregate level, and employed a model that controlled for socioeconomic characteristics, fit with longitudinal data, and included data that were independent of other data included in the universe of studies considered by Hanushek. These quality control measures pruned a significant number of studies used by Hanushek.[5]

Most of the studies Hanushek included in his analysis had serious data and methodological limitations, which have since been addressed in more recent work.[6] And pertaining to aggregate per-pupil spending measures, Greenwald, Hedges, and Laine found that among statistically significant findings, the vast majority were positive (11:1) and that most of the analyses that did not find a statistically discernible relationship between spending and outcomes still found a positive association. They concluded that "global resource variables such as PPE [per-pupil expenditures] show strong and consistent relations with achievement. In addition, resource variables that attempt to describe the quality of teachers (teacher ability, teacher education, and teacher experience) show very strong relations with student achievement." And digging deeper and exploring the relationship between a variety of resource and student outcome measures, they found that "a broad range of resources were positively related to student outcomes, with 'effect sizes' large enough to suggest that moderate increases in spending may be associated with significant increases in achievement."[7] This conclusion stands in sharp contrast to Hanushek's statement of uncertainty.

Other researchers have explored with greater precision the measures of financial inputs to schooling that are most strongly associated with variations in student outcomes. Largely confirming the meta-analyses of Greenwald, Hedges, and Laine, Harold Wenglinsky found that "per-pupil expenditures for instruction and the administration of school districts are associated with achievement because both result in reduced class size, which raises achievement."[8] More recent studies improved on earlier analyses by adjusting the value of the education dollar for regional cost variation, testing alternative "functional forms" of the relationship between financial inputs and student outcomes, and applying other statistical corrections for the measurement of inputs.[9] These studies have invariably found a positive, statistically significant (though at times small) relationship between student achievement gains and financial inputs. They also raised new, important issues around the complexities of attempting to identify a direct link between money and student outcomes, including equating the value of the dollar across widely varied geographic and economic contexts and accurately separating the role of expenditures from that of students' family backgrounds, which also play some role in determining local funding.

It is important to recognize that Hanushek's original conclusion was merely a statement of "uncertainty" about whether a *consistent* relationship exists between spending and student outcomes, one that is significant enough to be important. His conclusion was not that such a relationship doesn't exist. Nor was it a statement that schools with fewer resources are better or that reducing funding can be an effective way to improve schools. But it wasn't until the early 2000s that the uncertainty conjured by Hanushek lifted, following the publication of more rigorous studies by finance scholars using detailed data sets to examine more finely grained relationships between money and student outcomes.

HOW FUZZY PICTURES SOW THE SEEDS OF DOUBT

Most consequential debates over the efficacy of funding for improving school quality and student outcomes occur outside of academic journals and conferences—in state legislative testimony, in consultation with policy making bodies, and in school finance litigation adjudicated in state courts. In those contexts, debates over the nitty-gritty details of statistics and research methodology tend to be less compelling. Over the past few decades, a parallel universe of evidence has emerged with the purpose of convincing policy makers that there is no substantive connection between school spending, school quality, and student outcomes. One common approach is to kick up a cloud of doubt, to produce a scatterplot of data on school spending and student outcomes that appears to show little or no relationship between the two.

An example of this is Eric Hanushek's 2014 report prepared for *Connecticut Coalition for Justice in Education Funding v. Rell*, in which he included sixteen scatterplots of the relationship between Connecticut school district sending and student math and reading scores. Figure 3.1 captures how Hanushek showed "added" expenditure per pupil on the horizontal axis using district average test scores (math grade 4) adjusted for race, language, and disability populations. By rigorous research standards, these outcome adjustments are far from sufficient. The scatterplots present a shattered (or scattered) predisposition of the money-outcome relationship. Hanushek himself concluded that "when looking across Connecticut schools, there is no relationship between how much money is spent and student results, either for all students or for students from poor families. Additionally, at any level of spending, one sees a very wide difference in how well students in different districts perform—a range amounting to multiples of the standard deviation of performance. The Connecticut analysis reinforces the previous conclusions from national analysis about the lack of systematic relationship between spending and student performance."[10]

If Hanushek's scatterplots are to be believed, it stands to reason that any judge would be foolish to order the state to spend any more than it presently does on schools, or that the judge should be concerned with differences in spending across districts, since a wide variety of outcomes can be achieved at any given spending level. But this graph is wholly insufficient for drawing

FIGURE 3.1   Spending and math achievement gains, grade 4 poor students

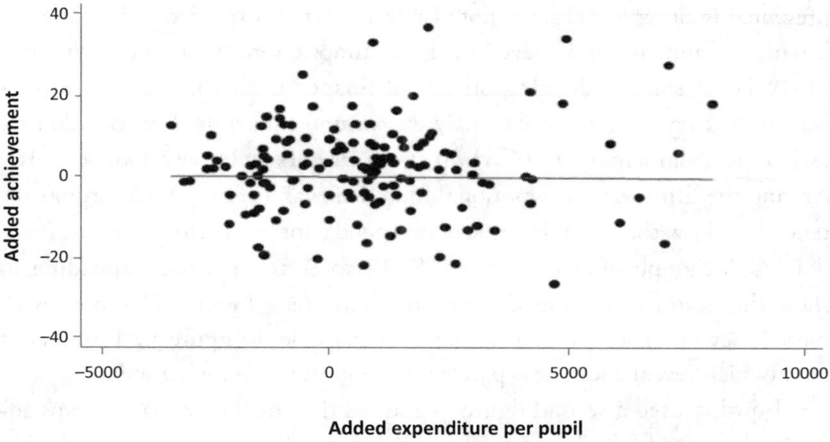

Note: Adjusted for Black, Hispanic, limited English proficiency (LEP), and special education students.

Source: "Expert Testimony of Eric Hanushek, *Connecticut Coalition for Justice in Education Funding v. State*, Submitted on Behalf of State/Defendants, 4/28/14," 29.

such conclusions, ignoring a variety of additional factors that mediate the relationship between school spending and student outcomes. Scatterplots are confusing and highly subjective. They are the ultimate Rorschach test of popular statistical analysis and should be viewed with appropriate scrutiny. Readers with at least some exposure to statistics, correlations, and scatterplots have predispositions to what visually constitutes a weak versus a strong correlation, as well as what they think they should be seeing for any given relationship. Knowing this, it becomes all too easy for the person creating the graph to confuse an audience. If readers assume that a certain relationship is supposed to be reasonably strong, they likely picture in their minds a scatterplot where the dots approximate an upward-sloping pattern. And if they do not see such a clear pattern, their expectation is undermined. Also, most scatterplots reduce visual relationships to two dimensions (three is possible but rare), setting aside the numerous other moderating factors and leaving readers with an unclear picture of when such factors are not or cannot be considered.

Such is the case with the frequent framing of the spending-outcomes relationship. The audience is told, "You might think (or have been led to believe) that more school spending leads to higher outcomes," which sets up the expectation of a simple, clear upward-sloping pattern when graphing spending (horizontal axis) and test scores (vertical axis). But when the actual pattern presented is either less clear or not visible at all, that expectation is shattered, leaving the audience to believe its prior assumption must have been wrong.

When I started blogging on school finance in 2009, one of my goals was to shed light on deceptive analyses. Around that time, Bob Bowdon released the documentary *The Cartel* that criticized New Jersey public schools.[11] Among the film's early promotional materials was a series of scatterplots intended to show that New Jersey schools spend a lot but perform poorly. Bowdon used a graph of states' average SAT scores and per-pupil spending to show that states which spend more on schools have lower SAT scores, with New Jersey being a particularly egregious example. In figure 3.2 I use newer data (which reveal a less clear pattern) to replicate Bowdon's graph.

Bowdon used a second figure to address the possibility that perhaps adjusting per-pupil spending for cost of living would be more reasonable, because it at least adjusts for the fact that the education dollar doesn't go as far in New Jersey as it might in New Mexico, where wages and prices of other school inputs are lower. But after this adjustment the audience is left to

FIGURE 3.2 The more a state spends on schools, the worse its students' SAT scores are

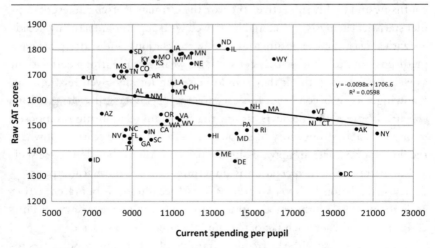

Sources: https://blog.prepscholar.com/average-sat-and-act-scores-by-stated-adjusted-for-participation-rate; Baker et al., *School Funding Fairness Data System*.

conclude that there is no relationship between spending and outcomes (see figure 3.3). So the audience first has its underlying assumption shattered by a graph showing the opposite of what they expected and is then led to believe that the presenter (Bowdon) is taking reasonable steps to moderate his claim. But this second claim is no more credible than the first.

Bowdon's graphs are examples of the two-dimension shortcoming. A really important consideration missing from these analyses (which I've included in figure 3.4) is that northeastern states that tend to be higher-spending states also tend to have much higher participation rates on the SAT. More kids take the SAT in these states, which means more kids from lower-income family backgrounds are taking the SAT. And where larger shares of the population take the SAT, average SAT scores tend to be lower. Bowdon's graphs hide this important reality. And even if corrected for the participation rate

FIGURE 3.3 After cost-of-living adjustments, education spending shows no correlation to SAT scores

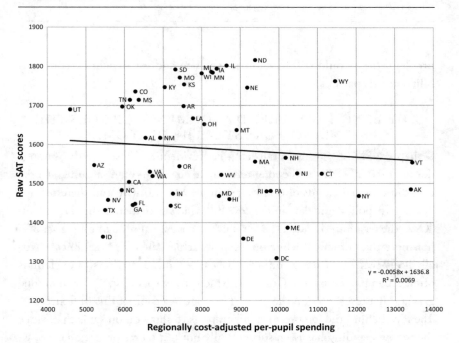

$$y = -0.0058x + 1636.8$$
$$R^2 = 0.0069$$

Regionally cost-adjusted per-pupil spending

Sources: https://blog.prepscholar.com/average-sat-and-act-scores-by-stated-adjusted-for-participation-rate; Baker et al., *School Funding Fairness Data System*.

FIGURE 3.4 Participation rates and average SAT scores

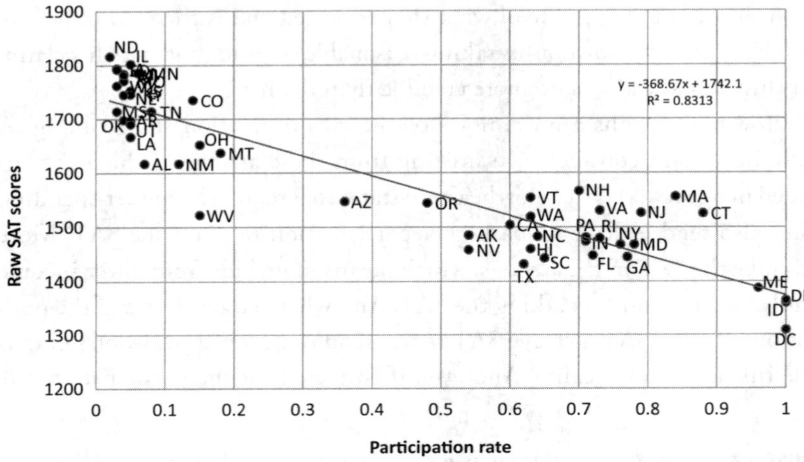

problem, they would still have other issues to address to achieve comparability, ceteris paribus.

THE LONG-TERM TREND ARGUMENT—UP GOES THE SPENDING, FLAT STAY THE OUTCOMES

Perhaps the most repeated and debunked evidentiary basis for the "money doesn't matter" claim is the long-term trend, or time-trend, argument. Like two-dimensional clouds of doubt, it's simple and intuitive and therefore appealing to policy and lay audiences. Bill Gates articulated this argument: "Over the past four decades, the per-student cost of running our K–12 schools has more than doubled, while our student achievement has remained virtually flat. Meanwhile, other countries have raced ahead."[12] This sort of claim is often accompanied by The Graph, in which rising spending is shown on one axis and flat test scores on the other. I recreate a version of this in figure 3.5.[13] The idea behind the long-term trend graph is to show on one axis that, since the 1970s, spending has risen substantially but test scores on national assessments (namely NAEP) have remained "virtually flat." Thus, it stands to reason that spending increases don't improve test scores.

FIGURE 3.5   The long-term trend

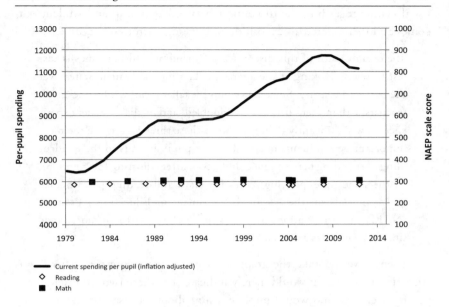

Source: NAEP long-term reading trend assessments for 1971, 1975, 1980, 1984, 1988, 1990, 1992, 1994, 1996, 1999, 2004, 2008, 2012.

Like my version, Gates's graph also has both NAEP scores and spending on the same vertical axis, using different measures. This approach is widely recognized as inappropriate, since it can too easily be constructed to show dramatic change on one scale (spending) and little change on the other (test scores). To illustrate this problem, my graph shows a spending range of $0–$12,000, a relatively fine grain size that will magnify the impact of even small increases in spending. By contrast, I set the scale for NAEP scores at 260–400, a range well beyond feasible gains. At this large grain size, even significant results will appear flat. Gates's use of this kind of graph gained notice from a blogger at Junk Charts, who opined that "Bill Gates should hire a statistical advisor."[14] As a graphic representation alone, the figure is meaningless and can certainly not be interpreted as Gates does.

Given how many times the long-term trend argument has been debunked, it's astounding that it never seems to die. With or without The Graph, the argument continues to make its way into public policy discourse, including in the context of school funding litigation. In his expert witness report to the court in the case of *Maisto v. State of New York*, Eric Hanushek laid out the usual claims regarding the disconnect between spending and student outcomes and then offered an exposition of the long-term trend argument.

> The overall truth of this disconnect of spending and outcomes is easiest to see by looking at the aggregate data for the United States over the past half century. Since 1960, pupil-teacher ratios fell by one-third, teachers with master's degrees over doubled, and median teacher experience grew significantly (Chart 1). Since these three factors are the most important determinants of spending per pupil, it leads to the quadrupling of spending between 1960 and 2009 (after adjusting for inflation). At the same time, plotting scores for math and reading performance of 17-year-olds on the National Assessment of Educational Progress (NAEP, or "The Nation's Report Card") shows virtually no change since 1970 (Charts 2 and 3).[15]

Even if we did take the graph at face value, as representing two concurrent, true trends, it would merely indicate that these two things are happening over time and would imply nothing about a causal (or lack thereof) relationship between the trends. Kirabo Jackson and colleagues make the following comparison:

> Consider the following true statistics: between 1960 and 2000 the rate of cigarette smoking for females decreased by more than 30 percent while the rate of deaths by lung cancer increased by more than 50 percent over the same time period. An analysis of these time trends might lead one to infer that smoking reduces lung cancer. However, most informed readers can point out numerous flaws in looking at this time trend evidence and concluding that "if smoking causes lung cancer, then there should have been a large corresponding reduction in cancer rates so that there can be no link between smoking and lung cancer."[16]

It may also be the case that the two trends illustrated in the graph aren't what they appear to be. Empirically, we should consider first that even the characterization of the trends in money, real resources (e.g., teachers), and outcomes might be incorrect or based on incorrect measurement. For example, the usual inflation adjustment, a consumer price index for all urban consumers, considers changes in the prices of a common set of goods and services. It is arguably far more appropriate to consider changes in the competitive wage required to recruit and retain a stable, quality workforce, all else equal. This is especially the case for an industry where over 80 percent of spending goes toward human resources and where the quality of the workforce matters greatly. I reiterate: outcomes have not been virtually flat.

An equally important issue is that the long-term trend claim is built on measuring only two things over time: spending and outcomes. The relevant framing of this issue is efficiency—Have US schools become less efficient over time? Have they spent more to achieve less, ceteris paribus? Ceteris paribus, or "with other conditions remaining the same," really matters. Framed from a productive efficiency standpoint, we should ask what outcomes are being achieved for any spending level or allocation of inputs given changes to the populations served by schools and other contextual factors that may affect the input-to-outcome relationship.

From a cost efficiency perspective, the goal would be to determine the spending levels required, given changes to the populations served by schools and other contextual factors that may affect the input-to-outcome relationship, to achieve existing outcome goals. Given that outcomes have increased over time, a system at constant efficiency would in fact have spent more to achieve those higher outcomes. It is, however, difficult to estimate precisely how much more should have been spent to achieve these outcome increases when evaluating national aggregate changes and with the diversity of the fifty-one systems that make up the whole.

IS US PUBLIC SCHOOLING THE LEAST EFFICIENT EDUCATIONAL SYSTEM IN THE WORLD?

What most commonly accompanies the long-term trend claim is the assertion that the United States spends more on education than other countries do but achieves less. Again, Bill Gates has gained attention for articulation of this claim: "Compared to other countries, America has spent more and achieved less."[17]

Gates did not support this contention with a graph, and many others who make this argument forgo empirical support altogether. But those who do introduce empirical support often turn to graphs that, at best and only with manipulative intervention, mildly support their case.[18] The "least efficient nation" claim generally rests on comparisons of per-pupil spending as reported to the Organisation for Economic Cooperation and Development (OECD) and on test scores from the Program for International Student Assessment

(PISA). According to figure 3.6, the United States appears to be about the second-highest-spending (not the highest, and not the most of "any society in human history") among the nations included, but a handful are in the same vicinity.[19] A trendline (the straight, steep line) drawn by hand to track the relationship between spending and test scores can show that the United States falls well off that line, spending well more than expected given its reading scores. In effect, however, this hand-drawn trendline ignores countries like Austria and Luxembourg, which are higher-spending and lower-performing (than the US) countries. But a trendline (straight or curved) fit to the data shows that the United States falls much closer to or even on that line representing the average outcomes given current spending.

Much like the long-term trend claim, when this achievement claim is coupled with graphs or references to data, it is invariably based on two imprecise and questionably accurate measures: national per-pupil expenditures as reported to the OECD and PISA outcomes. Also like the long-term trend, this claim should be evaluated by applying rigorous and thorough efficiency

FIGURE 3.6   International spending and reading scale scores

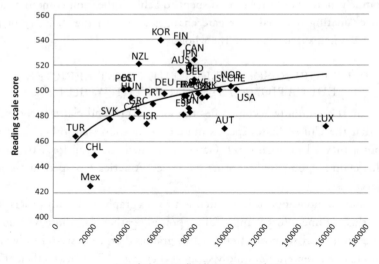

Cumulative spending between 6 and 15 years

Source: "Socio-Economic Indicators and the Relationship with Performance in Reading," in *PISA 2009 Results: What Students Know and Can Do* (Paris: OECD, 2010), http://dx.doi.org/10.1787/9789264091450-table76-en.

analysis, where the unit of analysis is "country." And multiple countries have to be compared and evaluated. But equating the relevant measures and contexts is tricky, to say the least.

If we want to make a legitimate comparison of the relative efficiency of national education systems, we have to begin by accurately and consistently measuring the financial inputs to those systems. Doing so requires first defining the scope of services and intended outcomes. What programs and services are being provided, and at what expense, toward achieving the outcome goals in question? We must, for example, be able to parse whether costs associated with employee health benefits and pensions are part of the education system expense (reported per-pupil spending), paid for by some other entity (national health-care system), or passed along to individuals. The case is similar for extracurricular activities (Are arts and sports included in school programs, or other community programs?), related health services for children with disabilities, and transportation. OECD per-pupil expenditure figures do not even attempt to achieve comparability in this regard.

Further, we must have a reasonable metric for adjusting the value of the education dollar for regional/international cost differences of recruiting and retaining comparably qualified personnel. In a 2016 policy brief, Mark Weber and I explained that, despite seemingly high expenditures, teacher wages in the United States are relatively noncompetitive (compared to nonteachers) when compared with other OECD nations.[20] Further, US class sizes at the primary level are relatively average and at the lower secondary (upper elementary/middle) level are relatively large. Even the amount we are spending in the United States is not sufficient to pay for real resources (teacher wages and quantities) comparable to those in other nations.

Once we get the financial input measurement right, we still have a long way to go toward making a valid efficiency comparison across nations. We must consider a plethora of exogenous factors that may further affect the value of the education dollar in the provision of programs and services, like economies of scale and population density. We must also consider differences in the student populations for which we're striving for constant outcomes or which we're measuring on a common instrument.

Figure 3.7 shows the relationship between a measure of relative poverty and PISA outcomes, indicating that the proportion of children in families having less than half the median income is correlated negatively with those scores. Relative poverty explains over 36 percent of the variation in national

FIGURE 3.7 Relative poverty and PISA

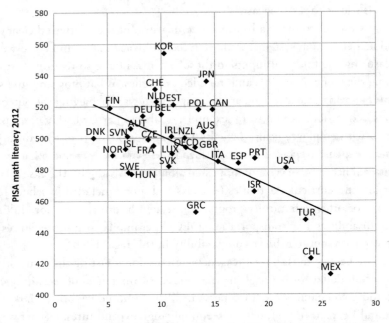

Share of children in families with less than 50 percent median income

Sources: http://nces.ed.gov/pubs2014/2014024_tables.pdf (table M4);provisional data from OECD income distribution and poverty database, www.oecd.org/els/social/inequality.

average PISA scores. More directly comparable and thorough measures of socioeconomic status are required for valid efficiency modeling. In addition, thorough efficiency comparisons require information on student disability status and language that are not consistently reported across nations. These are basic requirements for comparing relative efficiency of schools or districts within the same US metropolitan area or state; no less is expected when comparing Shanghai to France.[21]

On the flaws of international efficiency comparisons, Weber and I concluded that the OECD per-pupil spending measure, as incomparable as it is, shows that the United States may have higher per-pupil spending than many nations but that it falls right in line with expectations for nations of similar gross domestic product (GDP) per capita. We also found that the US is both a high-spending and a high-GDP country, but some of that high education spending may be a function of the scope of services and expenses included under the education umbrella. We also know that despite seemingly high spending levels in the US, teachers' wages are lower than they are in other professions, and the wage lag is not a result of providing relatively smaller class sizes. In fact, primary (ages 5–12) class sizes are average, and lower secondary (ages 12–16) class sizes are large. Our wage lag is, to an extent, a function of high nonteaching wages (related to our high GDP per capita), necessarily making it more expensive to recruit and retain a high-quality teacher workforce.

The United States is faced with a combination of seemingly high education expense (but noncompetitive compensation for its teachers, given large class sizes) and a high rate of child poverty. Again, it's hard to conceive how such a combination would render the US comparable in raw test scores to low-poverty nations like Korea and Finland or to small, segregated, homogeneous places like Singapore and Shanghai.[22] It is important to understand the magnitude and heterogeneity of the US education system in the context of OECD comparisons, which mainly involve more centralized and much smaller education systems. Lower-poverty, higher-spending states that have been included in international comparisons, like Connecticut and Massachusetts, do quite well, while lower-spending, higher-poverty states like Florida do not. This unsurprising finding tells us little about relative efficiency and doesn't provide much policy guidance for how we might make Florida more like Massachusetts.

DID NEW JERSEY AND KANSAS CITY PROVE THAT MONEY DOESN'T MATTER?

As an academic researcher in school finance, I have had the fortune of spending my career in the Kansas suburbs of Kansas City, Missouri, and in New Jersey, both of which are the most frequently cited illustrations for two key talking points: *courts should stay out of education reform* and *money is not the solution to educational shortcomings.*[23] Such arguments were built largely on two reports from the Cato Institute, a think tank favoring limited government and reduced spending on public education.[24] At the time of the publication of the Cato studies in the late 1990s, federal courts were beginning to back away from oversight in desegregation litigation, but state courts were becoming increasingly involved in managing school finance remedies.[25] The reports used the Kansas City Missouri School District (KCMSD), the site of a desegregation remedy, and the state of New Jersey, the site of a school finance case, as examples of why judicial interventions can never work, why they lead only to massive increases in spending with no positive effects.

These reports have become something approaching urban legend within school finance discussions, and they commonly resurface at opportune moments.[26] For example, in a Hoover Institution commentary regarding school funding litigation in New York State, Eric Hanushek noted that "one need only look at the results in Kansas City. A school desegregation ruling in the 1980s began a period of more than a decade when the schools had access to virtually unlimited state funds. The dreams of school personnel did not translate into any measurable gains in student performance, even as their schools moved to the very top of national spending."[27] And Hanushek and Al Lindseth make this same claim on multiple occasions in their book *Schoolhouses, Courthouses, and Statehouses*: "Perhaps the most dramatic test of whether spending more money leads to higher achievement occurred in the Kansas City, Missouri, school district from the mid-1980s to the mid-1990s." They cite (at least seven times) the Cato policy paper by Paul Ciotti—"As Paul Ciotti summed up the Kansas City debacle: 'The results were dismal. Test scores did not rise; the black-white gap did not diminish; and there was less, not greater, integration.'"[28]

The problems with the Cato manifesto on Kansas City are too numerous to fully critique here, but three points in particular underscore the weakness of the argument. First, Cato grossly overstates the amount spent in Kansas City, claiming it was more money per pupil than any of the other 280 largest districts in the country and that this funding persisted for more than a decade. Preston Green and I found, however, that "the KCMSD was a very high spending district for no more than five years, or the time in which one cohort of children is able to progress through five grade levels in the district. Further, when adjusted for student needs, the KCMSD's funding dropped below the metropolitan area average by 1998. This is hardly enough time to erase the generational poverty of the KCMSD or alter the residential structure and demographics of a school district that had been designed to be racially segregated until the 1960s."[29]

Second, much of the money was spent on a capital improvement plan involving the development of an interdistrict magnet program to achieve greater integration. The federal judge overseeing desegregation of the city's schools chose this path because of the constraints of prior desegregation litigation (*Milliken v. Bradley*). Specifically, the judge could not order suburban districts to participate in the solution, so instead he ordered them to adopt a policy of "desegregative attractiveness" to encourage suburban children to enroll in Kansas City schools. While the efficiency of this strategy can be criticized, it arose from constraints placed on desegregation orders. Thus, it is inappropriate to infer that this strategy, imposed under these constraints, provides proof that money doesn't matter for improving schools through state legislation, whether in response to court order or not. In fact, research on similar desegregative interdistrict magnet programs kept in place for longer durations has revealed positive effects on student outcomes.[30]

Third, the authors of the Cato Institute report based their assertions that Kansas City was a failed experiment on anecdotal descriptions of Kansas City alone, decrying the massive spending and poor outcomes but offering no counterfactual evidence against which to compare Kansas City and with no accounting for the multitude of factors that may have affected the efficacy of interventions or cost of improving student outcomes. In the years following the short-lived spending increase, after spending had stabilized, Preston Green and I found "regarding productive or cost efficiency, with specific emphasis on the Missouri Assessment Program, [that] the KCMSD is neither the most, nor the least efficient district in the immediate metropolitan area, no less the entire state."[31]

Frequent characterizations of New Jersey are no more valid. Hanushek and Lindseth relied on another *Cato Journal* article as a basis for their book's contentions about the failures of New Jersey school finance reforms: "One of the most comprehensive early studies . . . found 'no evidence of a positive effect of expenditures in New Jersey public high schools in urban districts with smaller per capita tax bases.'"[32] But the statistical analyses in the Cato report were particularly weak, relatively dated, and misaligned with the timing of the most significant New Jersey school finance reforms, which did not begin until 1998.[33] The authors examined data from three school years, 1988–89, 1992–93, and 1994–95, and emphasized high school outcomes (state exam and SAT scores) from 1994 to 1995.

In testimony, Hanushek has referenced a series of graphs (e.g., figure 3.8) that show New Jersey NAEP scores supposedly growing at a rate no greater than national averages, despite spending (supposedly, since no documentation provided) growing much faster due to judicial orders.[34] This is a New

FIGURE 3.8 Hanushek's testimony "proving" court-ordered spending yielded no gains in New Jersey

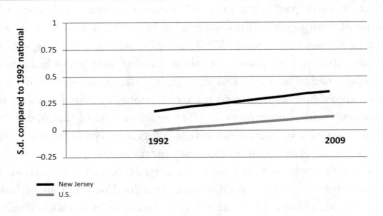

Source: Eric Hanushek, "Testimony in the Case of *Gannon v. Kansas* (Def. Exhibit #3), March 1, 2012," 35.

Jersey version of a graph presented to support the long-term trend argument. For starters, the vertical axis extends to a full standard deviation of test score change (an impossible feat to achieve on NAEP), with the visual effect of squashing the upward slope of both lines and making them look about the same.

In discussing this graph, and similar graphs of other test scores for other grades and subjects, Hanushek concluded that "the dramatic spending increases called for by the courts . . . have had little to no impacts on achievement. Compared to the rest of the nation, performance in New Jersey has not increased across most grades and racial groups . . . These results suggest caution in considering the ability of courts to improve educational outcomes."[35] He made similar claims in court cases challenging school spending equity and adequacy in Connecticut and New York State in 2014.[36] However, Hanushek's more rigorous analyses of state achievement growth rates on national assessments from 1992 to 2011 found that "the other seven states that rank among the top-10 improvers, all of which outpaced the United States as a whole, are Massachusetts, Louisiana, South Carolina, New Jersey, Kentucky, Arkansas, and Virginia."[37] Further, in that same report he noted that New Jersey has seen particularly strong growth in reducing the number of the lowest-performing students (those scoring at the "below basic" level), especially for eighth-grade math. In other words, Hanushek's own research provides perhaps the best refutation of his claims.

DOES HOW MONEY IS SPENT MATTER MORE THAN HOW MUCH IS SPENT?

Regarding New York State school finance litigation, Hanushek stated that "virtually all analysts now realize that how money is spent is much more important than how much is spent."[38] While the assertion that "how money is spent is important" is certainly valid, we cannot reasonably make the leap to assert that how money is spent is necessarily more important than how much money is available.[39] Yes, how money is spent matters, but if you don't have it, you can't spend it. Consider, for example, the trade-off between spending to pay teachers more competitive salaries to improve teacher quality versus spending to provide smaller class sizes. In many cases, schools and districts serving high-need student populations are faced with both noncompetitive salaries and larger class sizes, as compared to more advantaged surrounding districts.[40] Trading one for the other is not an option, or, in the best case, is a very constrained choice. It is unhelpful at best for public policy and is harmful to the children subjected to those policies to pretend without any compelling evidence that somewhere there exists a far cheaper way to achieve the same or better outcomes, and so we can cut our way down that more efficient path.

A common false-choice argument is that good teachers matter more than more money. In this view, we simply need good teachers and recruitment and retention (and dismissal) policies to achieve this goal, regardless of money. This argument falsely assumes that there is no connection whatsoever between the amount of available funding for salaries and benefits and the ability of schools and districts to recruit and retain a high-quality workforce. The level of teacher wages matters in at least two ways. First, among schools and districts in any given region, the salary a district can pay to a teacher with specific credentials affects which teachers that district can recruit and retain. So do working conditions, one of which is the total number of students for whom the teacher will be responsible and another is the student populations to be served. Schools in high-poverty neighborhoods need not only comparable wages to recruit and retain comparable teachers, but they need substantively higher wages. And second, the level of teacher salaries more generally, compared with other employment options requiring similar education levels, affects the quality of entrants into the teacher workforce. While the use of funds matters, and resources can surely be squandered inefficiently, the level of expenditures remains critically important for supporting sufficient numbers of high-quality teachers and other school staff.

STUDENT BACKGROUND MATTERS MUCH MORE THAN MONEY (SO WHY BOTHER?)

The argument that student background matters more than money originated in interpretations of the Coleman Report, which provided the first thorough, statistical documentation of the relationship between student and family background factors and student outcomes. Given the limitations of the data and methods available when the report was released in 1966, it makes sense that the study found few correlations between measured schooling resources and student outcomes. It was also a matter of expectations; many likely expected or even wished to see a stronger role for schools and resources in moderating disparities among children. After all, the study coincided with legislation that created the first substantial federal infusion of funding to support high-poverty schools: Title I of the Elementary and Secondary Education Act.

Because student backgrounds vary, because students are so unevenly sorted across schools, and because backgrounds and sorting lead to disparate outcomes, we must do everything we can to leverage resources to mitigate these disparities. For without equitable and adequate resources, there's little chance of achieving equal educational opportunity.

LESSONS LEARNED AND LOOKING FORWARD

There remain many questions about the most effective ways to leverage school funding to achieve desired outcomes. There are those who continue to opine in the public square and the courtroom that school finance reform—giving additional funding to districts serving high-need student populations—is neither the most effective nor the most efficient path toward improving schooling equity or adequacy.[41] But empirical evidence to support claims of more efficient alternatives remains elusive.

No rigorous empirical study validates the claim that increased funding for schools in general, or targeted to specific populations, has led to any substantive, measured reduction in student outcomes or other "harm." Arguably, if this were the case, it would open new doors to school finance litigation against states that choose to increase funding to schools. Twenty years ago, economist Richard Murnane summarized the issue exceptionally well: "In my view, it is simply indefensible to use the results of quantitative studies of the relationship between school resources and student achievement as a basis for concluding that additional funds cannot help public school districts. Equally disturbing is the claim that the removal of funds . . . typically does no harm."[42] This is as relevant today as it was then. The sources of doubt on the "does money matter" question are not credible.

While there remains much to debate, discuss, and empirically evaluate regarding the returns to each additional dollar spent in schools—and the strategies for improving educational efficiency, equity, and adequacy—we must be willing to cast aside the most inane arguments and sources of evidence on either side of the debate. Specifically, the following five sources of evidence no longer have a legitimate place in the debate over state school finance policy and whether and how money matters in K–12 education:

- vote counts of correlational studies between spending and outcomes without regard for rigor of the analyses and quality of the data on which they depend;
- the long-term trend argument that shows long-term spending going up and NAEP scores staying flat;
- international comparisons asserting that the United States spends more than other developed countries but achieves less on international assessments;
- anecdotal assertions that states like New Jersey and cities like Kansas City provide proof that massive infusions of funding have proven ineffective at improving student outcomes; and
- the assertion that how money is spent is much more important than how much is available.

Vote count tallies without study quality and rigor are of little use for understanding whether and discerning how money matters in schooling. The long-term trend argument is perhaps the most reiterated of all arguments that money doesn't matter, but it is built largely on deceptive, oversimplified, and largely wrong characterizations (accompanied by distorted visuals) of the long-term trends in student outcomes and school spending. Facile international comparisons are equally deceitful in that they fail to account for differences in student populations served and the related scope of educational and related services provided. They also fail to appropriately equate educational spending across nations, including the failure to account for the range of services and operating costs covered under "educational expense" in the United States versus other countries.

Finally, while the assertion that "how money is spent is important" is certainly valid, we cannot reasonably make the leap to assert that how money is spent is necessarily more important than how much money is available. Again, how money is spent matters; but if you don't have it, you can't spend it. As a panel of judges in Kansas noted so eloquently: "Simply, school opportunities do not repeat themselves and when the opportunity for a formal education passes, then for most, it is most likely gone. We all know that the struggle for an income very often—too often—overcomes the time needed to prepare intellectually for a better one. If the position advanced here is the State's full position, it is experimenting with our children which have no recourse from a failure of the experiment."[43]

CHAPTER 4

HOW SCHOOLS
USE MONEY

Elementary and secondary schooling, regardless of sector—public, publicly authorized and financed charter, or private—is a human resource–intensive industry. Quality schooling requires sufficient numbers of sufficiently trained teachers, support staff, administrators, and others to get the job done. There must be sufficient numbers of teachers and support staff to provide reasonable class sizes, relevant programs, and services. And teachers and support staff must be compensated competitively, with respect to other career options, to encourage our best and brightest to pursue careers in education.

The share of school spending allotted to salaries and benefits of employees has been remarkably stable from 1993 to 2015, at about 81 percent (figure 4.1). And while the share allocated to employee benefits has climbed (by about 6 percent), it has been offset by a commensurate decline in the share allocated to salaries and wages.

Substantially reducing the cost of education would thus require finding some way to change the delivery of education, thereby reducing the heavy reliance on human resources. In the broadest sense, *technological innovation for improving productivity and efficiency* refers to any change in the way things are done—the organization and deployment of staff, delivery of programs, use of materials, supplies, etc.—by the introduction of some new technology. It can be as simple as pens and pencils replacing slate tablets. The idea is that the introduction of new technology and any resulting change in the way things get done lead to improved efficiency—a lower cost to get the same outcomes or even better outcomes for the same cost. An extension of this concept, *disruptive innovation* refers to major shifts in the way things are done. Critics of public education systems assert that disruptive innovation is needed to completely overhaul our stagnant, costly, inefficient, and failing system.

FIGURE 4.1 Long-term trends on salaries and benefits as percentage of current spending

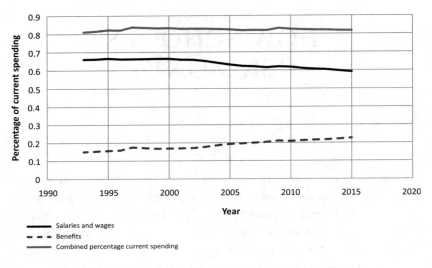

Source: Baker et al., *School Funding Fairness Data System.*

Modern edupreneurs and disrupters take a narrow view of technological substitution and innovation, equating technology almost exclusively with laptop and tablet computers as potential replacements for teachers, whether in the form of online schooling in its entirety or on a course-by-course basis ("unbundled schooling").[1] Fully online charter schools have expanded in many states and often operate as for-profit entities.[2] For example, the touted Rocketship model (named for a chain of charter schools) makes extensive use of "learning lab" time, in which groups of fifty to seventy or more students work on laptops under the supervision of uncertified "instructional lab specialists."[3] The overarching theme is that there must be some way to reduce the dependence on human resources to provide equal or better schooling, because human resources are an ongoing inefficient expense.

Arguments in favor of technological innovations and the potential they have to solve educational efficiencies sometimes verge on the absurd. For instance, in 2011, on the invitation of New York State Commissioner of Education John King, Marguerite Roza, a school finance advocate, presented the "Productivity Curve" graphic (figure 4.2) at a Board of Regents research symposium.[4] She used this graph to assert that, for example, for $20,000 per

FIGURE 4.2 Productivity curve illustration

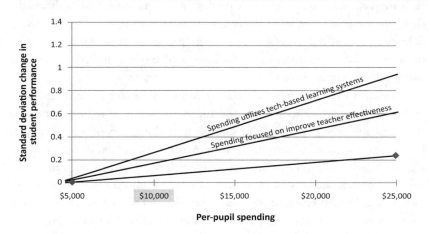

Source: Marguerite Roza presentation to New York Board of Regents, September 13, 2011, http://www.p12.nysed.gov/mgtserv/docs/School FinanceForHighAchievement.pdf.

pupil, tech-based learning systems could provide nearly four times the bang for the buck as the status quo and twice the bang for the buck as investing in improved teacher effectiveness. The most significant shortcoming of this graph, however, is that it's entirely speculative.[5] It was not based on any actual empirical evidence that such affects could be or have anywhere been achieved; it lacks any definition as to what "tech-based learning systems" or "improve teacher effectiveness" mean; and it provides no information on the expenditures or costs that might be associated with either the status quo or the proposed innovations. Despite these obvious shortcomings, Commissioner King used it in his presentations to district superintendents throughout the state.

So far, however, efforts to "disrupt" conventional schooling by replacing teachers with technology show little promise. In a comprehensive review of literature on the state of charter schooling in the United States, including online charter schooling, Dennis Epple, Richard Romano, and Ron Zimmer paint a rather ugly picture of the outcomes achieved by fully online "cyber" charter schools, noting that they "appear to be a failed innovation, delivering markedly poorer achievement outcomes than TPSs [traditional public schools]."[6] Perhaps we haven't figured out how to most effectively and efficiently deploy mass substitution of human resources with computing technology. Or maybe such mass substitution simply isn't productive. It's notable, and problematic, that expansion of these alternatives has not been accompanied by serious efficiency or cost-effectiveness analysis. Or it's possible that the outcome reductions measured are consistent with the associated expenditure reductions, that we're really doing less with less.

Successful and resource-rich schools, regardless of sector, continue to rely on human resource–intensive models and strategies of schooling. It may be that these resource-rich institutions simply have the luxury of operating inefficiently, investing excessively in their human resources (and elaborate facilities) with little budgetary pressure to seek efficient substitutes or to innovate. Yet, a 2017 meta-analysis of 101 studies of interventions for low-income children found human resource intensive strategies to be particularly effective.[7] And another 2017 study found that recession-era reductions in staffing were associated with negative achievement effects concentrated on low-income children in high-poverty schools.[8] Similar results have yet to be realized for investments in "tech-based solutions."

THE BASIC MODEL: FROM REVENUE SOURCES TO CLASSROOM RESOURCES

The model linking available revenue, schooling resources, and, ultimately, student outcomes remains relatively simple. Setting aside federal revenue (about 10 percent of revenue on average), figure 4.3 illustrates that the amount of revenue state and local education systems tend to have, on average, is a function of both fiscal capacity and fiscal effort. Some states put forth more effort than others, and some states have greater capacity to raise revenue. These varied capacities lead to vast differences in school funding across states and, consequently, to vast differences in classroom resources. And federal aid is far from sufficient to close these gaps. Similarly, within some states, local districts have widely varied capacities to raise revenue for their schools, and some differences in revenue also result from disparities in local effort. States' efforts to close these gaps vary.

Whether at the state level, on average, or at the local level, the revenue available dictates directly the amount of money that can be spent. Current operating expenditures are balanced primarily between the quantity of staff employed, often reflected in pupil-to-teacher ratios or class sizes, and the compensation of those employees, including salaries and benefits. Therein lies

FIGURE 4.3   The flow of revenue to expenditures to real resources

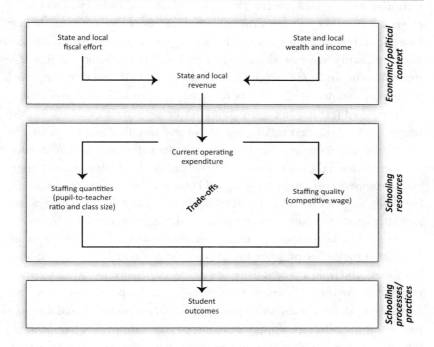

the primary trade-off in school district planning and budgeting. One could trade teachers for computers, but most schools do not, and those that do have not produced impressive results. With any given budget constraint, staffing numbers can be increased at the expense of wages, or vice versa. Whatever approach, the combination of the two must be sufficient to achieve desired outcomes. These revenue to expenditure flows matter in terms of equity, adequacy, and productivity and efficiency.

From an equity perspective, if revenue sources remain unequal, leading to unequal expenditures, those inequities will also lead to unequal staffing ratios and/or wages and, as a result, unequal school quality and outcomes. The argument that schools and districts with less money simply need to use it better (figure out how to hire better teachers in each position with lower total payroll) is an inequitable requirement. This argument is loosely based on the popular book and film *Moneyball*, which told the story of the (short-lived) success of the Oakland Athletics when management applied new metrics in recruiting undervalued players. The A's mined data on a variety of metrics of player contributions to team wins to identify cheaper players who might help take the team to the postseason. This strategy was necessitated by the vast payroll disparity in major league ball, as indicated in the book's subtitle: *The Art of Winning an Unfair Game*. It's up to the league to decide whether greater parity across teams—and thus a fairer game—is preferable (and profitable).

Public education, however, shouldn't be an unfair game. Resource-strapped school districts serving higher-poverty neighborhoods shouldn't be asked to be more creative with their resources than affluent suburban districts a few miles down the road are with theirs. Further, developing creative strategies to compete on an unfair playing field may reap some short-term rewards, but doing so never makes the game truly fair, and as others catch on to the new strategies, any short-term competitive advantage is negated.

From an adequacy perspective, sufficient funding is a necessary condition for hiring sufficient quantities of qualified personnel to achieve desired outcomes. And from a productivity and efficiency perspective, while we know that human resource–intensive strategies tend to be productive, as yet we have little evidence of substantial gains in efficiency from tech-based solutions that result in reduction of human resources. After all, resource-constrained schools and districts that already have large class sizes and noncompetitive wages are unable to trade one for the other. Put simply: if you don't have it, you can't spend it.

VARIATIONS IN REVENUE AND CLASSROOM RESOURCES ACROSS STATES

Across states, average state and local revenue are partly a function of differences in "effort" and "capacity."[9] Figure 4.4 shows the relationship across states in 2015 between the capacity measure, the GDPs and total state and local revenue per pupil. Differences in state GDPs explain about 42 percent of the differences in state and local revenue. Higher-capacity states like Massachusetts, Connecticut, New York, Wyoming, and Alaska tend to raise more revenue for schools. Vermont stands out as a state where capacity is below the median but revenue is very high. And Mississippi is a state with very low capacity and very low revenue.

Figure 4.5 shows the relationship between a common measure of effort and state and local revenue. The effort measure is the ratio of state and local

FIGURE 4.4   State GDP and revenue

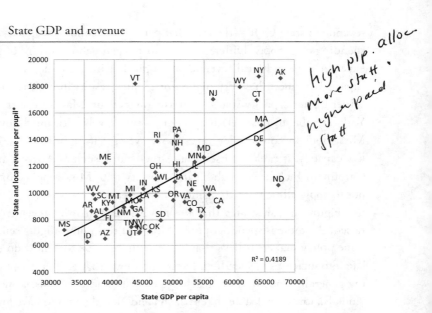

Note: *Per-pupil revenue projected for districts with more than 2,000 pupils, average population density, average labor costs, and 20 percent of children in poverty.

Source: Baker et al., *School Funding Fairness Data System*.

FIGURE 4.5   Fiscal effort and revenue

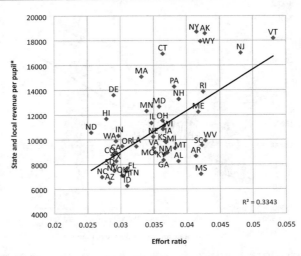

Note: *Per-pupil revenue projected for districts with more than 2,000 pupils, average population density, average labor costs, and 20 percent of children in poverty.

Source: Baker et al., *School Funding Fairness Data System*.

revenue to state GDP—that is, what percent of economic capacity are states spending on schools? Differences in effort explain about a third of the differences in state and local revenue per pupil. For instance, despite having low capacity, Vermont has very high effort, which results in high revenue levels. Other higher-capacity states, such as Connecticut, Massachusetts, and New York, are able to raise relatively high revenue levels with much lower effort. Mississippi, by contrast, leverages above-average effort, but because of its very low capacity, it can't dig itself out. Other states, such as Arizona and North Carolina, which have much greater capacity than Mississippi, simply choose not to apply effort toward raising school revenue.

Figure 4.6 illustrates that the more state and local revenue per pupil raised, the more is spent per pupil. Although this point might seem obvious, some policy makers believe that increases in revenue somehow do not translate into increases in spending. Figure 4.7 shows that greater per-pupil spending generally leads to more teachers per one hundred pupils. Low spending (and also low effort) states like Arizona and Nevada tend to have low staffing ratios compared to other states. Figure 4.8 shows that states spending more per pupil, on average, tend to have more competitive teacher wages. Here the

FIGURE 4.6 Revenue and spending

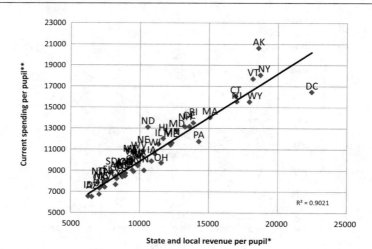

Notes: *Per-pupil revenue projected for districts with more than 2,000 pupils, average population density, average labor costs, and 20 percent of children in poverty. **Current spending per pupil projected for districts with more than 2,000 pupils, average population density, average labor costs, and 20 percent of children in poverty.

Source: Baker et al., School Funding Fairness Data System.

If want
to increase
personnel
pay less
+ opposite
true
fewer positions
More A

FIGURE 4.7 Spending and staffing ratios

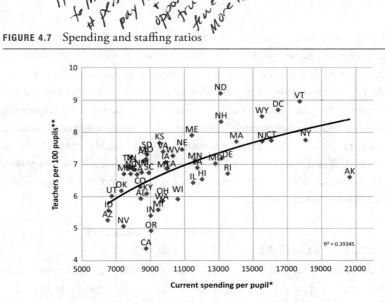

Notes: *Current spending per pupil projected for districts with more than 2,000 pupils, average population density, average labor costs, and 20 percent of children in poverty. **Teachers per 100 pupils projected for districts with more than 2,000 pupils, average population density, average labor costs, and 20 percent of children in poverty.

Source: Baker et al., *School Funding Fairness Data System*.

FIGURE 4.8 Spending and teacher salary competitiveness

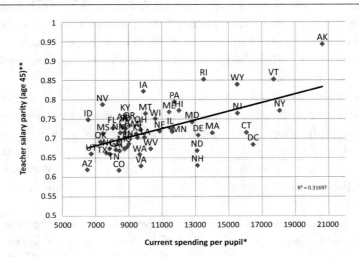

Notes: *Current spending per pupil projected for districts with more than 2,000 pupils, average population density, average labor costs, and 20 percent of children in poverty. **Teachers per 100 pupils projected for districts with more than 2,000 pupils, average population density, average labor costs, and 20 percent of children in poverty.

Source: Baker et al., *School Funding Fairness Data System*.

indicator of competitive wages is the ratio of salaries of elementary and secondary teachers to same-age, similarly educated nonteachers in the same labor market in each state. As indicated by decades of teacher labor market research, the relative competitiveness of teacher wages influences the quality of candidates who enter the profession.[10] Teacher compensation is especially poor in states like Arizona, which has among the lowest per-pupil spending in the nation. By contrast, teacher compensation is highly competitive in Vermont and Wyoming, both higher-spending states but also states where nonteacher compensation is not particularly high, as compared to New York, New Jersey, and Connecticut.

DISTRICT SPENDING TRANSLATES
TO REAL SCHOOL RESOURCES

Similar disparities play out at the local level, especially in those states that have done the least to resolve disparities between rich and poor districts. Year after year, "Is School Funding Fair?" identifies Illinois and Pennsylvania as among the most disparate states in the nation.[11] Specifically, in these states districts serving high-poverty student populations continue to have far fewer resources per pupil than do their more advantaged counterparts. Illinois serves as a good example of the relationship among district-level spending variation, school-site spending variation, and on-the-ground resources, including staffing assignments per pupil. If a district has sufficient revenue, that revenue can be used to support the schools in that district, leading to more and better paid teachers. And if a district does not have the resources, neither will its schools.

Over the past decade, federal policy (and the think tanks that inform it) have placed disproportionate emphasis on the need to resolve inequities in spending (particularly staffing expenditures) across schools within districts while ignoring inequities in spending between districts. Especially in highly inequitable states like Illinois, resolving between-school inequities in poorly funded school districts is akin to rearranging deck chairs on the *Costa Concordia*.[12]

Figure 4.9 shows the relationship between district-level operating expenditures per pupil and school site staffing expense per pupil for the Chicago metropolitan area in 2012. Only a few districts have large numbers of schools across which resources might vary (circle size indicates school enrollment). Chicago schools appear at approximately the $15,000 per-pupil point

FIGURE 4.9   School staffing and district operating spending 2015

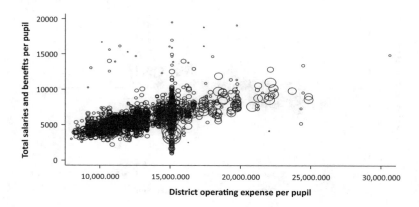

Sources: https://www.isbe.net/Pages/Operating-Expense-Per-Pupil.aspx; http://www.isbe.net/Pages/Educator-Employment-Information.aspx.

on the horizontal axis as a vertical pattern of circles. While there appears to be substantial variation in resources across schools, about half of that variation is a function of differences in student populations (special education in particular) and grade ranges served. On average, schools in districts that spend more per pupil overall also spend more per pupil at the school level on staffing. Forty-four percent of the variation in staffing expenditure across schools is driven by spending differences across districts, and about half of the remaining differences in staffing expenditure across schools are driven by the distribution of special education populations across schools and district targeting of staff to serve those children.[13] That is, much of the within-district variation that does exist makes sense: resources that flow to districts pay for staff that work in schools. If the district has more revenue coming in, it can spend more, and that spending shows up in the form of more and better paid teachers in schools. While Chicago is able to allocate more resources to some schools serving more children with disabilities, it does not have the resources, on average, districtwide to fund all of its schools adequately or equitably in comparison with more affluent surrounding suburban districts.

Figure 4.10 shows how, in the Chicago metropolitan area, differences in district-level operating expenditures lead to differences in competitive wages for teachers. Here, competitiveness of wages is measured in terms of the salaries

FIGURE 4.10 School salary competitiveness and district operating spending 2015

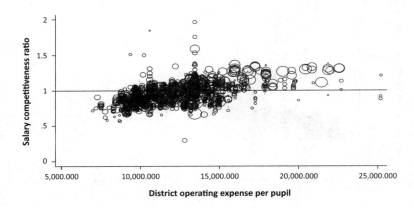

Sources: https://www.isbe.net/Pages/Operating-Expense-Per-Pupil.aspx; https://www.isbe.net/Pages/Educator-Employment-Information.aspx.

of teachers with specific numbers of years of experience and degree levels (contract hours and days per year, grade level taught, and job assignment) as compared to their peers in other schools in the Chicago metro area. Salary differentials may influence teacher sorting across schools and districts. Teachers in low spending districts tend to have salaries that are about 75 percent of the average teacher with similar credentials in a similar assignment. Teachers in high spending districts tend to have salaries that are roughly 25 percent higher than the average teacher in a similar position and with similar credentials.

Table 4.1 summarizes features of Illinois school districts, with advantaged districts identified as having high spending and high outcomes and the more disadvantaged as having low spending and low outcomes.[14] To identify advantaged and disadvantaged school districts, I adjusted spending for the costs of providing equal educational opportunity to all students. To arrive at equal opportunity adjustments, I applied a cost modeling method that estimates the differences in costs of achieving common outcome goals for children with varied educational needs and backgrounds, sorted across different school settings. In short, it costs more to achieve common outcomes in higher-poverty settings, in settings serving more children who are English language learners and more children with disabilities, in areas with higher labor costs, or in small districts lacking economies of scale.

TABLE 4.1   Advantaged and disadvantaged school districts in Illinois

	HIGH SPENDING/HIGH OUTCOME			LOW SPENDING/LOW OUTCOME		
	Elementary	Secondary	Unified	Elementary	Secondary	Unified
Districts	146	41	82	120	25	156
Enrollment						
2001	266,760	133,075	219,357	149,963	45,518	835,814
2009	261,869	150,754	251,432	148,739	51,790	813,820
Operating expenditure per pupil	$10,881	$14,215	$10,054	$9,175	$11,780	$10,505
Adjusted operating expenditure per pupil	$13,123	$13,681	$11,208	$7,485	$7,880	$7,290
Low income	15%	14%	13%	64%	57%	68%
Staff assignments per 1,000 pupils						
2001	76.66	76.01	71.76	70.31	73.50	68.56
2009	85.81	79.38	79.07	78.59	72.21	70.70
Relative teacher salaries				−$7,000	−$7,511	−$220

Note: Based on regression model, where salary = f (experience, degree level, assignment, contract months, core based statistical area, spending/outcome category, year) and including only full-time certified staff.

Source: Baker, "Unpacking the Consequences of Disparities in School District Financial Inputs."

I included in my analysis 146 high spending/high outcome elementary districts serving more than 250,000 children and 120 low spending/low outcome elementary districts serving about 150,000 children; 41 high spending/high outcome secondary districts serving up to 150,000 children and 25 low spending/low outcome secondary districts serving about 50,000 children; and 82 high spending/high outcome unified districts serving 250,000 children and 156 low spending/low outcomes districts serving more than 800,000 children, with about half of those children attending Chicago Public Schools. Even without any adjustment for costs or needs, the average per-pupil operating expenditures are lower in low spending/low outcome districts. The percentage of children who are low income is substantially higher in low spending/low outcome districts. Table 4.1 shows that the district operating expenditure advantages of the high spending/high outcome district schools translate directly to more staff per pupil and better paid staff per pupil. In 2009, high spending schools had 86 and 79 teacher assignments per 1,000 pupils in elementary and secondary schools, respectively, compared to 79 and 72 for low spending schools. Further, for teachers with similar training and experience in similar assignments, teachers in low spending schools were paid

$7,000–$7,500 less. Schools in financially advantaged districts had both more staff per pupil and were able to pay them more, and they served far less needy student populations.

DO CHARTER AND PRIVATE SCHOOLS USE THEIR RESOURCES DIFFERENTLY?

A common critique of traditional public schools is that, as bureaucratic public institutions operating under collective bargaining agreements with politically powerful labor unions, they are beholden to those unions and therefore inefficiently allocate resources toward increasing numbers of unionized staff and into salaries and benefits for those staff (typically favoring quantity over quality). And lacking any market competition, there is no need to seek more efficient alternatives. Charter schools, by contrast, are not beholden to all of the same bureaucratic structures and obligations and are subject to market competition. As such, the argument goes, if there are innovations out there that really can change the way schooling gets done, they'll emerge in the charter sector. And since private schools get the majority of their revenue from tuition-paying parent-consumers, they must be particularly responsive to local and regional competitive market pressures.

While modern charter schooling was conceived by some as a way to spur innovation—try new things, evaluate them, and inform the larger system—studies of the structure and practices of charter schooling find the sector as a whole not to be particularly "innovative."[15] Analyses by charter advocates at the American Enterprise Institute have found that the dominant form of specialized charter school is the "no-excuses model," which combines traditional curriculum and direct instruction with strict disciplinary policies and school uniforms, and in some cases extended school days and years.[16] Further, charter schools that raise substantial additional revenue through private giving tend to use that funding to provide smaller classes and pay teachers higher salaries for working longer school days and years.[17] But for those charters that have less and spend less, total costs are held down, when necessary, by employing relatively inexperienced, low-wage staff and dealing with high staff turnover rates.[18] In other words, the most common innovations arising from charter schooling are not especially innovative or informative around systemic, structural reform and provide few, if any, insights into scalable, more efficient resource use.

Studies of charter school effectiveness show vast differences across charter school operators (CMOs), or management companies, and across cities and regions. Charter schools in New York City have often demonstrated strong, positive results, as have major, established CMOs like the Knowledge Is Power Program (KIPP).[19] But a close look at high-profile charters in New York City indicates that their success reflects their access to additional resources and a fairly traditional approach to leveraging them.[20] Figure 4.11 compares the demographics of major charter school operators in New York City to those of district schools serving the same grade ranges in the same borough of the city. For each of these major operators, including KIPP schools, the share of low-income (those who qualified for free or reduced-price lunch), English language learners (ELLs), and children with disabilities is lower than for district schools, in some cases quite substantially. On average, these schools are serving far less needy and thus less costly student populations than are the district schools. Figure 4.12 shows the relative spending of these schools when compared with district schools in the same borough of New York City serving the same grade levels and similar students and with schools of similar size. Charter schools tend to be smaller and, because they lack economies of scale,

FIGURE 4.11   Student populations in New York City charter schools

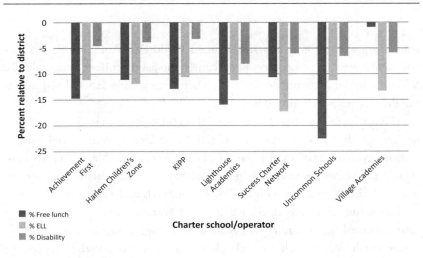

Source: Baker et al., "Charter School Expansion and Within-District Equity."

FIGURE 4.12   Per-pupil spending in New York City charter schools

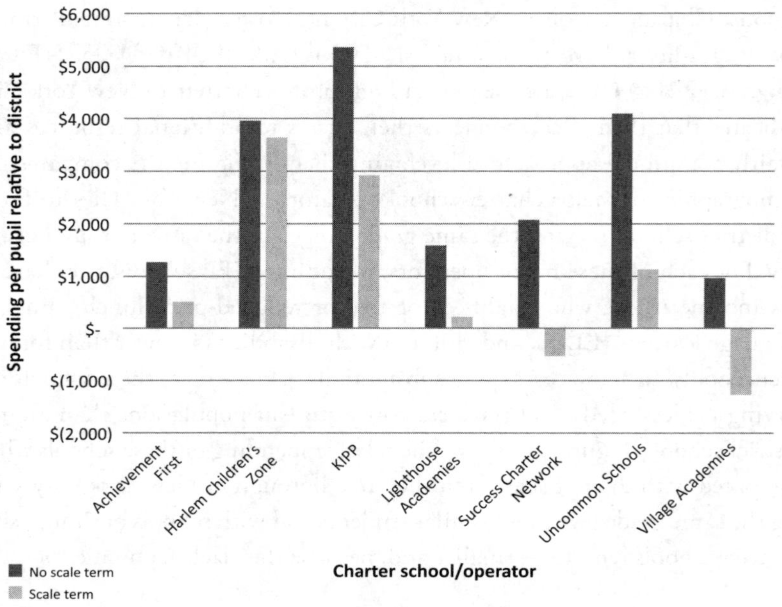

Source: Baker et al., "Charter School Expansion and Within-District Equity."

thus operate at a higher expense. Harlem Children's Zone, KIPP, and Uncommon Schools, for instance, significantly outspend similar district schools. Success Charter Network does as well, when setting aside scale-related spending differences, which might be considered inefficient.

Figure 4.13 shows that the additional spending relative to district schools (at least in Harlem Children's Zone, KIPP, and Uncommon Schools) translates into consistently smaller class sizes than in comparable district schools. Figure 4.14 shows the relative wages of teachers in these schools compared to wages of district teachers with similar degree levels and experience. Teachers in the charter schools tend to have far fewer average years of experience and thus lower average salaries. This is because of higher turnover rates among young teachers in the charter schools and also because, at the time of the study, many of the schools were only five to ten years old. The dark bars show the relative annual salary difference, and the lighter bars show the salary.

FIGURE 4.13   Class sizes in New York City charter schools

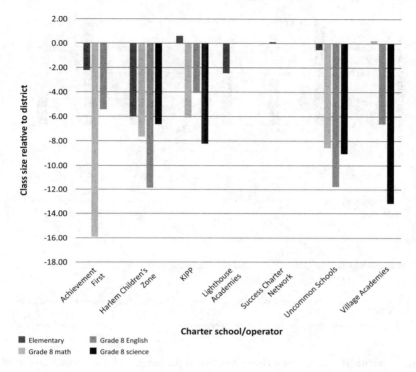

Sources: New York State Education Department, School Report Cards (Class Size); Baker et al., "Charter School Expansion and Within-District Equity."

The table shows that teachers in Achievement First and Uncommon Schools are paid substantially higher annual salaries than similar teachers in district schools; yet, a share of that difference is due to the longer school year. While the margins of difference are smaller for Harlem Children's Zone and KIPP schools, the patterns are similar. There exists a substantial annual salary differential, but nearly all of that salary differential is attributed to additional contracted months.

Collectively, these figures tell a story of high-profile, well-funded CMOs in New York City leveraging their additional resources in three logical and rather traditional ways: by hiring more staff per pupil in order to provide smaller class sizes; by paying their teachers more at any given level of experience and degree;

FIGURE 4.14   Relative salaries in New York City charter schools

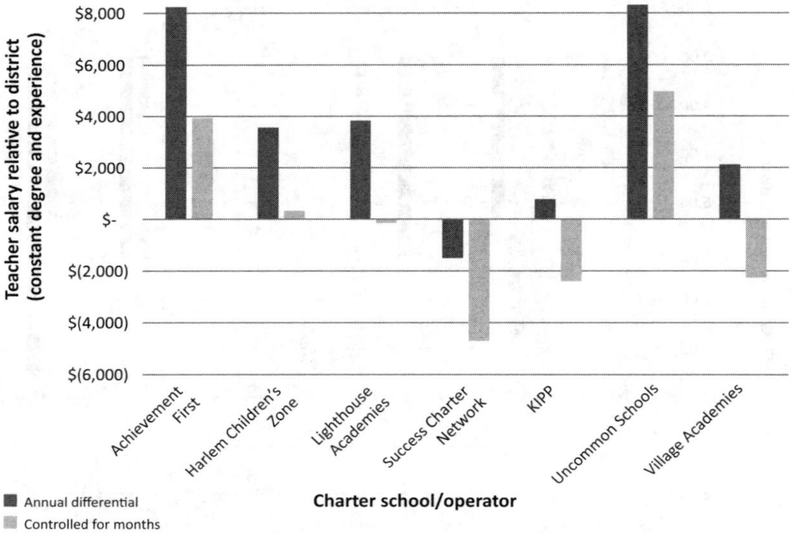

Sources: New York City Public Schools, Personnel Master File (Teacher Salary Data); Baker et al., "Charter School Expansion and Within-District Equity."

and, specifically, by paying them more to work longer school hours, days, and years. In other words, they pay more people for more time.

STUDIES OF CHARTER SCHOOL RESOURCE ALLOCATION

The New York City examples are somewhat unique, however. Not every city or state has these well-endowed high-flying charter operators, or the local philanthropies to support them. For example, Ohio charter schools are much less well-off, and Texas charter operators are a mixed bag.[21] Further, with these examples, I do not mean to imply that charter schools allocate dollars to human resources in exactly the same way as district schools do. Rather, the point here is that charter schools that have the resources and flexibility to make trade-offs often choose to spend money on logical things, such as competitive wages, more hours, and smaller classes.

Studies of resource allocation in charter schools have found some systematic differences between charter school and traditional district schools' spending, though they are hardly a result of technological innovation or creative resource substitution. In most cases, observed resource allocation differences are the result of structural constraints like operating at inefficient scale, with inadequate access to capital for acquisition and renovation of facilities, or simply being new and having larger numbers of new, young, and lower-paid employees.

Two studies of Michigan charter schools, which are fiscally independent of local public districts, found them to have particularly high administrative expenses and low direct instructional expenses. David Arsen and Yongmei Ni found that "controlling for factors that could affect resource allocation patterns between school types . . . charter schools on average spend $774 more per pupil per year on administration and $1,141 less on instruction than traditional public schools" and that "charter schools managed by EMOs spend significantly more on administration than self-managed charters (about $312 per pupil). This higher spending occurs in administrative functions traditionally performed at both the district central office and school building levels."[22]

A study by Oded Izraeli and Kevin Murphy found that from 1995–96 to 2005–06, district-operated schools in Michigan spent more on instruction per student than did charter schools, and the gap grew by about 5 percent to nearly 35 percent over the period studied. The spending gap for instructional spending was greater than the gap for general spending: the overall funding gap between district and charter schools was approximately $230; the spending gap for basic programs was $562 and for total instruction $910. The study's authors noted, "Much like a profit-maximizing firm, charter schools generate a surplus of revenue over expenditure."[23] Robert Bifulco and Randall Reback explored the complex relationship between fiscally dependent charter schools and their host districts in upstate New York cities. They found that having charter schools which are financial dependents of local districts ("fiscally dependent" or receiving revenue and administrative support as pass through from district hosts) but separately affiliated with outside management companies and governance structures can create excess and redundant costs.[24]

Others have explored teacher compensation in relation to instructional expense in charter schools. In their review of charter school research, Epple and colleagues conclude that, "on the whole, teachers in charter schools are less experienced, are less credentialed, are less white, and have fewer advanced degrees . . . They are paid less, their jobs are less secure, and they turnover [sic] with higher frequency."[25] Similarly, in a report on Texas charter schools' spending behavior, Taylor and colleagues explain that much of the difference between instructional and noninstructional expense across different types of charter and district schools is tied to differences in teacher compensation:

> Open-enrollment charter schools paid lower salaries, on average, than did traditional public school districts. Average teacher pay was 12% lower for teachers in open-enrollment charter schools than for teachers in traditional public school districts of comparable size, and adjusted for differences in local wage levels, average teacher pay was 24% lower. Average teacher salaries were lower not only because open-enrollment charter schools hired less experienced teachers, on average, but also because open-enrollment charter schools paid a smaller premium for additional years of teacher experience.[26]

Using two sources of Texas school expenditure data, table 4.2 provides an example of the very different approaches of two CMOs, KIPP and Harmony.[27] Specifically, the table contrasts the revenue and expenditures of charter schools relying primarily on revenue enhancement versus those relying on expenditure cutting to free up resources for "other" uses, presumably including innovation. KIPP's primary approach to supporting its various additional costs is one of revenue enhancement, whereas Harmony's is one of salary expense reduction.[28]

Publicly subsidized revenue in Texas's charter schools and urban districts are relatively consistent. Nonetheless, KIPP schools in Texas in 2013, on average, increased their operating expenses by nearly 20 percent. And while major urban district schools, other charter schools, and Harmony schools spent around $8,500 per pupil, KIPP schools reported spending $10,280—a conservative figure that likely misses some additional spending by the CMO's regional and national organizations on its Texas schools. Despite the higher revenue, table 4.2 shows that KIPP's instructional spending was second lowest among Texas charters. Harmony's was lowest: even though in comparison to urban district schools and other charters its total operating expense was lower, Harmony still spent a smaller percentage on instruction. KIPP's total payroll per pupil remained higher than Harmony's. Despite having the highest total operating expense, KIPP schools diverted the largest shares of its budget to central and school leadership activities. And while Harmony's central administrative expenses were lower than "other" charter schools as a share of operating expense, its "plant services" expenses were noticeably

TABLE 4.2   Characteristics of urban district and charter school operators in Texas

	Major urban district	Other charter	KIPP	Harmony
Students	967,480	140,646	12,220	24,616
Operating total	$8,429	$8,648	$10,280	$8,359
Instruction	$4,943	$4,470	$4,300	$4,118
Percent of operating				
Instruction	58.74%	52.55%	41.87%	50.15%
Central administration	5.07%	13.34%	14.85%	8.34%
School leadership	5.96%	8.07%	11.47%	10.19%
Plant services	10.97%	14.06%	13.60%	19.04%
Other	19.29%	11.99%	18.27%	12.31%
FAST TEXAS data by object				
Operating total	$8,349	$8,578	$10,161	$7,242
Payroll per pupil	$6,804	$5,314	$6,018	$4,139
Other operating	$1,682	$3,293	$4,191	$3,103
FAST TEXAS percent				
Payroll	63.70%	58.81%	55.44%	53.17%
FAST TEXAS workforce attributes				
% Teacher turnover rate	14.35	34.61	35.83	40.75
% 1 to 5 Years	25.30	43.75	57.88	58.13
Margin (relative to average charter)				
Instructional expense (based on snapshot)				$4,929,225
Salary expense (based on FAST TEXAS)				$10,059,091

Sources: Data from http://ritter.tea.state.tx.us;perfeport/snapshot/download.html; http://www.fastexas.org/results/downloads.php#district.

higher, approaching 20 percent of its operating expenses. Again, while these operating expenses are notably different both among charter operators and between charter operators and district schools, it is difficult to attribute these differences to disruptive innovation or technological substitution. In particular, KIPP, the more researched of the two CMOs, has maintained expenditure on personnel but shifted emphasis toward administrative personnel (school leadership).

ARE PRIVATE SCHOOLS DIFFERENT?

One difficulty in making private school–public school comparisons is that private schools, having fewer regulations, vary widely and vary regionally.

Also, there is much less evidence on private school spending, resource allocation, and teacher compensation, and charters' financial reporting is sparse, inconsistent, and decentralized. Like charters, private schools vary by their operator type. While many private school studies view schools only in terms of Catholic schools, other religious denomination schools, and nonreligious schools, these distinctions are not sufficiently fine grained.

In a 2009 study I collected IRS financial filings of 1,500 private schools nationally, combining those data with national surveys of private school teachers, school enrollments, and pupil-to-teacher ratios.[29] Table 4.3 summarizes the comparisons with public schools of major private schools by their primary affiliation. Catholic schools (parish elementary and middle schools and diocesan secondary schools), for example, had very low nominal tuition prices, but their per-pupil spending was much higher than their tuition, at $10,135, comparable to nearby district schools (metro area). Catholic schools had lower teacher salaries for similar teachers but comparable staffing ratios. At the bottom end were low tuition and relatively low spending schools belonging to dominant Christian schools associations. These lower spending schools managed to maintain reasonable staffing ratios, but with low salaries. At the other end of the spectrum were those schools belonging to the major independent schools associations (National Association of Independent Schools and regional affiliates, National Independent Private Schools Association), which include the most elite (and expensive) private independent day schools.[30] These were the schools for which the most comprehensive fiscal data were available. Tuition rates for these schools were nearly 50 percent higher than nearby public district's per-pupil spending, and per-pupil spending was nearly double nearby public district per-pupil spending. Institutions such as these have the opportunity to leverage resources creatively.

As table 4.3 shows, more elite private independent schools tend to spend their resource advantage primarily on dramatically reducing pupil-to-teacher ratios (<10:1 compared to nearly 17:1 for nearby district schools). While annual salaries for otherwise comparable teachers are somewhat lower for private independent school teachers, they are higher than for "other" private school teachers. Further, elite private independent schools tend to have shorter school years (by ten or more days) compared to district schools, and independent school teachers have much lower total student loads (number of students taught per day, week, or year) than their public district counterparts. Again, the financial resources translate to human resources, with some insightful

TABLE 4.3   Spending, salaries, and outcomes for private schools by affiliation

Affiliation	Tuition[a] nominal	Expend per pupil[b] nominal (CWI adjusted)	Teacher salary diff.[c] (rel. to public schools)	Pupil/Teacher All Prv. Sch. Surv.[d] (IRS 990 Data 2007)	% Teachers High/Most Selective Undergraduate Colleges[e]	Outcome differential— NAEP scale score relative to public schools (Lubienski & Lubienski, 2006) 4th/8th
Independent	$14,910	$20,131 ($14,940)	–$2,914	9.87 (9.02)	34.36%	NA
Hebrew	$9,622	$17,008 ($12,149)	–$9,162	10.14 (8.52)	24.14%	NA
Public	NA	$10,140 ($8,402)	Comparison Group	16.83	8.17%	Comparison Group
Catholic	$4,363	$10,135 ($7,743)	–$14,400	16.59 (13.52)	8.53%	–7.2/–3.8
Christian Association Schools (CAS)	$4,016	$7,118 ($5,727)	–$14,652	13.53 (13.30)	3.42%	–11.9/–10.6

Notes: [a]Average highest tuition charged by private schools in states included in this study [original document], not adjusted for regional cost variation, based on Schools and Staffing Survey (variable = TUITIN) of 2003–04. [b]Public expenditures based on Census Fiscal Survey 2005–06, weighted for student enrollment and including public school districts in states included in the present study [original document]. Nominal expenditures (not regionally adjusted) expressed outside of parentheses, and adjusted expenditures reported inside parentheses. Private school expenditures based on IRS 990 data set described in this report [original document]. [c]Relative teacher salary based on wage regression of public and private school teachers in the NCES Schools and Staffing Survey of 2003–04, as explained in the attached report [in original document]. Dollar values represent the amount over/under public school teacher salaries at same degree, experience, and location. [d]Based on pupil-to-teacher ratios for public school districts in states included in this study [original document], where public school pupil-to-teacher ratios are generated by dividing total teachers reported in the NCES Common Core of Data 2006–07 by total enrollments and where private school pupil-to-teacher ratios are drawn from the NCES Private School Survey variable indicating pupil-to-teacher ratio. Public and private ratios may not be directly comparable, but private school ratios are comparable across affiliations. [e]Based on competitiveness ratings from Barron's *Guide to the Most Competitive Colleges*, applied to undergraduate institutions attended by teachers in the 2003–04 NCES Schools and Staffing Survey.

Source: Baker, *Private Schooling in the US.*

differences in the trade-offs between staffing quantities and salaries and intertwined factors like numbers of students and courses taught.

One notable disruptive innovation of elite private schooling that continues to drive the human resource intensive model at the secondary level was the introduction in 1930 of Harkness tables—large oval tables that can seat fourteen (some up to eighteen). These tables, with their accompanying philosophy of encouraging student and faculty interaction, were gifted by wealthy philanthropist Edward Harkness to the elite New Hampshire boarding school Phillips Exeter Academy.[31] Harkness tables persist to this day as central to the teaching and learning philosophy of many elite private independent schools. But they are also a testament to the preference for a human resource–intensive model of schooling involving small interactive classes staffed with highly qualified academic instructors. To the extent that these schools also have the flexibility to introduce what modern edupreneurs might consider disruptive technologies (tablets and hand-held devices, cloud-based computing, interactive video, white boards, etc.), these schools are more likely to take a both-and rather than either-or path—that is, iPads around the Harkness table rather than in place of it.

LESSONS LEARNED AND LOOKING FORWARD

On average, the financial resources available to schools, whether public district, charter, or private, are generally spent on human resources. Financial resources determine the quantities of staff that can be hired or retained and the wages that can be paid—both of which matter.

All schools require sufficient resources to provide high-quality educational services and produce high outcomes. Understanding the baseline conditions and relationships of financing schools is necessary for moving forward.

- Schooling—whether traditional public, charter, or private—is resource intensive.
- When schools have more money, they invest it in more staff and wbetter pay for the staff.

As noted in this chapter, charter schools often divert resources from direct instruction and personnel not to achieve greater flexibility and adopt disruptive technologies, but because they lack economies of scale, and they also often lack access to capital needed to access necessary land and buildings.[32] My work on private schools has revealed significantly higher administrative expenses than for public schools partly due to scale differences, but also due to the choice to pay top administrators much higher salaries than superintendents of larger public districts earn.[33] Public systems enjoy the scale efficiencies that mitigate administrative and other overhead expenses, including construction, maintenance, and operations of capital.

Finally, despite much talk of creative, alternative, performance-based compensation for teachers, my related work on charter and private schools finds that the primary determinants of differences in pay across teachers are their years of experience, the degrees and credentials they hold, and the amount of time they are expected to work and students they are expected to serve.[34] Compensation for staffing across sectors remains largely a function of years of experience, credentials earned, and contractual hours worked.

This is how schools currently work in the United States (and around the world, for that matter). This isn't necessarily the way it should be or how it will always be. This is how schools use money, whether large public bureaucracies, publicly subsidized private operators, or fully independent private operators. Researchers, policy makers, pundits, pontificators, and even self-proclaimed thought leaders have yet to conjure some new "secret sauce" or technological innovation that will greatly improve equity, adequacy, and efficiency. Human resources matter, and equitable and adequate financial resources are necessary for hiring and retaining the teachers and other school staff necessary to achieve equal educational opportunity for all children.

CHAPTER 5

SCHOOL FINANCE REFORMS AND RESULTS

Research intended to advance policy must be designed appropriately to evaluate past policies or experimental alternatives. Rather than asking, by contemporaneous correlation, whether student background matters more than money, we should ask, given differences in student background, how money (and the resources that flow from it) can be leveraged to mitigate disparities resulting from student backgrounds. This chapter looks at some of the myths and misdirects of state school finance reform before moving on to review high-quality empirical research evaluating the influence of substantive and sustained reforms on short-term and long-run student outcomes, as well as research on the specific schooling resources that seem to matter.

It is important to continue to tighten our research designs around questions of *when, whether,* and *who.* In reviewing studies on the effects of past reforms, we should scrutinize closely whether studies sufficiently measure when and to what extent reforms are implemented and sustained. That's the *when* question, and it's a dynamic one. School finance reform doesn't just happen as a simple before-and-after condition. We also must scrutinize whether studies identify with sufficient precision the population affected by the reforms and the counterfactual population not affected. That's the *who* question. Though this may seem obvious, we must closely scrutinize *whether* substantive reform actually happened by measuring and tracking sufficiently precise indicators of the reforms. Finally, it's critically important to consider the translation of research findings into policy implications—that is, how empirical finding and research conclusion should influence policies moving forward.

STUDYING THE EFFECTS
OF SCHOOL FINANCE REFORMS

In 2011, Kevin Welner and I published a critique of the many attempts to discredit school finance reforms, including an appraisal of judicial intervention.[1] Recall that much of the debate over whether money matters and whether school finance reform can make a difference has occurred in the context of state courts, in front of judges faced with the difficult decision of whether or not to order the state legislature to remedy inequities or inadequacies in school funding. As such, much attention has been placed on court rulings and orders as first steps, or initiation points, in school finance reform.

In order to sufficiently inform policy advocates and policy makers, empirical studies need to make these connections, from (a) the filing of litigation challenging a state school finance system and the nature and source (who) of that filing; to (b) the resulting court ruling, if any, and substance of that ruling; to (c) whether any substantive and sustained legislative action followed the order; and (d) to what outcomes, short term and longer term, came of those reforms (figure 5.1). It's not useful to know whether the mere presence of a court order is associated with differences in or even changes to student outcomes without also knowing what happened as a result of the court order. It's important to know the conditions that led to the legal challenge, who brought the challenge, what claims were made and validated, and, if a court order was issued, what violations were identified and what the scope was of the reforms ordered. (Some judicial orders in state school finance cases are very limited in scope, such as ordering that the state improve equalization aid for capital outlay funds.)

Importantly, some of the most substantive state school finance reforms have not involved a court order at all or have involved a court order that isn't logged as an official ruling (e.g., *Mock v. Kansas*).[2] Understanding that some substantive reforms occur in the absence of court orders is important when conducting studies that assume states without such orders to be a nonreform comparison group, or counterfactual. Executive/Legislative response is critical, whether responding to judicial order or legislative action in the absence of a judicial order. Were there substantive policy changes measurable via indicators of "equity" and "adequacy" of financial inputs to schooling? Over what period did those changes scale up? Did they eventually scale down? Were the changes both substantive and sustained? Such questions help determine whether we can or should expect any improvements to student outcomes and

FIGURE 5.1   Evaluating school finance reforms

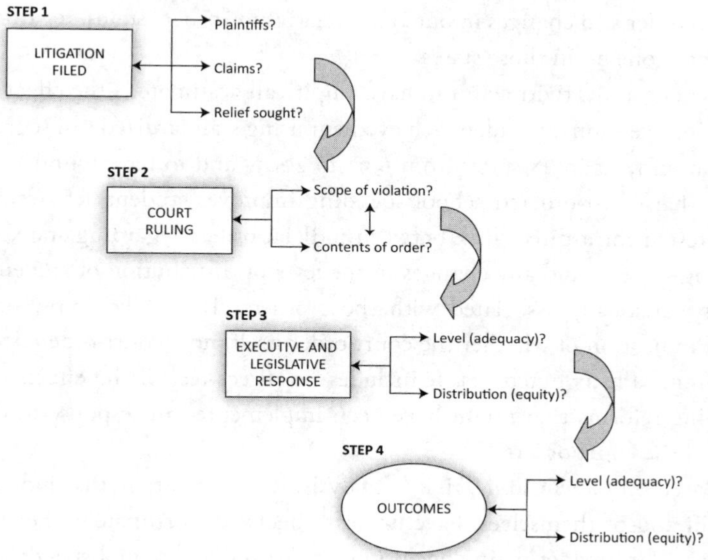

Source: Adapted from Baker and Welner, "School Finance and Courts."

school quality. If funding becomes more equitable one year or over three years and then reverts to its original state within the next five, the duration of treatment is relatively short, affecting only a few years of any one cohort of children's schooling. So while there may be measurable effects, they may be smaller than needed.

Jay Greene and Julie Trivitt provide one especially problematic example of a cross-state study that tests only the link between the occurrence of a judicial ruling on school funding and changes in student outcomes from before to after that occurrence. The authors find no association between judicial orders and outcome measures, thus concluding that court-ordered spending increases have no effect.[3] Specifically, they set up a statistical test of the relationship between the existence and type of court ruling issued in each state and student outcome measures for each state, without regard for whether substantive reforms followed the court ruling. Their models do not incorporate any measures of the actual reform legislation, or even indicate whether any reforms happened. Accordingly, the resulting empirical analysis addresses only whether there exists a direct link between the occurrence and type of a judicial order and changes in outcomes relative to "other" states, regardless of what has gone on in those states.

Greene and Trivitt claim to have empirically estimated "the effect of judicial intervention on student achievement using standardized test scores and graduation rates in 48 states from 1992 to 2005" and to have found "no evidence that court-ordered school spending improves student achievement."[4] They tested for a direct link between judicial orders regarding state school funding systems and any changes in the level or distribution of student outcomes statistically associated with those orders. The study simply offers a rough indication of whether the court order itself, not "court-ordered school spending," affects outcomes. It includes no direct test of the effects of any spending reforms that might have been implemented in response to one or more of the court orders.

Based on Greene and Trivitt's analysis, it's fair to argue that judicial orders, in and of themselves, have unclear effects. Unfortunately, the authors leapt to a far broader main conclusion: "court-ordered school spending" has no effect. Given that their analysis never measured "spending," this conclusion is unwarranted.

RECENT NATIONAL STUDIES
OF SCHOOL FINANCE REFORMS

New data, and increased availability of longer-term longitudinal data on both school district finances and student outcomes, have enabled a new wave of large-scale national analyses of the influence of state school finance reforms on student outcomes. There's been a recent flurry of new, rigorous national longitudinal studies testing relationships between school finance reform and student outcomes. To now, few rigorous large-scale attempts were made to link school finance reform to changes in the level and distribution of student outcomes. The most notable of the earlier studies was by David Card and Abigail Payne, who found "evidence that equalization of spending levels leads to a narrowing of test score outcomes across family background groups."[5]

Access to increased longitudinal data on both local district-level school finances and student outcomes has enabled this new wave of research.[6] A study by Kirabo Jackson, Rucker Johnson, and Claudia Persico looks at the long-term effects on high school graduation rates and future adult income of substantial infusions of funding to local public school districts through school finance reforms of the 1970s and 1980s.[7] The authors used data from the Panel Study of Income Dynamics (PSID) on approximately 15,000 sample members born between 1955 and 1985, who have been followed into adulthood through 2011.[8] Their analysis rests on the assumption that these children, and specific subgroups among them, were differentially affected by the infusions of resources resulting from school finance reforms that occurred during their K–12 schooling: some children received substantive infusions of additional resources, sustained over time, while others did not.

One methodological shortcoming of this long-term analysis is the imperfect connection the authors make between the treatment and the population that received that treatment.[9] Jackson and colleagues matched childhood address data to school district boundaries to identify whether a child attended a district likely subject to additional funding as a result of court-mandated school finance reform. While imperfect, because the authors could not track exactly which students received which resources and for how long, this approach creates a tighter link between the treatment and the treated than exists in many prior national, longitudinal, and even state-specific school finance analyses.[10] The study does a better job of addressing the *who* question than previous studies have. It also more thoroughly tackles the *whether* question by tracking the extent of actual resource infusion and the *when* question by linking the relevant cohorts of children to the period of time resource changes occurred.

Jackson and colleagues note that "the estimated effect of a 22 percent increase in per-pupil spending throughout all 12 school-age years for low-income children is large enough to eliminate the education gap between children from low-income and non-poor families."[11] This investment led to a 20 percentage point increase in graduation rates and, on average, an additional year of educational attainment for these children. Even lower levels of investment made a sizable difference: "increasing per-pupil spending by 10 percent in all 12 school-age years increases the probability of high school graduation by 7 percentage points for all students, by roughly 10 percentage points for low-income children, and by 2.5 percentage points for non-poor children."[12] They also observed positive effects on adult wages (a 13 percent increase in hourly wages) and a substantial decrease in adult poverty rates resulting from this investment.[13]

A similar recent study by Julien Lafortune, Jesse Rothstein, and Diane Schanzenbach evaluates the influence of adequacy-oriented school funding reforms during the 1990s and 2000s. Using NAEP data, the authors find that "reforms cause gradual increases in the relative achievement of students in low-income school districts, consistent with the goal of improving educational opportunity for these students. The implied effect of school resources on educational achievement is large."[14] In another national longitudinal analysis, Mark Weber and I note that states with greater overall investment in education, resulting in more intensive staffing per pupil, tend to have higher outcomes for low-income children, higher performance in schools serving low-income children, and smaller disparities between schools serving low-income children and schools serving more advantaged populations.[15] Christopher Candelaria and Kenneth Shores have found that there is a strong relationship between state school finance reforms and graduation rates. Seven years after the reforms, the poorest districts showed an average 12 percent increase in per-pupil spending and increases in graduation rates of between six and twelve percentage points.[16]

Finally, Kenneth Shores and Matthew Steinberg conducted an analysis of the effects of recessionary spending cuts between 2009 and 2013 on short-run student achievement outcomes, combining data from national district-level school finance surveys with a unique collection of student-level, nationally normed state assessment scores.[17] They found that the recession "significantly reduced student math and ELA achievement. Moreover, the recessionary effect on student achievement was concentrated among school districts serving more economically disadvantaged and minority students, indicating that the adverse effects of the recession were not distributed equally among the population of U.S. students. We also find that the academic impact of the recession was more severe for students who were older at the time of first exposure to the recession, compared to their younger counterparts."[18] Other studies have yielded similar findings regarding the impact of recessionary cuts on student outcomes, providing compelling new evidence of the large-scale achievement and economic benefits of substantive and sustained additional funding for schools serving higher-poverty student populations and demonstrate that a reduction in funding can cause harm.[19]

STUDIES OF STATE SCHOOL FINANCE REFORMS

Over the years, several state-specific studies of school finance reforms have validated the positive influence of those reforms on a variety of student outcomes. Among the most studied states are Michigan and Massachusetts, which implemented significant reforms in the early-to-mid-1990s and maintained them for a decade or more.[20]

Massachusetts

Even the most vocal critics of school finance reform concede that Massachusetts may have struck the right balance between funding and accountability reform.[21] In 1993, following the *McDuffy v. Secretary of Education* lawsuit, the state adopted a package of far-reaching education reforms that included a new education funding formula under Chapter 70 of the state code.[22] Chapter 70 established a "foundation budget" for all districts, which calculates expenditures for each district in eleven functional categories (e.g., administration, teachers, pupil services, professional development), adjusted for wage costs and for the higher costs of students in poverty, ELLs, and those identified for special education. The annual budget also calculates how much each district can afford to contribute (based on local revenues) and creates a fund of state aid to fill gaps when local revenue proves inadequate to meet the foundation level.[23]

Figure 5.2 shows the changes in revenue by source for high- poverty school districts in Massachusetts since 1993. State aid per pupil scaled up dramatically from 1995 through 2000 and then climbed more slowly through

FIGURE 5.2 State and local revenue for high-poverty Massachusetts school districts

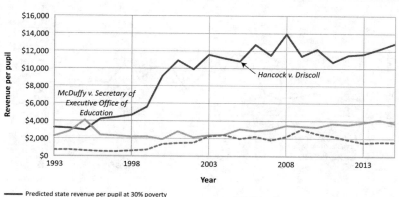

Source: Adapted from Baker and Welner, "School Finance and Courts."

2015. Figure 5.3 shows that these reforms had significant influence on the level and progressiveness of funding and staffing for Massachusetts school districts. That is, over the period when state aid to high-poverty schools was increased significantly, high-poverty districts received 40 percent more state and local revenue per pupil than low-poverty districts. This raised current spending and staffing ratios. Although the state still spends more on high-poverty than low-poverty districts, the degree of progressiveness has waned since 2008, as state aid has remained flat for high-poverty districts and local spending has increased for low-poverty districts.

Three studies of Massachusetts school finance reforms from the 1990s found positive effects on student performance. Thomas Downes, Jeffey Zabel, and Dana Ansel noted that the combination of funding and accountability reforms "has been successful in raising the achievement of students in the previously low-spending districts."[24] Jonathan Guryan found that increases in per-pupil spending led to significant improvement in overall mathematics, reading, science, and social studies test scores for students in grades 4 and 8.[25] And Phuong Nguyen-Hoang and John Yinger commented that "changes in the state education aid following the education reform resulted in significantly higher student performance."[26]

FIGURE 5.3   Progressiveness of funding in Massachusetts over time

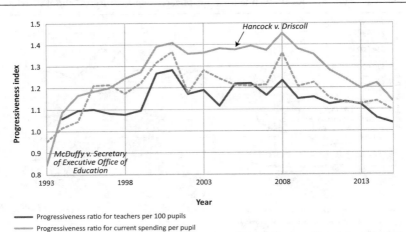

Source: Baker et al., *School Funding Fairness Data System.*

Michigan

In the early 1990s, Michigan eliminated the property tax as a source of school revenue and replaced it with state funds generated through the sales tax and a new tax earmarked for schools.[27] This plan, Proposal A, dramatically improved funding equity among school districts by creating a minimum per-pupil foundation allowance and by increasing funding for the low-revenue school districts, thereby reducing inequality in spending among rich and poor districts. Between 1993 and 2003, revenues and expenditures increased by 60 percent, and funds were more equitably distributed.

Studies of the 1990s-era reforms have shown positive effects on student performance in both the previously lowest-spending districts and lower-performing districts.[28] In her study, Latika Chaudhary concludes that "a 60% increase in spending increases the percent satisfactory score by one standard deviation. The positive impact of expenditures on test performance seems largely due to higher teacher salaries."[29] Specifically, she found that the infusion of new funding under Proposal A led primarily to increased teacher salaries and secondarily to reduced class sizes, and it was through these resource allocations that Michigan schools realized improved outcomes. These findings are entirely consistent with those of Jackson and colleagues in their national analysis, which reveal that funding increases tend to lead to increased staffing and more competitive compensation for teachers.[30]

Joydeep Roy found that Michigan's school finance reforms of the 1990s led to a significant increase among previously low-spending districts. Using analyses that measured both *whether* the policy resulted in changes in funding and *who* was affected, he concludes that Michigan's school finance plan "was quite successful in reducing interdistrict spending disparities. There was also a significant positive effect on student performance in the lowest-spending districts as measured in state tests."[31] Similarly, Leslie Papke notes that "increases in spending have nontrivial, statistically significant effects on math test pass rates, and the effects are largest for schools with initially poor performance."[32] Joshua Hyman also found positive effects of Michigan's school finance reforms but raises some concerns around their distribution. Much of the increase, he notes, was targeted at schools serving fewer low-income children. However, he did find that students exposed to "$1,000, or 12%, more spending per year during grades four through seven[,] experienced a 3.9 percentage point increase in the probability of enrolling in college, and a 2.5 percentage point increase in the probability of earning a degree."[33]

While these studies attempted to capture the effect of a disruptive reform like Proposal A, studies that came out of the conservative Michigan policy think tank Mackinac Center focused on the period 2007–13, when reforms were in retreat, and found no relationship between resources and student outcomes.[34] If the goal of policy makers moving forward is to implement a new, disruptive reform—one that alters both the level and distribution of school spending—the earlier studies on the effects of Proposal A are as relevant, if not more so, than a study over a period when no such reforms have been attempted.

Figure 5.4 shows the disruptive policy effect of Proposal A, which primarily involved a substitution of local property tax revenue with substantially increased state aid to schools, the effect of which was to marginally reduce overall disparity across Michigan districts. In particular, Proposal A leveled up revenues of low-property-wealth districts. The reform resulted in an initial stark change; but after about 2001, state aid began to taper off and local revenue increase. Figure 5.5 shows the mean and standard deviation of per-pupil

FIGURE 5.4 Michigan per-pupil revenue by source

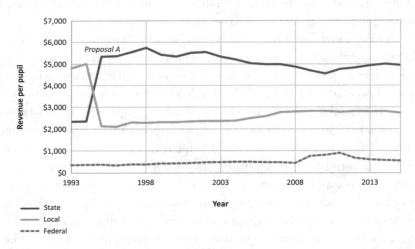

Note: State, local, and federal revenue is from the Census Fiscal Survey of Local Governments, adjusted for inflation and regional cost variation using the Education Comparable Wage Index (expressed in year 2000 dollars).

Sources: US Census Bureau, Fiscal Survey of Local Governments, Public School Finances, June 2017, http://www.census.gov/govs/school/; Education Comparable Wage Index, http://bush.tamu.edu/research/faculty/taylor_CWI/.

FIGURE 5.5   Spending equity in Michigan over time

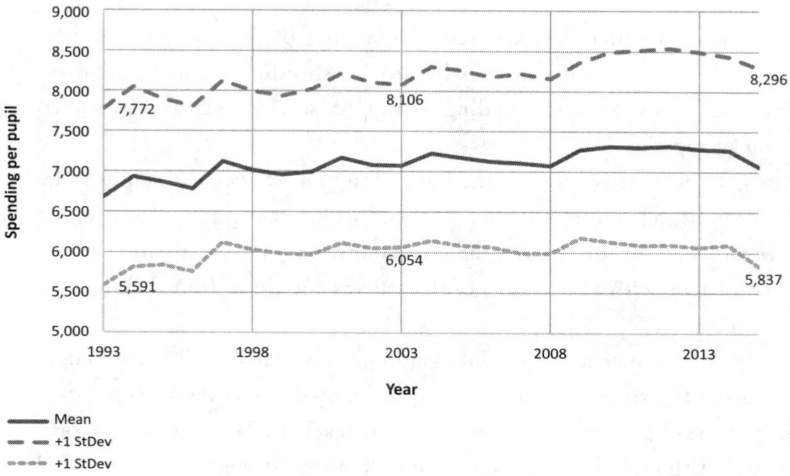

Note: Per-pupil spending is from the Census Fiscal Survey of Local Governments (PPCSTOT), adjusted for inflation and regional cost variation using the Education Comparable Wage Index (expressed in year 2000 dollars).

Sources: US Census Bureau, Fiscal Survey of Local Governments, Public School Finances, June 2017, http://www.census.gov/govs/school/; Education Comparable Wage Index, http://bush.tamu.edu/research/faculty/taylor_CWI.

spending across Michigan districts over time and thus offers a way of looking at resource equity. It reveals that differences between districts that were one standard deviation above and below the mean shrunk modestly from 1993 to 2003 and then reverted to their previous levels by 2013. So the period for which the Mackinac Center authors are studying the effect of funding is one in which disparity grew, in important contrast to the period studied by other researchers, which involved marginal reductions in disparities.

MORE TEACHERS, SMALLER CLASSES, AND BETTER PAY

Recent national studies have also shed light on the connections between financial inputs to school systems and real classroom resources. An important feature of the Jackson, Johnson, and Persico study is that it does explore the resultant shifts in specific schooling resources in response to shifts in funding. It finds that, for the most part, increased spending led to increases in typical schooling resources, including higher educator salaries, smaller classes, and longer school days and years. The authors explain some key points:

> "When a district increases school spending by $100 due to reforms, spending on capital increases by $10.60, spending on instruction increases by $66.80, and spending on support services increases by $40.80 on average."
>
> "The increases for instruction and support services (which includes expenditures to hire more teachers and/or increase teacher salary along with funds to hire more guidance counselors and social workers) are consistent with the large, positive effects for those from low-income families."
>
> "A 10% increase in school spending is associated with a 5.7% reduction in the student-teacher ratio (p-value < .01), 1.36 more school days (p-value < .01), and a 4% increase in base teacher salaries (p-value < .01)."
>
> "Although there may be other mechanisms through which increased school spending improves student outcomes, the results suggest that the positive effects are driven, at least in part, by some combination of reductions in class size, having more adults per student in schools, increases in instructional time, and increases in teacher salary that may have helped attract and retain a more highly qualified teaching workforce."[35]

In other words, traditional investments in schooling resources occurred as a result of court-imposed school finance reforms, and those changes in resources were likely responsible for the resultant long-term gains in student outcomes. Such findings are particularly consistent with recent summaries and updated analyses of data on class size reduction.

Kenneth Shores and Matthew Steinberg's study sheds light on the flip side—when funding decreases and staffing ratios increase and student outcomes suffer: "The recession's effects on student achievement were concentrated in districts with the largest reductions in teacher personnel, providing evidence that the effects we observe are driven, in part, by the recession's negative effects on school resources."[36] Further reinforcing the importance of human resources in schools, specifically high-intensity deployment of human resources, is a recent comprehensive meta-analysis of programs and strategies for improving outcomes for low-income children.[37] Examining 101 studies from the past fifteen years, the researchers found the largest effects on achievement were from interventions like tutoring, small-group instruction, and coaching or mentoring of children's teachers.

TEACHER QUALITY AND WAGES

The Coleman Report looked at a variety of specific schooling resource measures, most notably teacher characteristics, and found some positive relationships between these traits and student outcomes. A multitude of studies on the relationship between teacher characteristics and student outcomes has followed, producing mixed messages as to which characteristics matter most and by how much.[38] Inconsistent findings on the relationship between teacher "effectiveness" and how teachers get paid—by experience and education—have added fuel to the "money doesn't matter" fire. Since a large proportion of school spending necessarily goes to teacher compensation, and (according to this argument) since we're not paying teachers in a manner that reflects or incentivizes their productivity, then spending more money won't help.[39] The assertion is that money spent on the current system doesn't matter, but it could if the system were to change. Of course, in a sense, this is an argument that money *does* matter. But it also misses the important point about the role of experience and education in determining teachers' salaries and what that means for student outcomes.

While teacher salary schedules may determine pay differentials across teachers *within* districts, the simple fact is that *where* one teaches is also very important in determining how much the teacher makes.[40] Arguing over attributes that drive the raises in salary schedules also ignores the bigger question of whether paying teachers more in general might improve the quality of the workforce and, ultimately, student outcomes. Teacher pay is increasingly uncompetitive with salaries offered by other professions, and the gap between teachers and similarly educated nonteachers increases the longer they stay on the job.[41]

A substantial body of literature validates the conclusion that teachers' overall wages and relative wages affect the quality of those who choose to enter the profession, and whether they stay once they get in. For example, Richard Murnane and Randall Olsen found that salaries affect the decision to enter teaching and the duration of the teaching career.[42] David Figlio and Ronald Ferguson conclude that higher salaries are associated with more qualified teachers.[43] In addition, more recent studies have tackled the specific issues of relative pay noted previously. Susanna Loeb and Marianne Page show that "once we adjust for labor market factors, we estimate that raising teacher wages by 10 percent reduces high school dropout rates by 3 percent to 4 percent. Our findings suggest that previous studies have failed to produce robust estimates because they lack adequate controls for non-wage aspects of teaching and market differences in alternative occupational opportunities."[44] In short, while salaries are not the only factor involved, they do affect the quality of the teaching workforce, which in turn affects student outcomes. Research on evaluating spending constraints or reductions reveals the potential harm to teaching quality that comes from leveling down or reducing spending. For example, Figlio and Rueben note that "tax limits systematically reduce the average quality of education majors, as well as new public school teachers in states that have passed these limits."[45]

Teacher salaries also play a potentially important role in improving the *equity* of student outcomes. While several studies show that higher salaries relative to labor market norms can draw higher-quality candidates into the profession, the evidence also indicates that relative teacher salaries across schools and districts may influence the distribution of teaching quality. For example, Jan Ondrich, Emily Pas, and John Yinger find that "teachers in districts with higher salaries relative to non-teaching salaries in the same county are less likely to leave teaching and that a teacher is less likely to change districts when he or she teaches in a district near the top of the teacher salary distribution in that county."[46] Regarding teacher quality and school racial composition, Eric Hanushek, John Kain, and Steven Rivkin note that "a school with 10 percent more black students would require about 10 percent higher salaries in order to neutralize the increased probability of leaving."[47] Other studies, however, point to the limited capacity of salary differentials to counteract attrition by compensating for working conditions.[48]

In a perfect world, we could tie teacher pay directly to productivity, but contemporary efforts to do so—including performance bonuses based on student test results—have generally failed to produce concrete results in the United States.[49] And studies of individual and group financial incentives continue to find mixed to null effects, although alternative compensation models in some settings have yielded positive results.[50] Thomas Dee and James Wyckoff find some evidence that a comprehensive strategy combining teacher evaluation and financial incentives can yield marginal improvements to the average rate of student achievement growth among retained teachers.[51] Similarly, in a study of an Austin, Texas, pay-for-performance program, Ryan Balch and Matthew Springer find that the school district's "REACH program is associated with positive student test score gains in both math and reading during the initial year of implementation" and that test score gains "were maintained in the second year," though they found no "additional growth."[52] Aaron Sojourner and colleagues note: "Exploiting district variation in participation status and timing, we find evidence that [pay-for-performance]-centered [human resource management] reform raises students' achievement by 0.03 standard deviations."[53] In a more extreme application of financial incentives, characterized as "loss aversion," Roland Fryer and colleagues studied the effect of providing teachers' bonuses in advance and taking the money back if students did not improve sufficiently; this approach "yields math test score increases between 0.2 and 0.4 standard deviations. This effect is on par with the impact of increasing teacher quality by more than one standard deviation."[54]

Still missing in this literature, however, are cost-effectiveness comparisons of the alternatives. If we take the same total payroll dollars and allocate those dollars traditionally across teachers with incremental differences in salaries by experience and credentials held, as opposed to implementing those salaries and bonuses by the above alternatives (along with paying for the associated costs of the evaluation metrics used for allocating salaries), do we see differences in the production of student outcomes? Or, can comparable or better outcomes be achieved where the total costs of providing alternative compensation and producing measures for allocating *performance-based* compensation are equal to or less than current costs?

Assertions that performance-based pay is necessarily more cost-effective than traditional salary structures also falsely assume that traditional step-and-lane salary schedules are monolithic. In practice, salary differentials associated with experience and credentials vary widely. Some are compressed from top to bottom, while others are not, and they may favor experience over credentials, or vice versa. Matthew Hendricks explored these issues: "Increasing salaries for teachers with 3 or more years of experience differentially retains high-ability teachers, while higher salaries for teachers with 0–2 years of experience differentially retain low-ability teachers. This likely occurs because higher early-career salaries disrupt a positive sorting process that exists among novice teachers."[55] That is, one might restructure traditional salary schedules to achieve gains comparable to or greater than deeper structural

changes to compensation. Hendricks also found that changing salary structures may alter recruitment potential and the recruiting pool:

> Overall, a 1% increase in base salary for teachers of a particular expe-
> rience level increases the proportion of the targeted teachers hired by
> 0.04–0.08 percentage points. Pay increases have the largest effect on hire
> rates among teachers with 2–3 years of experience and the effect dimin-
> ishes with experience. I show that higher teacher salaries provide a dual
> benefit of retaining and attracting a more effective distribution of teach-
> ers. Districts may also improve student achievement growth at no cost
> by reshaping their salary schedules so that they are increasing and con-
> cave in teacher experience.[56]

In the wake of literature and policy rhetoric asserting the inefficiency of
paying teachers according to experience and credentials, some new studies
have surfaced which show that the gains in student outcomes resulting from
increased teacher experience may extend well beyond the first few years of
experience. Thus, it would not be entirely inefficient for salaries to continue
to scale upward with increased experience, especially given additional costs
of implementing alternative measures for determining salaries. Matthew
Wiswall notes that by "using an unrestricted experience model I find that for
mathematics achievement there are high returns to later career teaching experience, about twice as much dispersion in initial teacher quality as previously
estimated, and a pattern of negative selection where high quality teachers are
more likely to exit."[57] According to John Papay and Matthew Kraft, "Consistent with past research, we find that teachers experience rapid productivity
improvement early in their careers. However, we also find evidence of returns
to experience later in the career, indicating that teachers continue to build human capital beyond these first years."[58] And Helen Ladd and Lucy Sorensen
note: "Once we control statistically for the quality of individual teachers by
the use of teacher fixed effects, we find large returns to experience for middle
school teachers in the form both of higher test scores and improvements in
student behavior, with the clearest behavioral effects emerging for reductions
in student absenteeism. Moreover these returns extend well beyond the first
few years of teaching."[59]

Perhaps most importantly, the overall efficiency and effectiveness of
teacher compensation does not depend exclusively on the extent to which each
dollar allocated to any and every teacher's salary can be associated precisely

with a measurable, marginal gain to the test scores of children linked with that teacher. First, benefits of schooling extend beyond short-term achievement gains. Second, teacher compensation exists, and exerts whatever influence it may have, within a complex social and economic system. Thoughtful expositions considering these complex dynamics are few and far between. Two recent examples, however, include a largely theoretical piece supported by longitudinal descriptive data by Gregory Gilpin and Michael Kaganovich and a recent National Bureau of Economic Research paper by Jesse Rothstein.[60]

Gilpin and Kaganovich propose a general equilibrium model of teacher quantity and quality adopting the premise that teachers' relative wages (to other sectors) are critical to maintaining a quality teaching workforce. Additionally, compression of salaries (at the high end) may reduce retention and recruitment of talented teachers. Illustrated in their data, the long-term increase in total numbers of teachers and support staff has led to lower average salaries, thus potentially reducing teacher quality. But so, too, has growth in wages of competing sectors. The authors argue that growth in the competitive wage (the premium) for higher-ability teachers will likely outpace that for average-ability teachers. Because there's no readily available, cheaper substitute for high-quality teachers, the "real" value of the education dollar—education spending—is reduced: that dollar can buy fewer high-quality inputs over time. The cost of high-quality labor is increasing faster than are the resources required to pay the premium to simply maintain quality, and there exist no viable technological substitutes to offset those increases. As such, we can expect the real quality of educational inputs to decline. Because of the rise in premium for high ability, Gilpin and Kaganovich assert that "countering this trend would therefore require an increase in the share of GDP spent on basic education, assuming that the institutional setup of the school system remains unchanged."[61] In other words, because talent is becoming more expensive more rapidly in other sectors, more investment, as a share of GDP, may be required merely to maintain education quality. Gilpin and Kaganovich present a reasonable set of theoretical assumptions but do not take the next steps of empirical validation.

Rothstein critiques the presumption that tying teacher pay directly to measures of performance outcomes will necessarily improve efficiency of money allocated to compensation: "Simulations indicate that labor market interactions are important to the evaluation of alternative teacher contracts. Typical bonus policies have very small effects on selection. Firing policies can have larger effects, if accompanied by substantial salary increases. However, misalignment between productivity and measured performance nearly eliminates the benefits while preserving most of the costs."[62]

While we have some new evidence that alternative compensation methods and evaluation metrics may yield some positive results, we do not yet have a deeper understanding of the relative cost-effectiveness of alternatives. Further, we have some evidence that restructuring compensation—still based on traditional metrics (experience and credentials)—may have positive effects on teacher recruitment and retention. What we do know in each case is that the overall level of teacher compensation continues to matter for recruitment of talent into the teaching profession, relative to other labor market opportunities. Further, the relative compensation of teachers across settings within labor markets continues to matter. Adequate teacher compensation, and appropriate compensation across settings, is a prerequisite condition, whether continuing with traditional compensation strategies or testing alternative compensation schemes.

Despite all the uproar about paying teachers based on experience and education, and its misinterpretations in the context of the "Does money matter?" debate, this line of argument misses the point. To whatever degree teacher pay matters in attracting high-quality educators into the profession and retaining them, it's less about *how* they are paid than *how much*. Furthermore, the average salaries of teachers, with respect to other labor market opportunities, can substantively affect the quality of entrants into the profession, applicants to preparation programs, and student outcomes. Diminishing resources for schools can constrain salaries and reduce the quality of the labor supply. Further, salary differentials between schools and districts might help to recruit or retain teachers in high-need settings. In other words, resources used for teacher quality matter.

CLASS SIZE AND TEACHER QUANTITY

Reducing class size is often characterized as a particularly expensive use of additional school dollars.[63] But the question of whether it's disproportionately expensive must rely on detailed comparisons of alternative uses of the same dollars, or the effects on student outcomes of those alternative uses. Instead, most arguments against class size reduction frequently proceed by noting that there are significant costs to adding more teachers and classrooms (an unsurprising revelation), followed by a statement, often vague, as to the differences between the most and least "effective" teachers (as measured by their effects on test scores).[64] The problem here is that we cannot compare the cost-effectiveness of class size reduction with "improving teacher quality," which is an outcome, not a concrete policy with measurable costs and benefits.

What we do know, however, is that ample research indicates that children in smaller classes achieve better outcomes, both academic and otherwise, and that class size reduction can be an effective strategy for closing racial and socioeconomic achievement gaps.[65] For example, Alan Krueger, in a reanalysis of data from the large-scale randomized Tennessee Project STAR class size reduction study, concluded that "1) on average, performance on standardized tests increases by four percentile points the first year students attend small classes; 2) the test score advantage of students in small classes expands by about one percentile point per year in subsequent years; 3) teacher aides and measured teacher characteristics have little effect; 4) class size has a larger effect for minority students and those on free lunch."[66] Among more recent studies on the topic, also reevaluating the Tennessee STAR data, is Spyros Konstantopolous and Vicki Chung's:

> We used data from Project STAR and the Lasting Benefits Study to examine the long-term effects of small classes on the achievement gap in mathematics, reading, and science scores (Stanford Achievement Test). The results consistently indicated that all types of students benefit more in later grades from being in small classes in early grades. These positive effects are significant through grade 8. Longer periods in small classes produced higher increases in achievement in later grades for all types of students. For certain grades, in reading and science, low achievers seem to benefit more from being in small classes for longer periods. It appears that the lasting benefits of the cumulative effects of small classes may reduce the achievement gap in reading and science in some of the later grades.[67]

Researchers continue to revisit data from the Tennessee STAR study, which in more recent years has permitted them to explore long-term outcomes of those students experimentally subjected to smaller class sizes. For instance, according to Susan Dynarski, Joshua Hyman, and Diane Schanzenbach:

> Assignment to a small class increases the probability of attending college by 2.7 percentage points, with effects more than twice as large among blacks. Among students enrolled in the poorest third of schools, the

effect is 7.3 percentage points. Smaller classes increase the likelihood of earning a college degree by 1.6 percentage points and shift students towards high-earning fields such as STEM (science, technology, engineering and mathematics), business and economics. We find that test score effects at the time of the experiment are an excellent predictor of long-term improvements in postsecondary outcomes.[68]

There remain some naysayers on whether class size reduction yields cost-effective benefits in terms of student outcomes. But the findings on which these counterarguments are based often lack the weight of large-scale randomized studies, such as Tennessee's Project STAR, and rely instead on natural variations in class sizes across schools.[69] Assertions of excessive cost and inefficiency of class size reduction also often lack rigorous cost-effectiveness analysis. In a 2011 brief for the Center for American Progress, for example, Matthew Chingos asserted that class size reduction is the "most expensive school reform" but provided no direct cost or cost-effectiveness comparisons between class size reduction and other alternatives.[70] A more recent review by Chingos criticizes class size reduction as broad state-imposed policy, revisiting the costs and potential downsides of statewide class size reduction policies implemented in California and Florida.[71] Chingos suggests that estimates of long-term earnings of students subjected to class size reduction do not justify the cost, but he also acknowledges that sufficient direct comparisons between spending on class size reduction and other alternatives are few and far between.[72]

Dynarski and colleagues provide the most direct cost-effectiveness comparison of class size reduction policies with other options that had sufficient data on costs and outcome benefits: "A fair conclusion from this analysis is that the effects we find . . . of class size on college enrollment alone are not particularly large given the costs of the program. If focused on students in the poorest third of schools, then the cost-effectiveness of class size reduction is within the range of other interventions. There is no systematic evidence that early interventions pay off more than later ones when the outcome is limited to increased college attendance."[73]

It's true that a large body of the literature on the effectiveness of class size reduction relies on data from a relatively small group of sources, most notably the Tennessee STAR experiment.[74] Further, most class size reduction studies finding substantial benefits have focused on reduction in the early grades (K–3), and most of these programs are pilots implemented on a relatively small scale.[75] It's also true that reducing class size costs more than not reducing class size. But class size reductions, implemented effectively, have positive effects. As such, one can reasonably infer that using increased resources to reduce class sizes would have positive effects or, again, that resources matter.

While it's certainly plausible that other uses of the same money might be equally or even more effective, there is little evidence to support this. For example, while we are quite confident that higher teacher salaries lead to increases in the quality of applicants to the teaching profession and, thus, increases in student outcomes, we do not know whether the same money spent toward salary increases would achieve better or worse outcomes if it were spent toward reducing class size. Indeed, some have raised concerns that large-scale class size reductions can lead to unintended labor market consequences that offset some of the gains attributable to those reductions (such as the inability to recruit enough fully qualified teachers).[76] And many have argued for a more precise cost-benefit analysis.[77] Still, the preponderance of existing evidence suggests that the additional resources expended on class size reductions do result in positive effects.

LESSONS LEARNED AND LOOKING FORWARD

Rigorous, well-designed, and policy-relevant empirical research finds that:

- *money matters for schools and in determining school quality and student outcomes.* More specifically, substantive, sustained, and targeted state school finance reforms can significantly boost short-term and long-run student outcomes and reduce gaps among low-income students and their more advantaged peers.
- *money matters in commonsense ways.* Increased funding provides for additional staff, including reduced class sizes, longer school days and years, and more competitive compensation.
- *cuts do cause harm.* The equity of student outcomes is eroded by reducing equity of real resources across children of varied economic backgrounds.

These findings form the basis for understanding the current state of state school finance systems and how we got here, how we might more thoughtfully approach and rigorously evaluate the introduction of innovations, and the steps needed to ensure equitable and adequate resources for all children through substantive and sustained state school finance reforms.

CHAPTER 6

STATE FUNDING FORMULAS AND DISTRICT DISPARITIES

The level and distribution of school funding matters. Achieving competitive student outcomes depends on adequate school resources, including a competitively compensated teacher workforce. Closing achievement gaps between children from rich and poor neighborhoods requires progressive distribution of resources targeted toward children with greater educational needs. Both the adequacy of students' outcomes and improving the equity of those outcomes are in our national interest. But US public schooling remains primarily in the hands of states. On average, about 90 percent of funding for local public school systems and charter schools comes from state and local tax sources. How state and local revenue is raised and distributed is a function of seemingly complicated calculations usually adopted as legislation and often with the goal of achieving more equitable and adequate public schooling for the state's children.

State school finance formulas don't just happen in a vacuum. They are legislated. Acts or laws are adopted by state legislatures and sometimes grant flexibility to state departments of education regarding distribution of some of the state resources. The rules of the game, the calculations and distribution formulas for state aid, are the product of often contentious political deliberation and are frequently subject to state judicial oversight. In most states, the portion of school funding—the state aid formula—is the largest pot of money the state legislature has responsibility over. The state aid formula is the primary mechanism by which state legislators can bring resources to their constituents.

All states have some language in their constitution that speaks to their legislature's obligation for the provision of public schooling. Constitutional clauses may require provision of a thorough and efficient system of public schooling, a uniform system of public schooling, or suitable provision for financing the educational interests of the state. State courts do not preemptively exert their authority over a legislatures actions, but if any subset of the state's citizens feel that the education system does not meet the constitutional mandate, those citizens can bring suit against the state (legislature, governor, board of education) challenging the constitutional violation. And thus the courts are introduced as the arbitrator of the extent to which the state school finance formula does or does not provide for what the constitution requires. Judicial will to exert that oversight varies widely across states.

The earliest state aid programs for local public schools date back to the late 1700s (formalized into law in 1812) in New York State, beginning with flat allocations of aid intended to stimulate local communities to raise additional funds and provide schools.[1] This was mathematically pretty simple and was merely intended to encourage local jurisdictions to provide some type of publicly accessible common (lower grades) schooling. Realizing that towns often had varied abilities to raise funds on their own, states began allocating more aid to those with greater need as early as the 1850s.[2]

State governments and the constitutions that define and govern them have not been stagnant since each state's founding. Rather, they have evolved dramatically. For example, the current education articles of the Kansas and Connecticut constitutions came about in the mid-1960s. Both have been invoked in legal challenges in the decades that followed.

The hybrid state-local financing of public school systems and the associated mathematical formulas exist because most states delegated significant authority to local public school districts, municipalities, or counties to establish school systems and raise taxes for their infrastructure and operations. Southern states tend to operate county systems but often have segregated enclave school districts carved out of counties. Northeastern states tend to have clearer alignment of municipal governments and local public school districts, with many districts financed through municipal budgets (fiscal dependence). In other regions there exists a vast array of local public school district boundaries that vary in their contiguity with municipalities or counties, in some cases having no clear relation to either.

In most cases, the original tax of choice was the local property tax. These local (school district or municipality) and intermediate (county) units and the tax policies under which they operate are all functions of state laws. The boundaries of geographic spaces that make up those systems (and rules for changing those boundaries), the property types/classifications within those boundaries, the methods by which those properties are assigned taxable value, the procedures by which local voters or elected representatives determine the rates at which properties will be taxed, and whether there will be limits on the overall level of local taxation or growth in local taxation or spending—it's all a matter of state policy (including how much authority is granted to local jurisdictions).

It became increasingly apparent from the mid-1800s through mid-1900s that states would need to play some role in supporting local school systems where local property wealth and residents' incomes were insufficient. In 1924 George D. Strayer and Robert Haig laid out the conceptual framing and math for what they called a "foundation aid" formula:

> To carry into effect the principle of "equalization of educational opportunity" and "equalization of school support" as commonly understood it would be necessary (1) to establish schools or make other arrangements sufficient to furnish the children in every locality within the state with equal educational opportunities up to some prescribed minimum; (2) to raise the funds necessary for this purpose by local or state taxation adjusted in such manner as to bear upon the people in all localities at the same rate in relation to their tax-paying ability; and (3) to provide adequately either for the supervision and control of all the schools, or for their direct administration, by a state department of education.[3]

For Strayer and Haig, the notions of "equity" and "equal educational opportunity" were qualified by the phrase "up to some prescribed minimum," a minimum adequacy threshold arrived at based not on what goals were to be achieved but on how much funding was available. Thus, the modern state school aid formula was born.

Foundation aid formulas continue to evolve, becoming increasingly complex as we better understand the cost and cost variation of providing comparable schooling inputs across varied settings and as we better understand how to leverage resources to meet students' needs both individual and collectively.

Complexity also increases as astute politicians learn what levers they can tweak to bring resources back to their own districts. State school finance systems are necessarily arrived at via political deliberation (subject to judicial oversight), and so each and every calculation within them is subject to political negotiation. In our efforts to make these systems more rational, adequate, and equitable, the best we can hope to do is inform the political deliberation and judicial evaluation with the best available evidence. Our goal must be to bend state school finance policy in a more rationale direction. Accepting "less than perfect" does not mean normalizing egregious inequalities or uncritically ceding each and every act of legislative self-interest, however small.

BASIC DESIGN AND GOALS OF SCHOOL FUNDING FORMULAS

Modern state school finance formulas strive to achieve two simultaneous objectives: account for differences in the costs of achieving equal educational opportunity (to achieve desired outcomes) across schools, districts, and the children they serve; and account for differences in the ability of local public school districts to cover those costs. Local districts' ability to raise revenue might be a function of either or both local taxable property wealth and the incomes of local property owners, thus their ability to pay taxes on their properties.

Table 6.1 summarizes components of a typical state school finance formula and the roles of those components with respect to equity objectives. For example, many state school finance systems are built to some extent around foundation aid models like those originally proposed by Strayer and Haig, which have at their core a foundation funding level per pupil. It is generally assumed that the foundation level of funding per pupil represents the cost of minimally adequate educational services either in the district with lowest costs or for the child with no specialized needs. Alternatively, the foundation level might be set to represent the cost of educational services in the average educational setting, for a local public school district facing average cost pressures and serving an average student population. Without any other considerations (alterations or adjustments), the foundation level itself provides only for equity of nominal financial inputs. When the foundation level is sufficiently high and/or caps are placed on additional revenue raising, the foundation level might also provide for revenue neutrality by district wealth.

Many foundation aid formulas also contain adjustments for variations in input prices across districts, specifically adjustment variations in the compet-

TABLE 6.1 Components of foundation aid formulas and equity objectives

Foundation formula element	Purpose	Notes
Foundation level	Intended to represent cost of "adequate educational services" and/or cost of achieving "adequate educational outcomes" in either "average" or "lowest cost" district	Without other considerations, guarantees only equity of nominal financial inputs (equal dollars)
Input price (teacher wage) adjustment	Intended to provide local public school districts sufficient funding to purchase comparable "real resources"	May attempt to account for differences in competitive wages and other input prices across regions, or may also attempt to account for influence of local working conditions on wages required to hire high-quality teachers
Student need adjustments	Intended to provide for "equal educational opportunity" by providing financial resources to achieve appropriately differentiated programs (program intensity)	

itive wages of teachers and other school staff. These adjustments are intended to provide local public school districts with sufficient funding to purchase comparable "real resources," or comparable quantities of comparable quality teachers and other school staff. Finally, foundation aid formulas also contain numerous adjustments related to student needs, which can refer to either individual programmatic needs of specific students or collective needs of the student population served. For example, children identified as having one or more disabilities or with limited English proficiency (LEP) might require specific curricular and program supports, which are provided by specially trained staff at higher costs. And schools with high concentrations of children in poverty might more generally have to adjust their programs/service delivery model to provide smaller class sizes for early grades, additional tutoring support, and/or extended learning time, also at higher costs. These strategies are intended to yield more equal student outcomes, to close achievement gaps between low-income and higher-income students, or between those with learning disabilities and/or limited English proficiency and other children. These adjustments are intended to provide for equal opportunity to achieve desired, or state-mandated, outcome levels. As such, for a state school finance system to provide equal educational opportunity, that system must ensure sufficiently more resources in higher-need (higher-poverty) settings than in lower-need settings. I characterize such a system as *progressive*. By contrast, many state school finance systems barely achieve flat funding between high- and low-need settings, and still others remain regressive.

FIGURE 6.1   Hypothetical equalized need-based school finance system

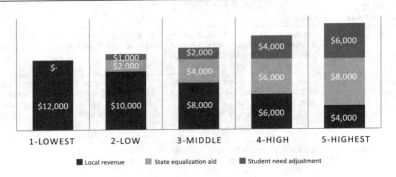

Source: Baker et al., *School Funding Fairness Data System.*

Figure 6.1 presents a hypothetical example of the distribution of state and local revenue per pupil across school districts, sorted by poverty concentration. The hypothetical relies on the simplified assumption that districts with weaker local revenue raising capacity also tend to be higher in poverty concentration. While that's not uniformly true, there is often some correlation between the two. Accepting this oversimplified characterization, figure 6.1 shows that the typical low-poverty district with high local fiscal capacity would likely raise the majority of the cost of providing its children with equal educational opportunity through local tax dollars. There may be some small share of state general aid, assuming that the total cost of providing equal educational opportunity exceeds the local resources raised with a fair tax rate.

A HYPOTHETICAL EQUALIZED NEED-BASED SCHOOL FINANCE SYSTEM

The typical implementation involves first calculating an "adequacy budget," or need- and cost-adjusted foundation level, for each local public school district or charter school:

adequacy budget (per pupil) = base + student need adjustment + geographic cost adjustments

Most state aid formulas set some basic target funding level. Student need adjustments are usually added through some student weighted count method (e.g., adding an additional .4 for each low-income student, counting that student as 1.4) and then totaled for a weighted student count. Geographic cost adjustments might include adjustments for the variations in competitive wages across schools and districts (usually an index multiplier) and/or adjustments to compensate for economies of scale and sparsity and remoteness of small rural districts.

The second step is to determine what share of the adequacy budget should be allocated as state aid:

state share = adequacy budget – local fair share

This step may follow Strayer and Haig's original foundation aid approach of determining local fair share by applying a uniform local property tax rate to each district and making up the difference with state aid. Or it may also include consideration of incomes of residents and other local economic factors.

Most of this implementation process applies only to state general aid formulas, which determine the core operating expenses for local public school systems—the money needed to keep the system running from year to year, to pay employees, to buy materials and supplies, to keep the lights on and buses running, etc. Certainly, running a school system takes more than this. It takes capital investment to finance construction of new facilities, to renovate and conduct major repairs, and to replace equipment (everything from heating and cooling systems to buses). Local districts vary in their ability to pay off capital debts and finance major long-term expenses, and states have been much less involved in providing for equitable capital financing. State legislatures do often distribute aid "outside the formula," but this aid can be subject to political whims and power plays.

EXAMPLES OF THE GOOD, THE BAD, AND THE UGLY

Often, the best way to evaluate a state school finance system is to examine the patterns of resources generated by that formula. A good start is listing and critiquing the individual ingredients—the calculations, the weights, the base spending figures—and attempt to interpret how those calculations will play out when applied to actual districts. An additional step is simulating the calculations across districts to observe how they play out, though it's often easier to start with the actual patterns of local revenue and state aid and current operating expenditures. Depending on the patterns revealed, then explore what factors make this system a good or bad one.

Beginning in 2010, in collaboration with the Education Law Center of New Jersey, I laid out a methodology and series of indicators for comparing state school finance systems using available national data sets. I based the method on the relatively straightforward premise that, all else equal, local public school districts serving higher concentrations of children from low income backgrounds should have access to higher state and local revenue per pupil than districts serving lower concentrations of children in poverty. By "all else equal" I mean that comparisons of resources between lower- and higher-poverty school districts are contingent on differences in labor costs and other factors, such as economies of scale and population density. State school finance systems should yield progressive distributions of state and local revenue, which should translate to progressive distributions of current spending per pupil, progressive distributions of staffing ratios, and competitive teacher wages. Other organizations, including the Urban Institute, have adopted similar approaches, acknowledging the basic need for funding distributions that are progressive with respect to child poverty.[4] Of course, progressiveness alone may not be sufficient. Progressive distributions of funding must be coupled with sufficient overall levels of funding to achieve the desired outcomes. No state has a perfect school finance system, but a few states stand out as providing sufficient levels of funding and reasonable degrees of progressiveness. Massachusetts and New Jersey are among the best examples.

Figure 6.2 provides a simple descriptive summary of local, state, and federal revenue per pupil for New Jersey school districts in 2015, by poverty quintile. Even New Jersey, though, does not achieve the hypothetical pattern presented in figure 6.1. New Jersey does provide substantively more state aid to its highest-poverty districts, but the progressiveness achieved by targeted state aid is partially offset by the high local revenue of these lowest-poverty districts, leaving districts caught in the middle with fewer resources (a U-shaped distribution rather than a smooth upward pattern from left to right).

Figure 6.3 tracks the per-pupil distributions of local revenue, state aid, and federal aid for the highest-poverty quintile of New Jersey districts from 1993 to 2015. It also includes the timing of state court rulings (*Abbott v. Burke*) pertaining to school funding, the most significant of these coming in 1997 (*Abbott IV*) and 1998 (*Abbott V*) and ordering specific programs and services be fully funded for many of the state's highest-poverty districts. State aid scaled up dramatically during this period but leveled off around 2005 and began to decline even before the economic downturn in 2008. In fact, the decline began

FIGURE 6.2 New Jersey revenue by source and by poverty group (quintiles), 2015

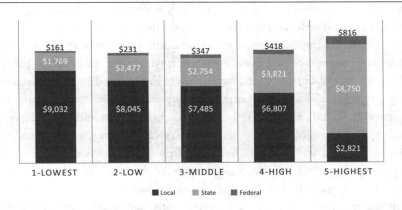

Source: Baker et al., *School Funding Fairness Data System.*

FIGURE 6.3 New Jersey revenue by source over time for high-poverty districts

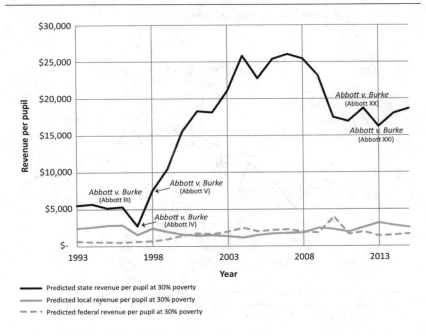

Source: Baker et al., *School Funding Fairness Data System.*

with the implementation of the state's new school finance formula that was designed to distribute resources more evenly statewide and less directly in response to court order and those who brought the original litigation.

Figure 6.4 tracks progressiveness indicators for New Jersey from 1993 to 2015, comparing the resources of high-poverty districts to those of low-poverty districts. An indicator of 1.4 indicates that a high-poverty district is expected to have 40 percent more resources than a low-poverty district, a progressive distribution. An indicator of .8 indicates that a high-poverty district is expected to have 80 percent of the resources of a low poverty district, a regressive distribution. In New Jersey, as state aid to high-poverty districts was dramatically scaled up, state and local revenue per pupil and current spending per pupil became progressively distributed. Progressiveness went as high as 1.5 by 2005 but has since fallen to about 1.2. Progressive state and local revenue led to progressive spending and, in turn, progressive distributions of staff. High-poverty districts were able to support higher staffing ratios than their lower-poverty neighbors. Again, staffing matters, especially in high-poverty settings.

FIGURE 6.4 New Jersey funding progressiveness over time

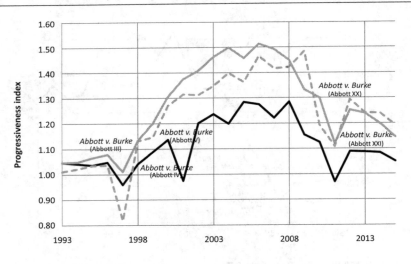

Source: Baker et al., *School Funding Fairness Data System*.

While the previous figures show the average patterns for New Jersey, figure 6.5 shows the actual distributions of per-pupil spending by district poverty level. To account for differences in competitive wages across labor markets (which also affects poverty measurement), each district's spending and poverty rates are compared to the average for other districts in the same labor market (in roughly the same metropolitan area). Each circle represents school district enrollments. Large circles are larger, often urban, districts. Districts in the upper-right quadrant have higher-than-average spending and higher-than-average poverty. Importantly, on average, across larger districts, higher-poverty districts tend to have higher per-pupil spending. However, this progressiveness is not as clean as assumed by previous simplified representations. Even New Jersey, which has among the most equitable state school finance systems in the country, suffers some pretty significant inequities. The upper-left quadrant shows that smaller, affluent suburban districts leverage their healthy property tax bases and local voter incomes to spend well above average for their labor markets while having very low poverty rates. Also, there are some high-poverty districts that appear to receive none of the benefits of progressive funding.

FIGURE 6.5   New Jersey 2015

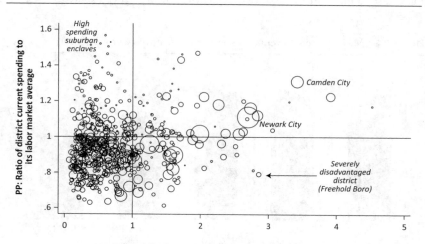

Source: Baker et al., *School Funding Fairness Data System.*

Figure 6.6 shows the distribution of local, state, and federal revenue per pupil for Massachusetts districts. The pattern for Massachusetts is more systematically progressive than that for New Jersey, but it's also less aggressive. Recall that the overall trajectory of Massachusetts school finance reforms is similar to that of New Jersey: state aid to high-poverty districts was scaled up during the 1990s, but that aid then flattened out and subsequently declined. The trajectory of progressiveness indicators follows a similar path. Progressiveness improved as aid increased and waned as aid fell.

Also like New Jersey, the pattern of progressiveness is imperfect (figure 6.7). It's critically important to look behind the statewide averages, because even in states with relatively fair state school finance systems, some districts get left out for a number of reasons. Massachusetts has several very-high-poverty midsized districts that have below-average funding. These tend to be small-to-midsized cities with increasingly low-income and racially and ethnically diverse populations. Massachusetts also has several smaller affluent districts that opt to significantly outspend those around them. Just because a state school finance system generally tilts in the right direction does not negate the possibility that the system deprives some students of their state constitutional rights to equitable or adequate education. Families of the children in Lowell, Everett, Malden, and Chelsea, in particular, might have a legitimate case to make in state court that their rights are being violated.

FIGURE 6.6 Massachusetts revenue by source and by poverty group (quintiles), 2015

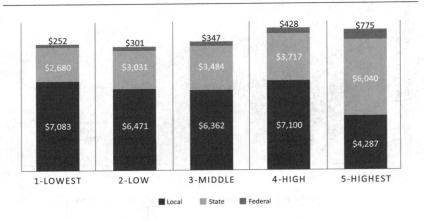

Source: Baker et al., *School Funding Fairness Data System.*

FIGURE 6.7   Massachusetts 2015

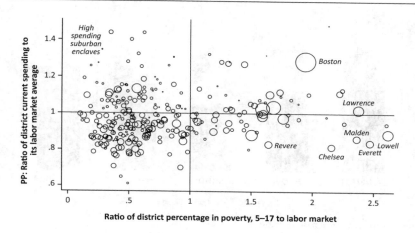

Source: Baker et al., *School Funding Fairness Data System.*

Illinois and Pennsylvania are two of the most regressively funded state school finance systems. Figure 6.8 shows the distribution of local, state, and federal revenue by poverty quintile for Illinois districts. In the lowest-poverty districts, local revenue is nearly double that of high-poverty districts, but these districts still receive substantial state aid per pupil. This occurs despite the fact that the available pool of state aid is insufficient to bring the highest-poverty districts to comparable (no less progressive) nominal spending per pupil. Even with federal aid, which is largely distributed with respect to poverty concentrations, Illinois high-poverty districts are left with fewer resources than their lower-poverty neighbors.

Figure 6.9 tracks the progressiveness indicators for Illinois revenue, spending, and staffing from 1993 to 2015. On average, per-pupil spending is relatively flat with respect to poverty (hovering around the 1.0 line) largely because federal aid, which is largely targeted based on poverty, tilts upward the regressive state and local revenue. State and local revenue per pupil is regressive throughout the period and becomes even more so over time. Staffing ratios follow a similar pattern. Arguably, the persistent regressiveness of school funding in Illinois is in part a function of the state court's refusal to intervene, as is the case in Pennsylvania. Yet, court rulings don't always make the difference. In New York State, for instance, the high court ruled that the state school finance

FIGURE 6.8 Illinois revenue by source and by poverty group (quintiles)

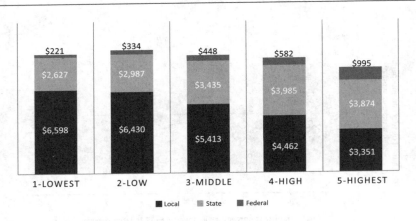

Source: Baker et al., *School Funding Fairness Data System.*

FIGURE 6.9 Illinois revenue and spending regressiveness over time

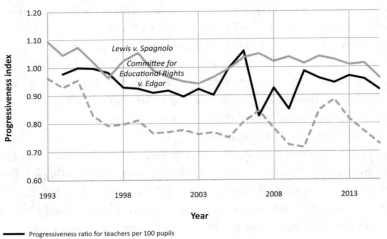

Source: Baker et al., *School Funding Fairness Data System.*

system provided inadequate resources for New York City Schools, yet the city continues to operate a largely regressive state school finance system.[5]

INEQUALITIES AND FINANCIALLY DISADVANTAGED DISTRICTS

In 2011, the Obama administration formed a national equity commission to explore fiscal inequities across US schools.[6] In one meeting of that commission, Eric Hanushek introduced a table from the National Center for Education Statistics (NCES) to assert that, on average, US states had already raised levels of spending in high-poverty districts to the point where, on average, high-poverty districts spend more than low-poverty districts—the implication being that school funding equity is not the problem, but, rather, the problem lies with inefficiency in high-poverty districts.. This statement is factually correct—states had increased spending in high-poverty districts, and, on average, high-poverty districts spend more than low-poverty districts—but the policy conclusions are not, as a close look at Table A-36-1 of the NCES 2010 "Condition of Education Report" reveals (figure 6.10).

However, there are a few problems with using this table to imply this, aside from the dollar figures not being adjusted for differences in labor costs across settings. While $10,978 (constant dollars) is in fact higher than $10,850, this is hardly enough to provide for the differences in programs and services needed to close achievement gaps between our highest- and lowest-poverty children. But perhaps most important, these broad national average figures hide substantial variation both across and within states. Many states have highly inequitable school funding systems, and many districts and the children they serve continue to be significantly disadvantaged by state school finance systems, ranging from imperfect to abhorrent.

In 2014 I produced a report for the Center for American Progress identifying "America's Most Financially Disadvantaged School Districts," which came about as an extension of a series of blog posts in which I identified "America's Most Screwed School Districts." It had become increasingly clear to me that the indicators we created for the *School Funding Fairness Data System*, while useful for describing overall patterns, were hiding important disparities within states behind the averages. For example, in Massachusetts and New Jersey, two of the most progressive state school finance systems, there are districts that are high in student poverty and have far fewer resources than

FIGURE 6.10 Current expenditures per pupil in fall enrollment (NCES Table A-36-1)

Table A-36-1. Current expenditures per student in fall enrollment in public school districts, by district poverty category: Selected school years, 1995–96 through 2006–07

District poverty category[a]	CURRENT EXPENDITURES PER STUDENT										Percent change from 1995–96 to 2006–07
	1995–96	1997–98	1999–2000	2000–01	2001–02	2002–03	2003–04	2004–05	2005–06	2006–07	
	[In current dollars]										
Total	$5,560	$6,023	$6,727	$7,200	$7,540	$7,870	$8,134	$8,540	$8,979	$9,501	70.9
Low	6,210	6,551	7,207	7,713	8,126	8,477	8,833	9,243	9,820	10,313	66.2
Middle low	5,414	5,853	6,604	7,032	7,345	7,640	7,862	8,202	8,543	9,070	67.5
Middle	5,186	5,621	6,194	6,601	6,951	7,215	7,455	7,725	8,111	8,731	68.3
Middle high	5,136	5,608	6,441	6,876	7,212	7,418	7,707	8,052	8,591	8,945	74.2
High	5,858	6,482	7,181	7,782	8,075	8,606	8,853	9,484	9,830	10,440	78.2
	[In constant 2008–09 dollars[b]]										
Total	$7,725	$7,994	$8,529	$8,828	$9,083	$9,277	$9,383	$9,564	$9,686	$9,991	29.3
Low	8,628	8,695	9,138	9,457	9,789	9,993	10,189	10,351	10,593	10,850	25.8
Middle low	7,523	7,769	8,373	8,621	8,849	9,005	9,069	9,184	9,216	9,538	26.8
Middle	7,206	7,460	7,854	8,092	8,374	8,505	8,600	8,651	8,750	9,181	27.4
Middle high	7,135	7,442	8,167	8,430	8,688	8,744	8,890	9,017	9,267	9,406	31.8
High	8,139	8,603	9,106	9,540	9,728	10,144	10,212	10,621	10,604	10,978	34.9

[a]Districts were ranked by the percentage of school-age children (five- to seventeen-year-olds) in poverty and then divided into five groups with approximately equal public school enrollments. For more information on poverty, see *supplemental note 1*.

[b]Expenditures have been adjusted for the effects of inflation using the Consumer Price Index (CPI) and are in constant 2008–09 dollars. For more information on using the CPI to adjust for inflation, see *supplemental note 10*.

Note: For more information on classifications of expenditures for elementary and secondary education, see *supplemental note 10*. For more information on the Common Core of Data (CCD), see *supplemental note 3*. Districts include elementary/secondary combined districts and separate elementary or secondary districts. They exclude Department of Defense districts and Bureau of Indian Education districts.

Source: U.S. Department of Commerce, Census Bureau, "Small Area Income and Poverty Estimates," 1995–96, 1997–98, and 1999–2000 through 2006–07, and U.S. Department of Education, National Center for Education Statistics (NCES), Common Core of Data (CCD); "School District Finance Survey (Form F-33)," 1995–96, 1997–98, and 1999–2000 through 2006–07.

the districts around them. That is, even in the most equitable state school finance systems, some districts, and the children they serve, are left out. These children should not be overlooked, and the disparities must not be ignored simply because the state system is generally fair.

It is important to understand that the value of any given level of education funding in any given location is relative. It does not matter whether a district spends $10,000 per pupil or $20,000 per pupil. What matters is how that funding compares to other districts operating in the same regional labor market and how that money relates to other conditions in the regional labor market. Relative funding matters because schooling is labor intensive. The quality of schooling depends largely on the ability of schools or districts to recruit and retain quality employees. The largest share of school districts' annual operating budgets is tied up in the salaries and wages of teachers and other school workers. The ability to recruit and retain teachers in a school district in any given labor market depends on the wage a district can pay to teachers relative to other surrounding schools or districts and relative to non-teaching alternatives in the same labor market.[7] Relative funding also matters because graduates' access to opportunities beyond high school is largely relative and regional, as the ability of graduates of one school district to gain access to higher education or the labor force depends on the regional pool in which the graduate must compete.[8]

Using 2015 fiscal and poverty data, table 6.2 lists K–12 unified districts that had less than 90 percent state and local revenue of their labor market average and more than 150 percent of the poverty rate. Other chronically underfunded high-poverty districts are in the margins of this analysis. Year after year Philadelphia and Chicago have appeared as the two most disadvantaged large urban districts. Other Pennsylvania cities, including Reading and Allentown, face even more dire conditions; and Illinois districts like Waukegan and Joliet also make the list year after year. While in Connecticut Hartford and New Haven have received additional aid in support of their magnet programs, creating an appearance of progressive funding in the state, other districts, including Bridgeport, Waterbury, and New Britain, have been entirely left out. Disparities of this type and magnitude are simply wrong, unfair, and they should be remedied.

High-poverty districts need equal resources as well as substantially more resources per pupil to achieve common outcomes for their students. One of the more rigorous studies to ask just how much more students need applied

TABLE 6.2   America's most financially disadvantaged districts, 2015

State	School district	Enrollment	Relative poverty	Relative revenue
Arizona	Sunnyside Unified District	17,168	156%	75%
California	Cajon Valley Union	16,601	157%	84%
California	Gilroy Unified	11,840	162%	74%
Connecticut	Bridgeport School District	21,047	254%	83%
Connecticut	New Britain School District	10,016	238%	75%
Connecticut	Waterbury School District	18,784	179%	83%
Georgia	Clayton County	53,367	171%	84%
Illinois	City of Chicago School District 299	392,558	161%	78%
Illinois	Joliet Public School District 86	11,781	157%	74%
Illinois	Waukegan Community Unit School District 60	17,042	208%	72%
Massachusetts	Brockton	17,186	150%	79%
Massachusetts	Lowell	14,075	262%	84%
Michigan	Kalamazoo Public Schools	12,456	154%	88%
Michigan	Warren Consolidated Schools	14,876	177%	88%
Missouri	St. Louis City	30,831	250%	85%
New Hampshire	Manchester School District	14,565	182%	81%
New Jersey	Union City School District	13,560	160%	86%
New York	Brentwood Union Free School District	18,648	214%	73%
New York	Schenectady City School District	10,066	227%	88%
North Carolina	Gaston County Schools	31,954	133%	85%
Ohio	Hamilton City	10,055	187%	79%
Oregon	Reynolds School District 7	11,750	184%	89%
Pennsylvania	Allentown City School District	16,483	237%	80%
Pennsylvania	Reading School District	17,303	233%	74%
South Carolina	Sumter 01	16,922	243%	86%
Tennessee	Shelby County	115,810	277%	85%

Source: Baker et al., *School Funding Fairness Data System.*

cost models to districts in New York State and found that the costs associated with each additional child in poverty (based on US Census poverty income level) were about two and a half times the costs of achieving the same outcome measures for children not in poverty.[9] Thus, a district serving 30 percent of children below the poverty line would have costs approximately 75 percent higher or 1.75 times (.3 x 2.5) per-pupil cost for a district with 0 percent census poverty.

As problematic as these disparities are, they still have their detractors and deniers, which is especially disheartening. Simply declaring repeatedly in 140 characters or less that such disparities don't exist or aren't relevant or important doesn't make it so. But it does introduce confusion into the debate, though the actual facts are clear and easily verifiable. Take a 2013 Twitter exchange between Andy Smarick, a fellow at the American Enterprise Institute, and Kombiz Lavasany, a research manager with the American Federation of Teachers.[10] In the exchange, Mr. Smarick—whose body of work contends that urban traditional public school districts don't and can't work and must be replaced with a portfolio of privately managed autonomous charter schools—tweeted, "No entity can fix Philly district or any urban district for that matter. Urban district is broken, can't be fixed, must be replaced." In response to prodding from Mr. Lavasany, Smarick went on to declare that money was clearly not the problem: "Philly's district = terrible for decades, families left, as a result it's bankrupt. Gotten huge state funding for yrs to prop it up"; "I know Philly gets among (if not THE) highest levels of funding from the state. I also know it's been losing thousands of students"; "And I know the state just bailed it out again. And now the district is asking for more money. Again."[11] The only hint at evidence here is Smarick's claim that Philadelphia's state aid is among the highest in the state—and that is true, because Philadelphia is by far the largest district in the state (several times larger than any other district).

Based on data from the *School Fairness Data System*, figure 6.11 shows Pennsylvania school districts arranged by their poverty rates and by per-pupil spending relative to districts in their surrounding labor market. Philadelphia, represented by the large circle in the lower right, had a little more than double the poverty rate of all districts in its area and less than 80 percent of the spending per pupil in 2015. Philadelphia is the classic case of a "screwed district."[12] Figure 6.12 shows the plight of Philadelphia Public Schools from 1993 to 2015. During this period, child poverty rates climbed from just under double the labor market average to over double the labor market average. Across two decades, Philadelphia received substantively less in per-pupil revenue and spent less per pupil on average than surrounding districts did, despite having much greater need and facing much higher costs. The Commonwealth of Pennsylvania has done little, if anything, for decades to "prop up" school spending in Philadelphia. Evidence-free bluster to the contrary is reckless and irresponsible.

Among the other financially disadvantaged districts of the Commonwealth are Reading and Allentown. Reading was the subject of a 2012 feature

FIGURE 6.11 Pennsylvania 2015

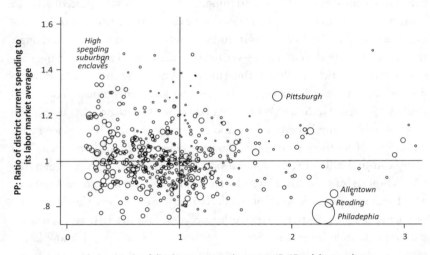

Ratio of district percentage in poverty, 5–17 to labor market

Source: Baker et al., *School Funding Fairness Data System.*

FIGURE 6.12 Philadelphia School District relative spending and relative child poverty 1993–2015

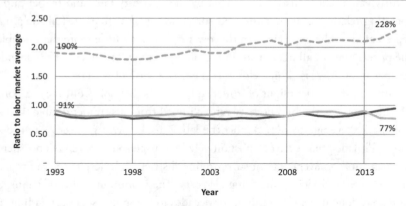

Year

- ——— PP: Ratio of district state/local revenue with federal impact aid to its labor market average
- ——— PP: Ratio of district current spending to its labor market average
- - - - Ratio of district % in poverty, 5–17 to labor market

Source: Baker et al., *School Funding Fairness Data System.*

article in the *Huffington Post* in which education writer Joy Resmovits detailed the ground-level impact of the city's school funding plight, including substantial staffing cuts and elimination of the district's preschool program.[13] Year after year Reading is also identified as among the nation's most financially disadvantaged school districts (high in poverty and low in funding).[14] Michael Q. McShane responded to the column, arguing that "Ms. Resmovits was right to point to Reading as an example of a property-poor district that cannot raise enough local funds to support education. However, as the 20-year changes in funding show, the state has worked to remedy this shortfall."[15] McShane's evidentiary basis for his claim was to show that the percent of Reading's funding coming from the state had increased over time and was greater than that of other districts, and thus the state was doing its part, and responsibility for any failures should fall squarely on Reading school district officials. While McShane's argument is more nuanced than Smarick's flat-out denial, it, too, is factually incorrect. There mere percent of a district's budget that comes from state sources is no indication of the overall adequacy of funding. A district spending $1 per pupil, with 90 cents coming from the state, would have a much greater state share than most Pennsylvania districts, but the per-pupil amount would clearly be insufficient. Figure 6.13 shows the relative insufficiency of Reading's per-pupil

FIGURE 6.13   Reading, PA, relative spending and relative child poverty 1993–2015

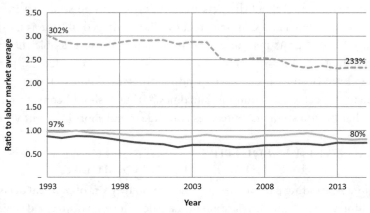

PP: Ratio of district state/local revenue with federal impact aid to its labor market average
PP: Ratio of district current spending to its labor market average
Ratio of district % in poverty, 5–17 to labor market

Source: Baker et al., *School Funding Fairness Data System*.

FIGURE 6.14   Relative poverty and spending in major urban districts

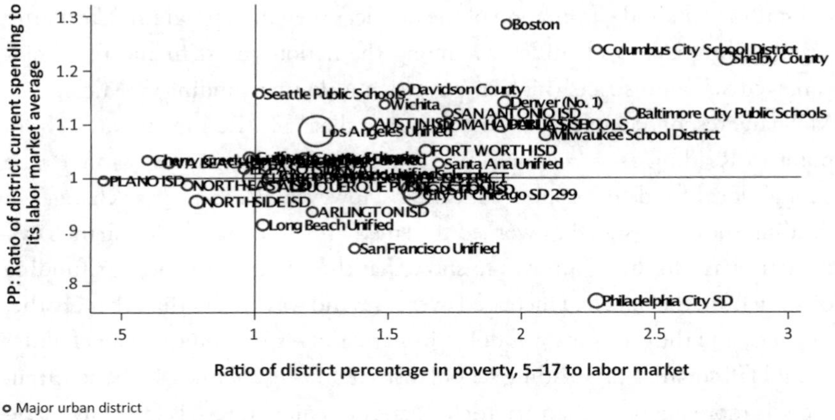

o Major urban district

Source: Baker et al., *School Funding Fairness Data System.*

revenue over time. Reading is an especially flagrant case of savage school funding inequalities. Reading is a midsized city district with nearly 250 percent of the poverty rate and about 73.6 percent of the state and local revenue per pupil of the surrounding labor market.

Figure 6.14 shows the relative poverty and relative state and local revenue for large city school districts (with 50,000 or more students) in 2013. Again, Philadelphia and Chicago are most disadvantaged. Boston is most advantaged here, but its margin of poverty difference is still double that of its surroundings, and its margin of revenue difference is only about 30 percent higher. Even Boston's progressive spending differential falls well short of cost estimates for achieving common outcomes.[16] Thus it should come as no surprise that Boston students' outcomes continue to fall short in recent years.

STEALTH INEQUITIES AND STRUCTURAL FLAWS IN SCHOOL FUNDING FORMULAS

Inequitable funding patterns are the result of many years of political decisions regarding the level and distribution of state aid. The level of state aid available is subject to political preferences regarding tax policies, since it takes higher taxes to raise more revenue. And then the distribution of state aid is subject to the constant tug-of-war among legislators with interest in appeasing their constituents, often forming alliances with other districts across the state that stand to benefit from similar changes or from preserving existing provisions of state aid formulas. Many of the most egregious disparities continue to exist as a function of the simple failure to raise and distribute sufficient state aid to offset vast disparities in local property tax revenue. Yet, even though high-poverty districts do not get enough aid to bring them even with low-poverty districts, those districts are still receiving substantial state aid.

Not surprisingly, state legislators advocating for their districts seek to preserve past funding streams and look for ways to advocate for more funding.[17] Consider Kansas, which permits the sixteen districts with the most expensive residential properties to levy a special local tax to raise more revenue because it costs more to hire teachers in neighborhoods with high-priced houses.[18] This has particularly negative equity consequences in the Kansas City metropolitan area, where housing price variation is influenced by decades of racial restrictions in property deeds.[19] Permitting districts with high-priced houses to raise more revenue means permitting districts that are predominantly White, largely due to decades of racial restrictions in home deeds, to raise more revenue than neighboring minority districts with the specific purpose of raising teachers' salaries. Similarly, Arizona's state school finance formula includes an adjustment for districts with more experienced teachers (higher than state average experience), who are more likely to serve in low-needs districts but includes no adjustment for the greater needs of low-income students.[20]

In 2012 Sean Corcoran and I prepared a report for the Center for American Progress on features of state school finance formulas that, with a certain stealth, reinforce rather than mitigate inequity.[21] In some cases, these provisions drive aid to districts that can more than pay their own way with their own source revenue. These provisions often emerge anew or persist as an untouchable third rail, as political trade-offs made to generate sufficient votes to get a formula passed in a state legislature. Table 6.3 is an overview of the types of provisions we identified through in-depth analyses of six focus states' school finance formulas: Illinois, New York, Pennsylvania, North Carolina, Missouri, Texas. While a general aid formula in its purest implementation would have a state-sharing ratio that drops to $0 aid (or a 0 percent state share) for districts with sufficient local capacity, many, if not most, state aid formulas include minimum aid provisions and/or other adjustments to state sharing ratios that allow districts to receive the "greater of x or y" or "no less

TABLE 6.3 Stealth provisions in state aid formulas

	Adjustments to state aid ratio (and minimum aid)		Unequalized (or ad hoc) categorical aid		Tax relief provisions	
	Note	Amount	Note	Amount	Note	Amount
Illinois[a]	Alternative aid formulas including flat minimum[b]	Minimum = $218 per pupil plus hold harmless aid[c]	Mandatory (state formula) and discretionary (ISBE distributed) categorical grants			
New York[d]	Minimum foundation aid and other adjustments	Minimum = $500 per aid able pupil unit			STAR[e]	
Pennsylvania	Minimum basic funding aid ratio[f]	15% of foundation target	Special education (US Census)[g]	$400+ per ADM		
North Carolina	Minimum aid through personnel ratio formula					
Missouri[h]	Hold harmless (transition to SB287 from SB380)		Classroom Trust Fund	$435 per ADA	Proposition C (1982)	$786–$818 per WADA (10% of state and local revenue)
Texas[i]	Available school fund	Approximately $250 per pupil minimum; $466 per pupil in 2010–11[j]	NIFA		ASATR[k]	Fills gap between revenue at compressed rate and target revenue

Notes: STAR, New York State School Tax Relief; WADA, weighted average daily attendance; ADA, average daily attendance; ADM, average daily membership; ASATR, Additional State Aid for Tax Reduction; NIFA, New Instructional Facilities Allotment.

Sources: [a]Illinois State Board of Education. General State Aid Overview. http://www.isbe.state.il.us/funding/pdf/gsa_overview.pdf. [b]The second formula is the "Alternate" formula. Districts qualifying for this formula have available local resources per pupil of at least 93% but less than 175% of the foundation level. The third formula is the "Flat Grant" formula. Districts qualifying for this formula have available local resources per pupil of at least 175% of the foundation level. [c]A hold-harmless provision is included in Section 18-8.05(J) of the School Code, http://www.isbe.state.il.us/funding/html/gsa.htm. [d]"New York State Education Department Primer on State Aid," http://www.oms.nysed.gov/faru/PDFDocuments/Primer11-12D.pdf. [e]"STAR," New York State Department of Taxation and Finance, http://www.tax.ny.gov/pit/property/star/index.htm. [f]"Basic Education Funding History," Pennsylvania, Department of Education, http://www.portal.state.pa.us/portal/server.pt?open=514&objID=509059&mode=2. [g]"Special Education Funding History," Pennsylvania Department of Education, http://www.portal.state.pa.us/portal/server.pt?open=514&objID=509062&mode=2. [h]Missouri Senate Bill 287, http://www.senate.mo.gov/07info/pdf-bill/intro/SB287.pdf. [i]"School Finance 101 (Overview of Foundation School Program)," Texas Association of School Boards, http://www.tasbo.org/files-public/publications/TEA/School_Finance_101.pdf. [j]"Available School Fund," http://www.tea.state.tx.us/WorkArea/linkit.aspx?LinkIdentifier=id&ItemID=2147499903&libID=2147499900. [k]Texas school finance topics overviews at http://www.tea.state.tx.us/index2.aspx?id=2147499540.

than z." These types of provisions produce the distributions of general aid to low-need, high-capacity districts. Such provisions may also adjust upward the aid for districts that would otherwise receive less aid.

Another similar type of adjustment to state general aid, often used when changes are made to a state school finance system, is the hold-harmless provision. These provisions take many forms, but the general idea is that no district should receive either less state aid or less in total funding than it received in some baseline comparison year. Thus, if a state is transitioning from a formula that had a minimum aid provision to one that does not, the state adopts a 100 percent hold-harmless state aid provision and essentially maintains the previous minimum aid provision. There's no more minimum aid, per se, but no district shall receive less than the minimum aid they received under the previous formula.

In addition to these provisions of states' general aid formulas, many states also have multiple funding formulas operating simultaneously. There may be one general aid formula and several additional aid formulas. It may be that the general aid formula is adjusted for differences in local capacity to pay for the services to be funded by that formula but that some or all of the other aid formulas are not adjusted for differences in local capacity. Additional aid may be allocated in flat block grants across districts, regardless of differences in student populations, regional costs, or local capacity. Alternatively, many of these additional grants may be allocated according to needs but not adjusted for local capacity. Further, some of these grants may be allocated entirely at the discretion of state agencies. In some states the general aid formula may constitute a relatively small part of the overall distribution of state aid. Consequently, while the general aid formula may be progressive and work to improve equity and adequacy overall, the other types of aid (outside the general formula funds) may completely erase any improvements made with general aid.

One particularly problematic category of aid provisions plays a significant disequalizing role in three of our six focus states: state aid for property tax reduction. On its face, it could make sense to allocate state aid to support reduction of local property taxes. In fact, state aid generally does just that. If a district receives more in state aid, then that district can provide the same level of service while raising less in local revenue, or it can provide a higher level of service while raising the same in local revenue. State equalization aid is generally distributed to permit lower fiscal capacity school districts to have comparable total revenue with a tax effort that is fair or comparable to the tax effort of higher fiscal capacity districts. In many states, however, it remains the case that poorer, lower fiscal capacity districts continue to levy much higher nominal tax rates than do higher fiscal capacity districts while still having lower total revenue per pupil. At the same time, in these states affluent local public school districts in particular can still raise far more through taxes than they need to operate their school systems.

It is important to remember that state general aid is partly intended to be allocated in inverse proportion to local capacity, which is usually measured in terms of taxable property wealth. That is, state general equalization aid is intended to allow districts, regardless of their property wealth, to raise the revenue they need and to make sure that high-need, low wealth districts are not forced to tax themselves at unfairly high rates. General equalization aid is property tax relief for those who need it most. Thus, there should be little or no reason to provide separate funding streams for property tax relief, especially in inverse relation to the general equalization aid formula. Yet some states have done just that—target tax relief aid to those with the greatest local fiscal capacity and the fewest additional need and cost pressures. These tax-relief aid programs are, in effect, *unequalization* aid.

New York State, for example, operates its property tax relief program as an entirely separate formula, while Texas embeds its property tax relief aid within its general aid formula and focuses on "compressing" (Texan for cutting or reducing) local property taxes of districts. Missouri's property tax relief aid is the least regressive among the three states with such provisions and is based on a referendum passed in 1982 that set aside a special fund derived from a 1 percent statewide sales tax.

There is a special irony to state aid for tax relief as applied in New York and Texas. Recall that the primary goals of state school finance formulas are to efficiently promote equity and adequacy. Yet, state aid for tax relief generally erodes equity and does little, if anything, to advance adequacy. Further, studies of the effects of New York's tax relief program also find that it promotes inefficient spending among already high-spending, affluent suburban school districts. Tae Ho Eom and Ross Rubenstein "find evidence that, all else constant, the exemptions have reduced efficiency in districts with larger exemptions, but the effects appear to diminish as taxpayers become accustomed to the exemptions."[22] Jonah Rockoff similarly finds that New York's STAR subsidies encouraged additional spending. He did not explore directly the efficiency consequences, noting, "Tax-price reductions for homeowners in New York State led to an increase in local school district expenditures, crowded out a significant portion of the intended tax relief, and raised taxes for other property owners."[23]

In addition to those policies listed in table 6.3, there are a number of other provisions that contribute to inequities by reducing support to high-need districts. For example, three of the states we studied distributed their state aid primarily on the basis of average daily attendance rather than enrollment or membership. Districts with higher poverty and minority concentration rates tend to also have lower attendance rates, often for reasons beyond the districts' control. Using attendance as the base count method for driving school funding reduces aid to these districts, thus serving effectively as an *unpoverty* weight. Also, states may tweak their need weighting systems in a number of ways to make them not play out as expected. Missouri, for example, provides additional need weighting only above the statewide average for any given need measure, so there is no need differentiation for districts from o percent low income to the statewide average (or o percent LEP/ELL to the statewide average). The weight only kicks in above that level. This approach serves to preserve more aid for the least-needy districts and provide less differentiation of aid for the neediest districts.

THE LIMITED ROLE OF FEDERAL AID

The majority of federal aid that reaches schools and districts is distributed through Title I of what was originally known as the Elementary and Secondary Education Act. This funding is distributed to states and passed along to districts and schools through a series of formulas with the primary directive of providing additional revenue to support programs in high-poverty districts and schools. Figure 6.15 shows the geographic distribution of federal aid as a percent of total revenue. Low-income districts in the Southeast and Southwest receive the largest shares of their revenue from federal sources, while districts in the Northeast receive relatively small shares.

Most federal entitlement programs like Title I, which use poverty data as a basis for allocation, use the US Census Bureau income thresholds for poverty measurement, which account for income and family size. But this poverty measure does not account for differences in income that might be needed for providing similar quality of living from one region to the next. Clearly, a $20,000 income for a family of four provides for a vastly different quality of life in El Paso than in New York City. Similarly, to provide for equal input purchasing power, state school finance formulas often include adjustments for regional differences in competitive wages. Federal Title I aid does not do this, though portions of the aid are adjusted for less logical factors, such as providing more to states that spend more on their own (state spending factor).

Some have argued that even while federal Title I aid does go disproportionately to states with higher census poverty rates, that distribution is not

FIGURE 6.15   Share of revenue from federal sources

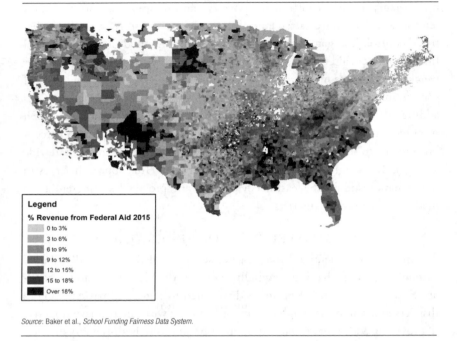

Legend

% Revenue from Federal Aid 2015
- 0 to 3%
- 3 to 6%
- 6 to 9%
- 9 to 12%
- 12 to 15%
- 15 to 18%
- Over 18%

Source: Baker et al., *School Funding Fairness Data System.*

progressive enough—too much aid goes to northeastern states and large cities and too little to southern and rural districts.[24] Lori Taylor, researchers at the American Institutes for Research, and I collaborated to evaluate whether these assumptions were correct if we first adjusted poverty thresholds regionally to make poverty measurement more comparable across settings and then adjusted the value of Title I dollars for differences in competitive wages.[25] Table 6.4 shows an abbreviated version of our findings, comparing Title I allocations per low-income pupil without any adjustments and then with both adjustments for metropolitan areas (around cities of 50,000 or more), micropolitan areas (around cities of 10,000–50,000), and rural areas.

What we found was the opposite of what others had asserted. Without adjustments, it appears that Title I aid per low-income pupil is highest in metropolitan areas in the Northeast. After applying both adjustments, however, it turns out that metropolitan areas in the Northeast are receiving

TABLE 6.4   Federal Title I revenue per child in poverty with and without adjustment

Region	Title I district revenue per poverty pupil			NCES CWI adjusted Title I district revenue per cost-adjusted poverty pupil		
	Metro	Micro	Rural	Metro	Micro	Rural
Appalachia Kentucky, Tennessee, Virginia, West Virginia	$1,420	$1,216	$1,465	$1,258	$1,601	$1,922
Central Colorado, Kansas, Missouri, Nebraska, North Dakota, South Dakota, Wyoming	$1,343	$1,686	$1,620	$1,396	$2,562	$2,577
Mid-Atlantic Delaware, Maryland, Pennsylvania, New Jersey	$1,665	$1,470	$1,700	$1,260	$1,768	$2,211
Midwest Illinois, Indiana, Iowa, Michigan, Minnesota, Ohio, Wisconsin	$1,484	$1,296	$1,279	$1,301	$1,701	$1,779
Northeast Connecticut, Maine, Massachusetts, New Hampshire, New York, Rhode Island, Vermont	$1,867	$1,514	$1,526	$1,311	$1,725	$2,059
Northwest Alaska, Idaho, Montana, Oregon, Washington	$1,443	$1,474	$1,717	$1,301	$1,897	$2,329
Southeast Alabama, Florida, Georgia, Mississippi, North Carolina, South Carolina	$1,418	$1,339	$1,402	$1,454	$1,770	$1,979
Southwest Arkansas, Louisiana, New Mexico, Oklahoma, Texas	$1,267	$1,398	$1,462	$1,254	$2,161	$2,423
West Arizona, California, Nevada, Utah	$1,368	$1,271	$1,216	$1,061	$1,723	$1,654

Note: Based on tabulation of district level data, weighted for student enrollment.

Source: Data from 2007–8, 2008–9, and 2009–10, Baker et al., "Adjusted Poverty Measures and the Distribution of Title I Aid."

relatively average to low Title I funding and that rural and micropolitan areas are receiving a disproportionate share (more than $2,000 per pupil in many cases). So despite all the attention given to Beltway deliberations over Title I aid formulas and related regulations, the effect of Title I funding on state school finance progressiveness is relatively modest. It's really up to the states to ensure equitable and adequate funding, and it will likely remain that way for the foreseeable future.

FIGURE 6.16 Federal aid and progressiveness in Massachusetts

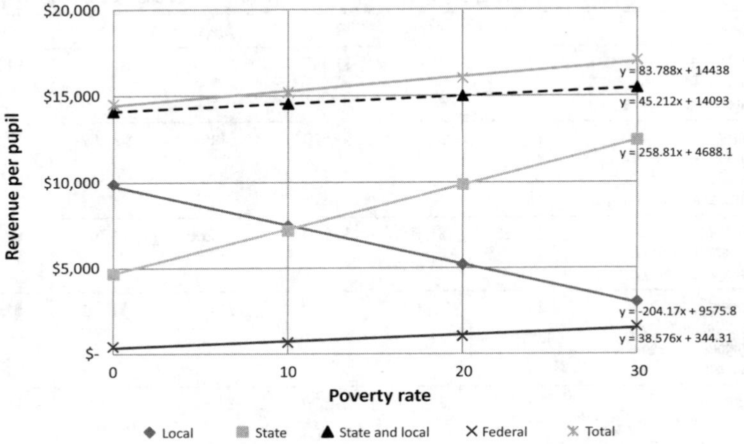

Source: Baker et al., *School Funding Fairness Data System.*

By way of example, figure 6.16 breaks down the progressiveness of revenue components for the Commonwealth of Massachusetts. The "local" component reveals a downward sloping trend, starting at $9,911 for the 0 percent poverty district to $3,765 for the 30 percent poverty district. The related equation suggests that an additional 1 percent of children in poverty is associated with $204 less in local revenue per pupil. State aid counters this regressiveness by adding, on average, $259 per each additional 1 percent child poverty rate. State and local revenue combined are thus mildly progressive, with an additional $45 per pupil for each additional 1 percent of children in poverty. Federal aid tilts the slope upward to an additional combined (local, state, and federal) $84 per pupil for each additional 1 percent child poverty rate.

When applied to a highly regressive state like Illinois, federal aid is insufficient to produce an overall progressive distribution (figure 6.17). For local revenue, each additional 1 percent of children in poverty is associated with $190 less in per-pupil revenue. State aid only partly offsets this disparity, providing an additional $88 per pupil for each additional 1 percent of children in poverty. Thus, combined state and local revenue remains regressive, with $127 less in revenue for each additional 1 percent of children in poverty. Federal aid

FIGURE 6.17   Federal aid and progressiveness in Illinois

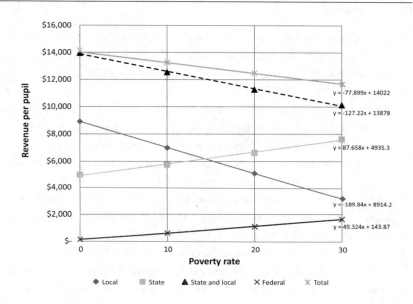

$y = -77.899x + 14022$

$y = -127.22x + 13878$

$y = 87.658x + 4935.3$

$y = -189.84x + 8914.2$

$y = 49.324x + 143.87$

Legend: ◆ Local   ■ State   ▲ State and local   ✕ Federal   ✕ Total

Source: Baker et al., *School Funding Fairness Data System.*

partially closes this gap, reducing it to $78 less in revenue for each additional 1 percent of children in poverty, but it can neither eliminate the state-imposed disparity nor reverse it to yield a progressive system.

LESSONS LEARNED AND LOOKING FORWARD

State school finance systems are messy. They are products of contentious, sometimes ugly legislative deliberations and court battles. But they're what we're stuck with. Resolving the shortcomings of the fifty-one public education systems in the United States requires that we move toward more equitable and adequate financing built on informed conceptual frameworks and guided by reasonable empirical analysis and evidence. Equitable and adequate financing is a prerequisite condition for the provision of equal educational opportunity to all children. Because the federal role is, and will likely remain, limited and political and politicized, moving forward requires action within and across states.

There are few common conclusions that can be drawn across state school finance systems:

- State school finance systems vary widely, with some states doing quite well (Massachusetts and New Jersey) both in overall level and progressiveness of funding, and others doing very poorly (Illinois and Pennsylvania).
- Whether in a progressively or regressively funded system, some districts are still being left out, so we must continue to look out for these districts and be vocal advocates for the children they serve.
- We know what a good school finance system looks like, generally, and should make efforts to inform state legislative processes in this regard.
- Despite significant common ground on principles of school funding equity, there will be those who deny and distract, aiding and abetting state legislatures in the maintenance of inequalities.
- State school finance systems are necessarily the product of political deliberations and thus have the potential for judicial oversight, where the role of advocates and analysts is to create pressure and introduce evidence to "bend" these systems toward equity and adequacy.

An examination of state school finance systems necessarily leads to a discussion of how the Great Recession and shifting policy environment around public school finance adversely affected most of these systems and, perhaps more importantly, what can be learned from this period.

CHAPTER 7

THE EROSION OF
EQUITY AND ADEQUACY

Much of the decay of state school finance systems had its origins in the economic downturn that hit most states in 2007–09. As soon as the recession hit, many states' school finance formulas were either dismantled or frozen in time: state lawmakers simply stopped using the legislated equations and overrode them, offering instead, "You'll get x percent less than you got last year." In some cases, freezes were coupled with new legislation limiting revenue or spending growth from that point forward, including new limits on local districts' ability to raise property taxes to offset state aid reductions. These self-inflicted state spending limits served to constrain legislators from ever returning to fully funding the formula adopted prior to the recession. They also froze in place any disparities that existed at the time the limits were imposed. Only recently have some states begun to either reinstate formulas or adopt new formulas similar to what were in place prior to the recession. Keep in mind, however, that foundation levels and need and cost adjustments of those formulas are now over a decade old.

Funding levels in some states have also been affected by the political claim that choice solves all ills and can serve as a substitute for adequate resources. The thinking is that if we provide enough choices, adequate, even excellent, options will necessarily emerge, and students and their families can simply choose the excellent schools. Regardless of how much money we provide through public financing, someone somewhere will figure out how to run an excellent school with that funding, and that school will be able to scale itself to serve all those who wish to attend, eventually replacing at lower cost the more expensive but inadequate current system. Everyone wins.

Everyone receives adequate schooling equitably by way of access to great choices. But it doesn't work that way. The "best" choices are often those that can garner additional resources. And the "best" choices will always have limited availability due to numerous constraints on scaling up, including access to supplemental resources.

Yet, the myth that it might work has arguably fueled even greater systemwide resource deprivation in states that have most expanded choice. The creation of dual systems of education serving common geographic spaces is further eroding equity and, to an extent, efficiency. Specifically, charter school expansion and citywide choice models, lacking advanced planning and sufficient regulation, complicate equitable resource distribution across schools and children, including access to space and transportation. Managing equity in a competitive system using alternative models of governance and operations for both day-to-day activities of schooling and for access to and maintenance of capital assets (land, buildings, equipment) is complex, to say the least. Policy makers have managed those complexities poorly and have allowed the dual systems to exacerbate rather than ameliorate inequality.[1]

DECLINING EFFORT AND RESOURCES
(AND FAILURE TO REBOUND)

Much of the political rhetoric during the "new normal" and recession eras centered on claims that all state's citizens are simply being taxed to death—taxes are way too high and are crushing states' economic productivity potential! Such was the basis for Governor Brownback's tax cut experiment in Kansas. Further, it was argued by many, without empirical validation, that these taxes had crept upward for decades, and at the state and local level the primary cause was the burgeoning cost of our grossly inefficient public schooling system.

In most states the percent of aggregate personal income allocated through state and local revenue to public school systems has declined since 2007. In some states that decline has been substantial. The *School Funding Fairness Data System* includes two measures of "effort." The first expresses state and local revenue for schools as a percent of a state's economic capacity, measured by state GDP. The second measures state and local revenue for schools as a percent of aggregate personal income. Both are expressions of states' "effort" to generate revenue for elementary and secondary education. Figure 7.1 shows that in Michigan effort was near 5.5 percent (relatively high among states) in

FIGURE 7.1 Effort in 2007 against change in effort 2007–15

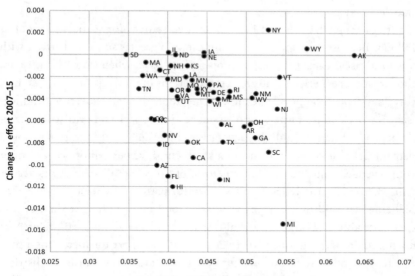

Source: Baker et al., *School Funding Fairness Data System.*

2007 but dropped by greater than 1.4 percent between 2007 and 2014. That drop is substantial, and Michigan's school funding formula took the hit, substantively erasing the gains of 1990s-era reforms. Texas, Indiana, Oklahoma, Georgia, Florida, and many other states also significantly reduced the share of aggregate income allocated to public schooling, inclusive of public financing of charter schools. In addition to state economic capacity, state effort explains a comparable share of school revenue. Effort matters. Yet despite the economic rebound in recent years, effort continues to decline.

When effort declines, so does revenue—in particular, state revenue that is largely intended to improve equity across local public school districts. State revenue is derived mainly from income and sales taxes (the balance depending on the state). The impact of the recession on public school systems came in two waves: first, it hit personal income, corporate income, and the tax revenue derived from these income sources; and second, states failed to revisit school funding as their economies began to recover. Sales tax revenue also took a hit during the recession. And due to the unique conditions leading to the recession, specifically the collapse of housing markets, property tax revenue declined as well.

In general, the ebb and flow of revenue sources for schools play out as follows. Because state aid is largely allocated in greater sums to districts with less local fiscal capacity (weaker property tax base) when state aid dries up, those districts experience the greatest reductions in total resources. Of course, this does depend on how state aid cuts are applied. Many governors and legislatures cut a constant percent of state aid from districts. For districts heavily dependent on state aid, this meant very large cuts; and for districts not as dependent on state aid, this meant a small cut. Five percent of 60 percent of your revenue is much more than 5 percent of 5 percent! New Jersey's governor Chris Christie actually levied a less harmful pattern of cuts across districts, reducing state aid by 5 percent of district total budgets (rather than of district state aid). In both cases, local districts tend to rely on local preferences for maintaining programs and services to rally support for increasing property taxes to offset state aid loss. Offsetting state aid losses is easier in districts with greater fiscal capacity, especially when their cuts are smaller (more affluent citizens and stronger tax base). As such, inequity expands.

For the first two years of the recession, the federal government distributed "fiscal stabilization" aid under the American Recovery and Reinvestment Act (ARRA). But that aid was insufficient to compensate fully for state aid reductions. Further, it was allocated for only two years, leaving behind significant budget holes, which would be felt most by districts in greatest need of aid once the federal funding was gone. The interplay of local, state, and federal revenue is critical to maintaining equitable and adequate funding systems. And understanding that interplay is critical to paving the path forward for sustainable, equitable, and adequate education systems. In 2014 I published an empirical analysis of the first part of the recession's effect on schools, the role of declining state aid on changes to revenue and spending progressiveness (fairness) across states.[2]

> The recent recession yielded an unprecedented decline in public school funding fairness. 36 states had a three year average reduction in current spending fairness between 2008–09 and 2010–11 and 32 states had a three year average reduction in state and local revenue fairness over that same time period. Over the entire 19 year period, only 15 states saw an

overall decline in spending fairness. In years prior to 2008 (starting in 1993) only 11 states saw an overall decline in spending fairness.

Declining funding fairness during the downturn resulted in part from cuts to state aid but also from a shifting role for federal aid. Further, during the period from 2007–2011, local public school districts' ability to offset losses to state aid varied. During the period from 2007–2011 compared to earlier periods, we saw the largest number of states where low poverty districts had local revenue changes moving in the opposite direction of state aid and the smallest number of states where high poverty districts showed the same inverse relationship. That is, during the downturn, low poverty districts compensated strongly for cuts to state aid while high poverty districts were unable to do the same.

In general, over the long haul, increases to state aid levels help to improve spending fairness. We see less clear evidence of shifts in state aid fairness resulting in shifts to spending fairness. We do, however, see that changes to local revenue fairness contribute to spending fairness. That is, this direct relationship suggests either or both that as local revenue becomes more disparate, so too does spending, and as local revenue becomes less disparate so too does spending. Despite a generally positive role for state aid improving spending equity, the role of state aid is not uniformly positive. In a number of states (16), changes in state revenue appear inversely associated with changes in spending fairness, suggesting a tendency either of state revenue increases to be targeted to less needy districts or state revenue decreases to be targeted to more needy districts.

Federal aid also seems to contribute to spending fairness. Changes to federal revenue fairness (targeting) contribute positively to spending fairness and changes to federal revenue levels also contribute to spending fairness. But, while the change in spending fairness resulting from a $1 increases in federal aid may be stronger in magnitude than the response to state aid, the overall level of federal aid is much smaller and therefore its overall effect on equity more modest.

While estimates herein shed some light on nationally representative patterns, above all else the findings herein highlight the heterogeneity of school finance across states. Yes, the recent downturn led to significant declines in funding fairness across a majority of states. Yes, state aid, on average, helps improve fairness. Yes, fairness of spending is compromised by disparity in access to local revenue. But, these relationships vary widely across states and defy simple classifications. In several states, abrupt policy decisions led to reclassification (Vermont and New Hampshire) or substitution (Michigan) of state and local revenue sources distorting the interplay between state and local revenue. Yet none of these cases led to sustained, substantive improvements to spending equity.

While equity overall took a hit between 1997 and 2011, the initial state of funding equity varied widely at the outset of the period, with Massachusetts and New Jersey being among the most progressively funded states in 2007. Thus, they arguably had further to fall. Funding equity for many states has barely budged over time, and remained persistently regressive, for example in Illinois, New York and Pennsylvania. Potential influences on these patterns are also evasive and widely varied. In Missouri, we see the 1990s influence of desegregation orders, which capitalized on the state's matching aid program to generate additional revenue in Kansas City and St. Louis driving spending progressiveness, but when the state adopts a need weighted foundation aid formula in 2006, spending continues to become more regressive. We see the more logical influence of school finance reforms in Massachusetts in the early 1990s and in New Jersey in the late 1990s, following court order, targeting additional funds to needy districts yielding an overall pattern of progressiveness. Court order in New York State (2006) appears to have had little or no influence on equity and the influence of court orders over time in Kansas has moved the needle only slightly. Better understanding role of judicial involvement requires significant additional exploration of these data linked to information on both judicial activity and legislative reforms.

Figure 7.2 shows the long-term trends of state aid and local revenue for high-poverty school districts in four states that, during the period 2007–15, implemented significant school finance reforms. Following a 2002 state supreme court decision in *Lakeview v. Huckabee*, Arkansas significantly scaled up state aid to schools while leveling down local revenue. State aid increased in Arkansas through the mid-2000s but has since leveled off.[3] Similarly, state aid to high-poverty districts in Kansas scaled up initially with the adoption of the 1992 School District Finance Act, and local contributions in high-poverty districts declined. As state aid declined in the late 1990s, local revenue began to climb, but within state-imposed limits. New lawsuits (e.g., *Montoy v.*

FIGURE 7.2 State aid and local revenue per pupil (constant year 2000 dollars) for highest-poverty quintile of school districts

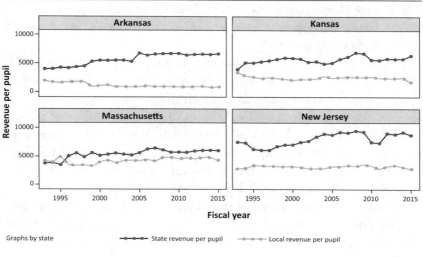

Graphs by state   ●━━● State revenue per pupil   ●━━● Local revenue per pupil

Source: Baker et al., *School Funding Fairness Data System*.

Kansas) led to judicial pressure in the mid-2000s, which led to increased state aid.[4] However, the recession and Governor Brownback's tax plan led to subsequent significant reductions in state aid. Massachusetts and New Jersey both scaled up state aid in the 1990s for high-poverty districts, which then leveled off in the mid-2000s. State aid in New Jersey took a significant hit during the recession but partially rebounded thereafter.

In Kansas, Arkansas, and Massachusetts, state aid per pupil in high-poverty districts leveled off around $6,000, but in New Jersey it reached nearly $10,000 per pupil. Kansas school finance reform was designed to embed a significant ongoing, prescribed local role involving a minimum required property tax levy and cap on additional local property taxes. During the late 1990s that minimum local contribution was repeatedly reduced, and for a period of time state aid increased to offset the difference. But in the late 1990s and early 2000s, state aid fell short. From the 1990s through the 2000s, the cap on local revenue that could be raised above the state foundation level was increased, appeasing more affluent districts but leading to increased inequity and new legal challenges.[5] Those challenges led to aid increases from 2005 to about 2008, when the recession hit. The 1998 *Abbott v. Burke* ruling in New Jersey placed the burden on the state specifically to fully fund specific programs and services needed for the largest high-poverty districts (and a few others in the Plaintiff class).[6] As such, the local role in these districts was minimized, even though the statewide average local share in New Jersey remains higher than average nationally.

Figure 7.3 displays the state and local revenue per pupil for the lowest-poverty quintile of districts for the same states. In Arkansas, higher- and lower-poverty districts experienced a similar shift in state and local revenue, with state revenue largely replacing local revenue. In Kansas, while state aid was substantively scaled up in high-poverty districts, state and local revenue for low-poverty districts remained relatively equal. In New Jersey and Massachusetts, low-poverty districts rely heavily on local revenue, with state aid playing a relatively small and constant role over time in both states.

There exists a common belief that because state aid is generally distributed with the goal of improving equity, states that have a larger share of total education spending from the state must be more equitable. As such, school funding advocacy organizations often point to state aid share as an important

FIGURE 7.3   State aid and local revenue per pupil (constant year 2000 dollars) for lowest-poverty quintile of school districts

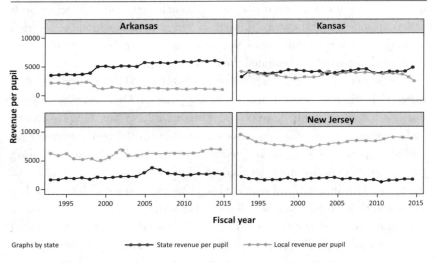

Source: Baker et al., *School Funding Fairness Data System.*

indicator of equity or even adequacy.[7] But state aid share isn't really a good indication of either. First, many of the worst-funded state education systems have relatively high shares of total resources coming from the state but the total amount of funding is very low—the state amount is low and the local amount even lower. This makes for a disconnect between state share and adequacy.

It also turns out that state share is not strongly associated with funding fairness, or progressiveness. Figure 7.4 shows the relationship between state and local revenue progressiveness and the percent of revenue received from the state for relatively high-poverty districts. States with a higher state share—even specifically for relatively high-poverty districts—do not necessarily have more progressive funding. Funding is relatively progressive in New Jersey, which has an above-average state share for high-poverty districts. But many states, such as Kansas, New Mexico, Arkansas, and Vermont, have a much higher state share and less progressive funding. Progressiveness depends not only on how much money is coming from the state but how well targeted that money is.

FIGURE 7.4 State share of revenue for a district with 20 percent of children in poverty and revenue progressiveness

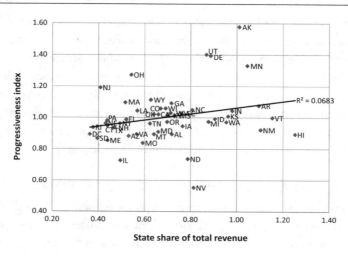

Source: Baker et al., School Funding Fairness Data System.

FIGURE 7.5 State share of revenue and progressiveness of funding in New Jersey 1993–2015

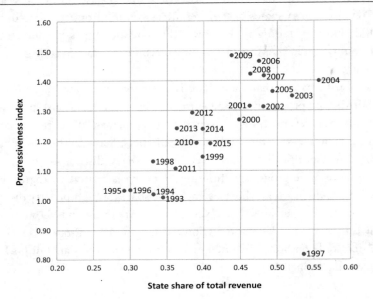

Source: Baker et al., *School Funding Fairness Data System.*

Because state aid in New Jersey is progressively targeted, increases and decreases to state aid translate to increase or decreases in progressiveness (figure 7.5). From 1998 through the mid-2000s, New Jersey's share for relatively high-poverty districts climbed, as did its progressiveness. The years 2004–09 saw high state shares and progressiveness. But in 2010–15 state support waned, as did progressiveness. So while higher state share doesn't necessarily lead to more equitable or adequate funding, appropriately distributed and robust state aid can enhance both equity and adequacy.

BALANCING THE REVENUE PORTFOLIO

Three levels of government involvement in public schooling coupled with the layered tax revenue sources derived from those levels makes for a complicated system. However, there are some virtues to this school finance layer cake, as flawed and politically divisive as it may be. Most notably, it provides a more balanced portfolio of revenue than would a single, dedicated source model.

A balanced revenue portfolio provides opportunity for more stable revenue sources to buffer losses from more volatile sources.

Most local revenue for schools comes from property taxes levied on residential, commercial, industrial, farm, and other properties. In most cases, these properties at least hold their value over time, and since reappraisal cycles for property values take time, any losses (or gains) to local property tax revenue do not occur immediately. State tax revenue comes from income taxes and sales taxes, with some states having a relative balance between the two, while other states are far more heavily dependent on income tax revenue (e.g., Massachusetts and California) and still others are without income taxes and thus dependent on sales tax revenue (e.g., Texas and Florida).

Rob Tannenwald, of the Federal Reserve Bank of Boston, wrote a handful of insightful analyses of state tax systems in the early 2000s, following the economic dip after the September 11 attacks. Even prior to the downturn, Tannenwald observed that state tax systems were becoming obsolete because sales taxes were levied primarily on goods and based on in-state brick-and-mortar retail sales while the nation's production was shifting from goods to services and interstate electronic commerce was expanding rapidly.[8] Also, the share of income that was from earned wages was declining, with investment returns and other forms of income increasing. The potential danger of this trend, he noted, was that wage income tended to be more stable and other income more volatile, which might be especially problematic in states most reliant on income tax revenue and in states where a lower share of income was from wages. The results were observable during the 2001–03 downturn and can be seen in figure 7.6, which portrays total tax revenue by source as a percent of prior year revenue from the same source—that is, percent change year after year (adjusted for inflation). While there had been a similar economic downturn in the early 1990s, it did not result in the same loss of income tax revenue. At the time, a much larger share of income was in the form of wage income. Luckily, during the early 2000s property tax revenue continued to grow, in part because of the housing bubble, and served as an important buffer during the post-9/11 downturn.

Figure 7.6 also shows that income tax revenue dipped again during the 2007–09 recession. Sales tax revenue dipped more during this period, but not by as much as income tax revenue. Property tax revenue did not dip until after income tax revenue had begun to rebound. So, had state school finance systems been 100 percent reliant on income taxes alone, or on income

FIGURE 7.6   Volatility of tax revenues by source

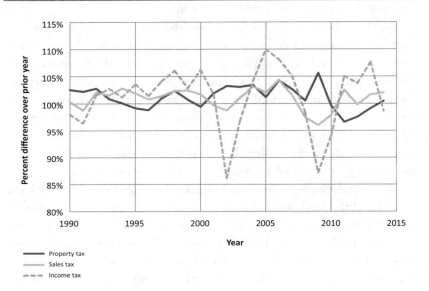

Sources: *State and Local Government Finance Data Query System*, The Urban Institute–Brookings Institution Tax Policy Center, http://www .taxpolicycenter.org/slf-dqs/pages.cfm; US Census Bureau, *Annual Survey of State and Local Government Finances, Government Finances*, Vol. 4, and *Census of Governments* (1990–2014).

and sales taxes alone, total reductions in school funding may have been far more severe.

WITHIN-DISTRICT EQUITY AND EXPANDED CHOICE

The 1990s saw a flurry of studies that began to explore equity of resources across schools within districts. These studies revealed significant variation in spending across schools, raising the legitimate concern regarding the effectiveness of state school finance formulas alone for resolving resource inequities down to the level of schools and students, since those policies are most often focused on districts as a unit of governance. After all, in a state like New York, a single district might serve over a third of all pupils across more than a thousand schools. Getting enough money to New York City to achieve equity with other districts statewide was one thing; but ensuring that the resources flowed equitably to children across schools within this very large socially, economically, and racially diverse city was another thing entirely.

Over the next decade, through the late 2000s, within-district inequality became a convenient scapegoat issue for federal policy makers, one informed by Beltway think tanks.[9] The message that emerged was that due to years of litigation and pressure by state courts, states had largely met their obligations to resolve disparities between local public school districts and that the bulk of remaining disparities were those that persist within school districts.[10] In this view, the most useful exertion of federal pressure is on local district officials and their corrupt policies that drive more money to schools in rich neighborhoods within districts and away from poor neighborhoods within the same districts.

The political convenience of focusing on within-district equity was that federal policy and funding could be leveraged to place pressure on local bureaucrats—namely, school superintendents and local boards of education—to fix their inequitable budget allocations, regardless of how much money was available. It was a simple, revenue-neutral solution, one that avoided federal officials having to place any pressure on state legislatures and governors to fund more equitable statewide formulas, which might require raising taxes. These federal policies exist today in the form of "comparability" regulations, which require that local school districts can show that poor schools receive resources at least comparable to those of rich schools in order to qualify to receive federal Title I funding.[11] Title I has long required that districts supplement, not supplant, state and local resources with Title I funds for high-poverty schools.

Indeed, it is important that we consider not only the delivery of resources from states to local districts but also how those resources reach schools and children. But federal attention on within-district disparities without regard for between-district disparities has created an unfortunate distraction from the larger issue: many high-need school districts lack sufficient resources to provide their students equal educational opportunity and have limited capacity to reshuffle those resources from poor to poorer schools within their highly segregated boundaries.

Assertions that the remaining dominant disparities in school finance are those across schools within a district are based on analyses that range from merely insufficient to flawed and outright deceitful.[12] Additionally, the argument falsely presumes that there exist large numbers of school districts around the country that have both rich and poor neighborhoods within their boundaries and many schools sorted among them. Except in southern states operating county systems, most racial and economic segregation exists across school district boundaries, not across schools within districts. Further, in many states there are relatively few districts that actually have large numbers of schools, and even fewer where there is large variation in poverty across those schools.

Table 7.1 shows that 21 states have less than half of their students attending districts with 10 or more schools. Vermont has none, and 15 states have more than one-third of their students attending districts with fewer than 5 schools. Mark Weber and I have illustrated that if we look across schools statewide, variations in district spending strongly dictate statewide variations in school spending: "District spending variation explains an important, policy relevant share of school staffing expenditures in 13 states. In many states, including Illinois and New York, a nearly 1:1 relationship exists between district spending variation and school site spending variation."[13] In other words, if a district has more money, so do the schools within that district.

TABLE 7.1   Distribution of students by numbers of schools per district

State	Total students	DISTRICTS WITH <5 SCHOOLS		DISTRICTS >10 SCHOOLS	
		Number	Share	Number	Share
Alaska	128,500	13,325	10.4%	110,218	85.8%
Alabama	715,618	105,756	14.8%	494,717	69.1%
Arkansas	467,372	216,091	46.2%	170,500	36.5%
Arizona	1,030,659	224,630	21.8%	657,757	63.8%
California	6,067,005	513,735	8.5%	4,844,091	79.8%
Colorado	834,909	69,625	8.3%	716,041	85.8%
Connecticut	550,112	155,430	28.3%	266,437	48.4%
District of Columbia	66,304	15,426	23.3%	43,530	65.7%
Delaware	127,615	22,369	17.5%	84,207	66.0%
Florida	2,615,008	14,351	0.5%	2,565,337	98.1%
Georgia	1,656,816	197,258	11.9%	1,285,984	77.6%
Hawaii	179,493			179,493	100.0%
Iowa	473,258	231,584	48.9%	170,372	36.0%
Idaho	271,398	56,209	20.7%	176,645	65.1%
Illinois	2,034,620	771,708	37.9%	998,525	49.1%
Indiana	1,014,850	322,583	31.8%	460,774	45.4%
Kansas	470,430	144,963	30.8%	240,674	51.2%

TABLE 7.1 *Continued*

State	Total students	DISTRICTS WITH <5 SCHOOLS		DISTRICTS >10 SCHOOLS	
		Number	Share	Number	Share
Kentucky	666,217	133,387	20.0%	390,523	58.6%
Louisiana	666,595	33,696	5.1%	583,557	87.5%
Massachusetts	928,826	307,105	33.1%	338,025	36.4%
Maryland	849,176	240*	0.0%	833,812	98.2%
Maine	173,079	72,860	42.1%	21,323	12.3%
Michigan	1,463,719	485,479	33.2%	580,359	39.6%
Minnesota	765,971	268,359	35.0%	353,087	46.1%
Missouri	897,145	319,563	35.6%	413,777	46.1%
Mississippi	474,942	155,462	32.7%	182,525	38.4%
Montana	137,716	98,984	71.9%	27,625	20.1%
North Carolina	1,471,917	85,196	5.8%	1,321,518	89.8%
North Dakota	94,792	41,239	43.5%	42,924	45.3%
Nebraska	294,883	96,787	32.8%	161,453	54.8%
New Hampshire	184,248	104,941	57.0%	36,659	19.9%
New Jersey	1,324,287	511,489	38.6%	457,087	34.5%
New Mexico	325,813	31,959	9.8%	266,834	81.9%
Nevada	434,314	3,042	0.7%	417,825	96.2%
New York	2,651,363	761,881	28.7%	1,400,489	52.8%
Ohio	1,681,521	743,631	44.2%	512,413	30.5%
Oklahoma	637,140	273,295	42.9%	270,207	42.4%
Oregon	524,470	73,271	14.0%	346,619	66.1%
Pennsylvania	1,729,448	662,191	38.3%	631,841	36.5%
Rhode Island	134,681	24,786	18.4%	61,513	45.7%
South Carolina	698,472	44,381	6.4%	586,258	83.9%
South Dakota	121,062	55,107	45.5%	40,851	33.7%
Tennessee	981,295	65,538	6.7%	753,632	76.8%
Texas	4,865,252	766,257	15.7%	3,659,655	75.2%
Utah	578,186	47,322	8.2%	507,033	87.7%
Virginia	1,240,510	89,808	7.2%	1,026,530	82.8%
Vermont	78,804	75,183	95.4%		
Washington	1,026,819	131,305	12.8%	732,068	71.3%
West Virginia	276,028	14,481	5.2%	224,178	81.2%
Wyoming	86,629	16,026	18.5%	51,065	58.9%

Note: *SEED School listed as independent of district governance.

Source: Baker and Weber, "State School Finance Inequities."

EVALUATING SPENDING VARIATION ACROSS SCHOOLS

In a 2012 article I illustrated what I refer to as the "deck chairs in Dallas" problem—which may as well be deck chairs in Chicago or Philadelphia or many other high-poverty, under-resourced districts across the nation. The deck chairs problem exists where a high-poverty district is surrounded by lower-poverty districts and has, on average, fewer per-pupil resources than surrounding districts. Further, even the lowest-poverty schools within the high-poverty district tend to be about as high in poverty as the highest-poverty schools in surrounding districts. It's often the case that these schools are only a few blocks apart. Figure 7.7 shows a flat distribution by poverty across schools in the surrounding districts and a regressive distribution in the low-income urban core district. Certainly, this is problematic. It's not easily solved, however, because shifting that regressive distribution within the district to a progressive one means spending much less on the lowest-poverty schools, which are still higher in poverty than schools in other districts with more resources and that are only a few blocks away. Figure 7.8 shows the actual 2007 school site expenditures for schools in the Dallas/Fort Worth metropolitan area. The figure shows that the overall pattern across schools surrounding Dallas is progressive. Fort Worth schools, on average, also fall within that pattern. Dallas schools, however, fall almost entirely toward the higher-poverty end of the distribution (greater than 80 percent low income) and are consistently below the average per-pupil spending of other schools in the metropolitan area.

FIGURE 7.7 Reconciling within and between district spending disparities

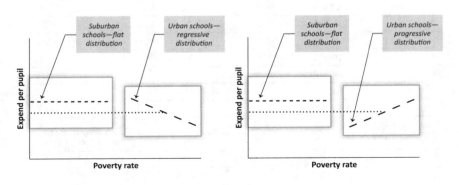

Source: Adapted from Baker and Weber, "State School Finance Inequities."

FIGURE 7.8   Rearranging deck chairs in Dallas

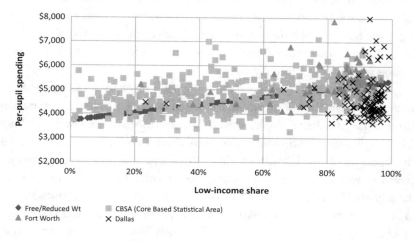

Source: Adapted from Baker, "Rearranging Deck Chairs in Dallas."

When evaluating within-district spending, we must take steps to separate "good variation" from "bad variation," or "equity-enhancing variation" from "equity-eroding variation." The same is true for between-district spending differences. In our school funding fairness work, we generate estimates of progressiveness of state school funding systems using a regression model, which estimates the relationship between census poverty rates and district revenue (and spending) while accounting for variation in competitive wages across regions, district enrollment size (economies of scale), and population sparsity. Failure to account for any of these relevant factors influencing spending variation can lead to erroneous conclusions.

An example of one such erroneous conclusion from school-level analyses is a 2007 study by researchers from the Buckeye Institute in Ohio, who counted the districts where there existed a positive versus negative correlation between low-income student concentrations and per-pupil spending across schools within those districts. They found that most of the seventy high-poverty districts studied did not have clear positive correlations between school spending and low-income shares.[14] Most of what they actually found was that school districts with one or a few elementary schools, a middle school, and a high school often had higher per-pupil spending in the high school, and that the high school often had lower shares of children reported as qualifying for free or reduced-price lunch.[15] This is important to understand because this is a common pattern that comes with a variety of explanations, including fewer families applying for subsidized lunch at the secondary level. However, it's not evidence that Ohio districts were shortchanging higher-poverty schools to favor lower poverty ones.

A more egregious example of faulty conclusions drawn from poor analysis comes from the New York–based charter school advocacy organization Families for Excellent Schools, which released a report arguing that New York City's highest-funded middle schools were also its worst. The press release for the report proclaimed, "At the middle school level, the bottom 50 schools received an average $30,256 per pupil, compared with $16,277 at the top 50 middle schools."[16] The goal of the report was to advocate that these funds should instead be directed toward charter school expansion, since it was clear, from this finding, that the district simply didn't know how to leverage resources to improve student achievement. But this "study" missed the simple fact that in New York City, like most large districts, the primary driver of differences in spending across schools within districts is the share of children with disabilities served in the schools. Children with disabilities significantly influence staffing ratios and thus school-level spending. Also, schools with more children with disabilities tend to have lower average test scores.

So what is the right approach for characterizing good and bad disparities across schools within districts? There is a common set of factors that should typically be included in any model of within-district school-level spending variation.[17] First, we must consider the grade-level issue, because there exist differences in both spending approaches across grade levels and student need measures (e.g., free or reduced-price lunch). It's not that we have any real basis for assuming that elementary school costs more than high school, or vice versa, but direct comparisons ignoring grade level are problematic and can lead to invalid conclusions (e.g., the Buckeye Institute report).

While district size and population sparsity are typically considered when evaluating district spending, one could argue that there should not exist inefficiently small (and thus higher spending) schools in densely populated urban contexts because they drain resources from other schools. It's inequitable variation, not equitable variation. Perhaps most importantly, the distribution of children with disabilities across schools must be considered, preferably with attention paid to which schools are serving children with more severe disabilities, which require even more direct instructional and related services and support personnel.

Tables 7.2 and 7.3 present results of regression models of school spending in New York City and New York State in 2015. I use these models to characterize the average patterns across all schools in each district. Often, statistical models like these are used for drawing inferences about relationships; but here the models describe actual patterns across all schools. For example, in table 7.2, for New York City, moving from 0 percent to 100 percent children in middle grades, per-pupil spending drops by $779. Moving from 0 percent to 100 percent children in secondary grades, per-pupil spending decreases by $757. This means that in terms of grade levels, elementary schools have the highest per-pupil spending rates. (The average regular New York City elementary school spent about $21,229 per pupil in 2015.) Moving from a school with 0 percent to 100 percent low-income children increases spending by about $2,000 per pupil (about a 10 percent margin). Moving from a school with 0 percent to 100 percent children in special education, spending per pupil doubles. Most schools fall between 0 percent and 30 percent children in special education, so the practical difference is about one-third of the $25,159 spent on each pupil. Importantly, these factors explain over 60 percent of the variations in spending across New York City schools. Most of the variation in spending is rational, explainable variation. Yet, a sizeable share is not and should be vetted further.

By contrast, table 7.3 shows a model applied to statewide, interdistrict spending variation in New York in 2015. Here, I also include factors for

TABLE 7.2   Model of school site spending in New York City, 2015

	Coefficient (difference)	Standard Error
Grade level		
% grades 6–8	–$779	$163
% grades 9–12	–$757	$142
Student need		
% subsidized lunch	**$2,008**	**$297**
% special education	**$25,159**	**$1,174**
School size (enrollment)	–$2,635	$85
Constant	$34,319	$653
Adjusted R–squared =		0.6148

Sources: Data from New York City Department of Education School Site Budgets, http://schools.nyc.gov/Offices/DBOR/SBER/default.htm); and New York State Department of Education School Report Card Data, School Enrollment Characteristics, https://data.nysed.gov/.

TABLE 7.3   Model of statewide current spending per pupil for New York State districts, 2015

DV = current spending per pupil	Coefficient	Standard error
Student needs		
% poverty (census)	−$11,783	$1,876
% ELL	$8,938	$2,864
% special education	$16,365	$4,272
Competitive wage variation	$9,081	$987
Population density	−$335	$131
<100	$21,779	$15,164
101–300	−$1,337	$5,284
201–600	$563	$4,626
601–1200	−$1,617	$1,989
1201–1500	−$418	$2,443
1501–2000	−$3,679	$1,946
Unified K–12 district	$368	$944
Interaction with population density		
<100	$1,620	$2,886
101–300	$3,044	$1,147
201–600	$742	$1,028
601–1200	$688	$378
1201–1500	$296	$424
1501–2000	$868	$317
Constant	$5,349	$1,445
R–squared = 0.4538		

Sources: Data from New York State Education Department, Fiscal Analysis and Research Unit, Fiscal Profiles, www.oms.nysed.gov/faru/; https://data.nysed.gov/.

regional wage variation and for economies of scale and population sparsity. As such, this even richer model should be able to explain even more variation if that variation is rationally related to cost and need factors. But the state-level model only yields about 45 percent variation explained by rational factors. More disturbingly, the state model reveals an overall statewide pattern of regressive interdistrict disparity, wherein a district with 100 percent poverty would be expected to have nearly $12,000 less in per-pupil spending than a district with 0 percent poverty. So, spending disparities within New York City are less of a problem than spending disparities statewide. New York City intradistrict funding is mildly progressive, whereas statewide interdistrict funding is regressive.

CHARTER EXPANSION AND INTRADISTRICT EQUITY

In an equitable system, after accounting for the relevant factors, there should not be any difference in spending between charter schools and district schools. Otherwise, charter schooling introduces inequity. Baltimore, unlike New York City, does spend more in schools serving more secondary-level students. Again, the margins of difference related to special education are the greatest but are somewhat buffered where the share of students who have mild disabilities is greater.

As shown in table 7.4, it appears that, on average, schools serving more low-income children have lower per-pupil spending, which means that Baltimore school funding is flat to regressive. But when taking charter schools into account, charters, on average, spend slightly more ($249) per pupil than otherwise similar district schools, and that spending with respect to low-income children is slightly progressive (a $183 per-pupil increase moving from 0 percent to 100 percent low income). The reason this pattern flips when accounting for charter schools is that Baltimore charters serve, on average, fewer low-income students and spend slightly more per pupil than district schools do. They introduce an inequity to the system. This finding is common across urban schooling systems that include a mix of charter and district schools.

TABLE 7.4 Model of school site spending in Baltimore, 2013–15

	Coefficient (difference)	Standard error	Coefficient (difference)	Standard error
Grade distribution				
% grades 6–8	$409	$276	$395	$276
% grades 9–12	$1,798	$232	$1,839	$234
Student needs				
% nonsevere special education	−$974	$603	−$1,164	$621
% all special education	$18,666	$1,416	$18,425	$1,427
% ELL	$554	$892	$548	$891
% low income	−$79	$542	$183	$579
Charter school			$249	$196
Year				
Year 2014	$481	$163	$480	$163
Year 2015	$506	$166	$498	$166
Constant	$10,071	$765	$9,973	$769
R–Squared	0.486		0.488	

Source: Data from Levin et al., "Study of Funding."

Based on a 2015 study of charter schools in New York City and Houston, Ken Libby, Katy Wiley, and I found that New York City charter schools served fewer needy student populations than nearby district schools do and, on average, after accounting for student population differences, spent significantly more per pupil than district schools. Even more striking were the differences in spending within the charter sector, between schools having substantial private contributions versus those receiving far less outside of their public subsidies.[18] In a follow-up study, Mark Weber and I found that for-profit charter operators, on average, divert more money from direct classroom services, leading to even greater variation across schools in jurisdictions with a mix of district, for-profit charter, and nonprofit charter schools.[19]

In ongoing work, Mark Weber, Ajay Srikanth, and I are finding that across large school districts that have sizeable and growing charter sectors, student sorting by demographics is exacerbated and school spending variations are increased. That is, expanded chartering seems to be leading to increased inequality across schools within common geographic spaces. Using data from two waves of the Civil Rights Data Collection, we again find that, controlling for the factors listed previously, New York City charter schools spend far more than district schools serving similar populations (figure 7.9).

FIGURE 7.9 Charter school spending per pupil relative to host district for large districts

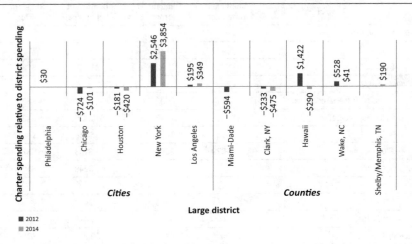

Source: Baker et al., School Level Data Panel, *School Funding Fairness Data System*.

Results are mixed for other large school districts, with district schools out-spending charters in some contexts and charter schools outspending district schools in others. But inequities are inequities, in whichever direction they fall.

INCOMPATIBLE POLICY PREFERENCES:
COMPARABILITY AND EXPANDED CHOICE

Tightening comparability regulations governing within-district equity, or progressiveness, while at the same time pushing for expanded choice and diversification of operators and governing bodies are entirely incompatible policies, because the former, choice, erodes the latter, equity. In some states, charter schools are governed by and financed through local district budgets, providing the opportunity for districts to use common formulas for funding both district and charter schools. In other states, fully independent charter schools may be authorized to operate within district spaces but outside of their control or financing. Some states (like Texas) have both.

Expanding the mix of providers and provider types in a common space is more likely to result in increased variations in quality and spending than in convergence toward equity. Private providers have widely varied access to outside resources and thus highly unequal opportunities for "revenue enhancement." The incentive for school operators is to pursue whatever means necessary to be the preferred school of choice (for the preferred students)—*not* to spend only what is needed to provide equal opportunity to achieve common outcomes.

Expanding choice also means accepting the presence of inefficiently small startups, at least for a period of time. The continued shifting of students from one sector to another within the same geographic space means accepting inequities and inefficiencies associated with growth-related costs in one sector and stranded expenses in another. For a system to be equitable, policy makers must figure out how to manage these inequities. Thus far, they've largely ignored them.

Much of the expansion of charter schooling occurred during the recession. States added schools while reducing overall funding, making inequitable choices on top of already unequal and inadequate systems. Expanded charter schooling was a centerpiece of the Duncan/Obama education reform platform that coincided with the recession and new normal era. Cursory descriptive analyses, as well as more complex longitudinal models, suggest that states which most expanded their charter sectors are also the states which most reduced their overall effort toward financing public education. This is a disturbing finding in part because charter schools also rely on public financing. So reducing public financing affects negatively both district and charter schools. Also, increasing the number of schools, holding enrollments constant, or shifting students from one sector to another creates additional costs, at least in the short run.[20] It is conceivable that state policy makers who have an ideological preference for school choice and assume that a competitive market-based system can "do more with less" apply that same ideology to state tax and spending policies. Or it just may be that states where legislators prefer choice and charter schools are also states where legislators prefer not to raise taxes or spend money on schools in general, whatever the type.

For example, figure 7.10 shows that states with very high charter market shares had in 2015 the lowest effort rates for financing public education (inclusive of charter spending). Focusing on four high charter market share states—Arizona, Colorado, Michigan, and Ohio—figure 7.11 shows that beginning in 2009, as charter market shares accelerated beyond 5 percent, state and local efforts toward financing public schools dropped precipitously. All four states have charter market shares above 5 percent in the most recent data years, with Colorado and Arizona above 10 percent. Michigan and Arizona

FIGURE 7.10 State charter enrollment share and fiscal effort

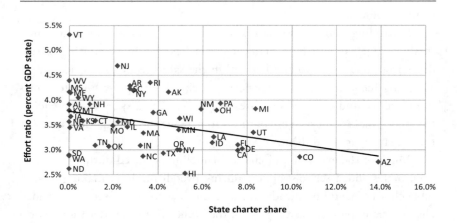

Source: Baker et al., *School Funding Fairness Data System.*

FIGURE 7.11   Charter enrollment share and fiscal effort

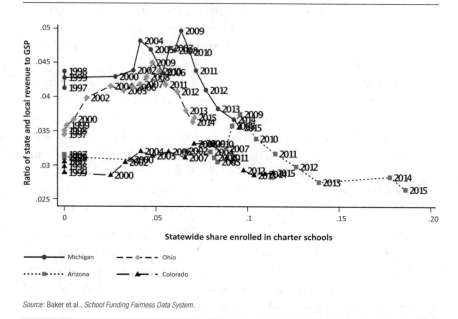

Source: Baker et al., *School Funding Fairness Data System*.

saw the greatest drop in effort, but effort also declined in the Colorado and Ohio. Whether there is causal relationship between charter market share and state effort, or these patterns merely exist as a function of shared ideologies of state policy makers, these patterns are problematic for both charter and district schools in these states.

LESSONS LEARNED AND LOOKING FORWARD

Although the recession did significant damage to state school finance formulas and funding equity, state economies have been on the rebound since about 2012, and some states are beginning to revisit their school finance formulas, considering both structural overhauls and infusion of additional funding. Still, by 2015

- most states had begun putting forth less effort to finance their education systems than they did a decade ago;
- many of those systems had become much less equitable than they were a decade ago;

- while allocating fewer resources, states had raised outcome standards without considering the costs of achieving those standards, thus setting up their schools for failure (the goals in 2017 were much higher than they were in 2007, but, in too many cases, the resources available were lower);
- an emphasis had been placed on within-district disparities, an unfortunate distraction from the bigger problem of between-district disparities and generally inadequate funding to achieve modern outcome goals; and
- policy preferences, such as taking a hard line on within-district inequity while promoting expansion of inequitable choices, also began diverting attention and resources away from the equitable provision of publicly provided schooling and into increased transportation, administration, and transition-related costs of operating expanded choice systems.

Advancing the state of our public education system, inclusive of choice systems, requires more consistent focus on equity and adequacy goals. Equitable and adequate resources are a prerequisite condition, regardless of the delivery system, and there are no substitutes for them. Achieving equity and adequacy in systems with multiple methods of delivery will necessarily be more complicated than doing so with a single model. The virtue of testing alternative models lies in the possibility that we might eventually find new efficiencies and more cost-effective methods, programs, and services. Maintenance of an adequate and equitable system over time will require stable and sufficient revenue, most likely derived from a balanced portfolio of major tax revenue sources.

CHAPTER 8

EVALUATING
EDUCATION INNOVATIONS

Methods used for evaluating the productivity, efficiency, and cost-effectiveness of potential education innovations have a long, rich history in scholarly literature that seems to have been all but forgotten in the past decade or so. Worse, in many cases the rigorous methods of the past have been replaced by pure speculation and unfounded claims devoid of either conceptual foundation or empirical evidence related to productivity and efficiency.

I began studying school finance in 1994 while a doctoral student at Teachers College at Columbia University, and one of my early introductions to the field and its literature was a 1995 symposium I attended. Sponsored by the New York State Regents, the Cost-Effectiveness in Education symposium featured research papers presented by faculty and graduate students from universities across the state, which were then released as a report to the Board of Regents in March 1996.[1] These state-supported research studies included research advancing the application of conceptual models and statistical methods for studying cost-effectiveness and efficiency of local public school districts. They represented the highest levels of empirical and conceptual rigor and were conducted by leading researchers in the field. The studies were part of an ongoing research consortium among scholars from Cornell, Syracuse, SUNY Albany, and NYU. Over time, research emanating from this group broke ground in analyses of equity, efficiency, resource allocation, and the use of state longitudinal data systems to study teacher labor markets.[2] Similarly, around the same time, in Texas, state agencies and academic researchers were collaborating to better understand variations in labor costs to inform recalibration of the state school finance formula and to more broadly inform the field of school finance. In the early 2000s, the Texas legislature established the Texas School Finance Project, in which I was involved with researchers from Texas A&M University in reviewing empirical methods and conducting empirical analyses to guide development of a more cost-based, efficient state school finance formula.[3] These state-supported efforts served to significantly advance our knowledge of education costs, cost analysis, cost variation, and efficiency through the production of numerous prominent and frequently cited reports.[4]

Research emanating from New York and Texas also found its way into national symposia sponsored by the US Department of Education and was released in two different recurring (1995–2005) report series: *Developments in School Finance* and *Selected Papers in School Finance.* The reports tackled with empirical rigor such issues as the development of national indices to capture variation in teacher wages from region to region, labor market to labor market, and district to district; the application of statistical modeling techniques to estimate costs of achieving common outcome goals; and statistical tests of the reliability and validity of estimates of school performance and efficiency.[5] These were the very types of analyses needed to inform state school finance polices and to advance the art and science of evaluating education reforms for their potential to improve equity, productivity, and efficiency. But these efforts largely disappeared over the next decade. More disconcerting, these efforts were replaced by far less rigorous, often purely speculative policy papers free of any substantive empirical analysis and devoid of any conceptual framework. Some of the more common policy proposals that have emerged for improving schooling productivity and efficiency include:

- expanding charter schooling and hoping that by granting greater flexibility in a competitive context, some operators will develop innovations that lead to greater efficiency;
- identifying "great teachers" and putting them in front of larger classes (up to one hundred students) while dismissing "bad" teachers, thereby reducing overall labor expenses;
- tying teacher compensation to performance metrics;
- replacing LIFO (last in first out) with quality-based dismissal in cases of reductions in force (RIFs); and
- finding technology-based substitutions.[6]

These proposals are mainly focused on expanded chartering and adopting new teacher evaluations and compensation and dismissal policies tied to student outcome measures. All are candidates for rigorous evaluation, but, to date, we have made little progress in this regard. It's essential to remember that equitable and adequate financing are prerequisite conditions for our education systems, regardless of how we choose to deliver those systems.

A COST ANALYSIS OF INNOVATIONS

Cost analyses come in a few flavors; cost-effectiveness analysis and cost-benefit analysis are two of the more common varieties. Cost-effectiveness analysis compares policy options on the basis of total costs. More specifically, it compares the spending required under specific circumstances to fully implement and maintain each option while also considering the effects of each option on a common set of measures. (Multiple options may, and arguably should, be compared, but there must be at least two.) Ultimately, the goal is to arrive at a cost-effectiveness index or ratio for each alternative to determine which provides the greatest effect for a constant level of spending.

The accuracy of cost-effectiveness analyses is contingent, in part, on carefully considering all direct and indirect expenditures required for the implementation and maintenance of each option. Consider an attempt to examine the cost-effectiveness of vouchers set at half the amount allotted to public schools per pupil. Assume, as is generally the case, that the measured outcomes are not significantly different for those students who are given the voucher. Then assume that the private school expenditures are the same as those for the comparison public schools, with the difference between the voucher amount and those expenditures being picked up through donations and supplemental tuition charged to the voucher parents. One cannot claim greater cost-effectiveness for voucher subsidies in this case, since another party is picking up the difference. One can still argue that this voucher policy is wise, but the argument cannot be one of cost-effectiveness. Note also that the expenditure required to implement program alternatives may vary widely depending on setting or location. Labor costs may vary widely, and availability of appropriately trained staff may also vary, as might the cost of building space and materials. If space requirements are much greater for one alternative, while personnel requirements are greater for the second, it is conceivable that the relative cost-effectiveness of the two alternatives could flip when evaluated in urban versus rural settings. There are few one-size-fits-all answers.

Cost-effectiveness analysis also requires having common outcome measures across alternative programs. This is relatively straightforward when comparing educational programs geared toward specific reading or math skills. But policy alternatives rarely focus on precisely the same outcomes. As such, cost-effectiveness analysis may require additional consideration of which outcomes have greater value, which are preferred over others. Hank Levin and Patrick McEwan discuss these issues in terms of "cost-utility" analysis.[7] For example, assume a cost-effectiveness analysis of two math programs, A and B, each of which focuses on two goals, conceptual understanding and more basic skills. Assume also that both require comparable levels of expenditure to implement and maintain and that both yield the same average combined scores of conceptual and basic-skills assessments. Program A, however, produces higher conceptual understanding scores, while Program B produces higher basic-skills scores. If school officials or state policy makers believe conceptual understanding to be more important, a weight might be assigned that favors the program that led to greater conceptual understanding, and vice versa.

In contrast to cost-effectiveness analysis, cost-benefit analysis involves dollar-to-dollar comparisons, both in the short term and long term. Instead of examining the estimated education outcome effect of implementing and maintaining a given option, cost-benefit analysis examines the economic effects. But, like cost-efficiency analysis, cost-benefit analysis requires comparing alternatives. Again, the baseline option is generally the status quo, which is not assumed to be the worst possible alternative. Cost-benefit analysis can be used to search for immediate, or short-term, cost savings. For example, a school in need of computers might use this approach in deciding whether to buy or lease them; or a district might use the approach to decide whether to purchase buses or contract-out busing services. For a legitimate comparison, one must assume that the quality of service remains constant: the quality of computers or busing is equal if purchased, leased, or contracted, including service, maintenance, and all related issues. All else being equal, if the expenses incurred under one option are lower than under another, that option produces cost savings.

Cost-benefit analysis can also be applied to big-picture education policy questions, such as comparing the costs of implementing major reform strategies like class size reduction or early childhood programs versus raising existing teachers' salaries or measuring the long-term economic benefits of those different programmatic options. This is also referred to as "return-on-investment analysis." While cost-effectiveness and cost-benefit analyses are arguably underused in education policy research, a handful of particularly useful examples of their effectiveness include:

- determining whether certain comprehensive school reform models are more cost-effective than others;[8]
- determining whether computer-assisted instruction is more cost-effective than alternatives like peer tutoring;[9]
- considering National Board Certification for teachers (or having other standard certifications) as an alternative in terms of estimated effects and costs;[10] and
- evaluating the long-term benefits and associated costs of participation in certain early childhood programs.[11]

Another useful example is economists Brian Jacob and Jonah Rockoff's policy brief on the potential costs and benefits of seemingly mundane organizational changes to the delivery of public education, including: school start times for older students, based on research on learning outcomes by time of day; school grade configurations, based on an increased body of evidence relating grade configurations, location transitions, and student outcomes; and more effective management of teacher assignments.[12]

Cost Analysis of Layoff Policies

Among the recent popular policy proposals is that to alleviate severe fiscal stress requiring budget reductions which cut into personnel, districts should be able to dismiss teachers based on their effectiveness rather than on their years of service. This is what proponents refer to as "quality-based" layoffs, rather than LIFO.[13] This proposal seems logical, and we would expect it to compare favorably, relative to seniority-based layoffs, in both cost-benefit and cost-effectiveness analyses. However, anticipating the potential magnitude of those benefits and effects is difficult. The proposal is often pitched as a major money saver and as also likely to yield huge positive effects in terms of student outcome gains. It is often pitched as a game changer for the overall quality of public education systems: the effectiveness of the systems will be greatly improved and the costs of providing public education reduced.

With this thinking, if we lay off based on quality, we'll have better teachers left (greater effectiveness) and will have saved either a significant amount of money or a significant number of teachers. If we are determined to lay off *x* teachers, it will save more money to lay off more senior, and more expensive, teachers than to lay off novice, and less expensive, teachers. However, the more likely scenario is that we are faced with cutting *x* percent of the staffing budget, so the difference will be in the number of teachers we need to lay off in order to achieve that x percent. And so the benefit difference might be measured in terms of the change in average class size resulting from laying off teachers by "quality" measures versus laying off teachers by seniority. The effectiveness of the alternatives might then be measured in terms of the student outcomes, which presumably would be greater where students are provide both smaller classes and higher-quality teachers.

First, reductions in teacher workforce don't happen very often or in very many places. The conditions that warrant downsizing include severe fiscal constraint and/or a dramatic decline in enrollment. This proposed solution to fiscal woes was popularized during the recession, when staffing reductions were more common. Second, this proposal presumes that administrators have no latitude whatsoever in whom they choose to dismiss or how they deal with budget reductions. Often, the first rounds of staffing reductions include elective and extracurricular positions. This means that the teachers who are least likely to be cut are those in core curricular areas. Yet, it is only the classroom teachers involved in the direct delivery of reading/language arts and math curriculum between grades 4 and 8 who are likely to have attached to them the types of "quality" metrics often cited for use in "quality-based" layoffs.[14]

Following is a simplified calculation of the benefit differences of alternative dismissal patterns within a fixed budget cut (in this case 5 percent) assuming that the full amount would be cut from core classroom teachers (a highly unlikely scenario). Here, the "benefit" is measured only in terms of spending difference, regardless of potential changes to effectiveness. This illustration arguably maximizes the possible benefits of quality-based versus seniority-based layoffs.

Seniority-based layoffs begin with letting go of the least-experienced, junior teachers as necessary to achieve 5 percent savings to the staffing budget. Quality-based layoffs are more difficult to estimate because most districts do not have in place rigorous teacher evaluation systems sufficient to justify dismissal decisions. Herein lies the most significant complication with implementing this seemingly obvious win-win alternative. Teacher quality metrics, where they do exist, are very imprecise and often inaccurate. It's not as simple as just identifying "bad" teachers and dismissing them instead of dismissing bright, young, energetic future stars of the teaching world. In expediting quality-based layoffs, districts likely revert to relying heavily on some form of student-test-score-driven teacher effectiveness rating.[15] Yet, even in reliable models of this type, there may exist a 35 percent chance of identifying an average teacher as "bad" and a 20 percent chance of identifying a good teacher as "bad."[16] Misclassifications of this type compromise the cost-effectiveness of this alternative. We cannot simply assume that seniority-based layoffs lead invariably to the dismissal of good teachers and that quality-based layoffs always protect good teachers from layoff. Any legitimate cost-benefit or cost effectiveness analysis must consider that real-world metrics for applying this policy have high error rates and that even when using quality-based layoff policies, some, if not many, high-quality teachers will be laid off.

In general, test-score-driven (value-added model) ratings fall somewhat randomly across the experience distribution, though novice teachers are often more likely to receive lower ratings. As such, more "new" teachers would likely be dismissed under a ratings-based system as well.[17] In this example, I assume that quality-based firings are random by experience, rather than concentrated among newer teachers who might also be dismissed under LIFO policies. Thus, the estimated benefits are overstated.

In table 8.1 I apply fixed budget cuts to elementary classroom teachers in Newark, New Jersey, public schools (NPS) using salaries only for illustrative purposes (one can make many arguments about how to parse out fixed versus variable benefits costs or deferred benefits versus short-run cost differences for pensions and deferred sick pay, etc.). NPS starts with just over one thousand elementary classroom teachers in and assumes an average class size of twenty-five. The number of teachers is real (per state data), but I've simplified the class sizes. I also assume that all students and classroom space to be interchangeable. A 5 percent cut is about $3.7 million of the salary expense. Assume that we've already done our best to cut elsewhere in the district budget (perhaps more than 5 percent across other areas) but are left with the painful reality of still having to cut 5 percent from core classroom teachers in grades K–8. We're hoping for some dramatic saving, or at least benefits revealed in terms of keeping class sizes in check.

If we lay off only the least-experienced teachers to achieve the 5 percent cut, we lay off only teachers with three or fewer years' experience when using the Newark data. These are actually the teachers most likely to have

TABLE 8.1   Staffing cut scenarios for Newark Public Schools, 2009–10

Option 1: Cut 5%	
Total salaries (elementary classroom)	$74,661,971
5% cut	$3,733,099
Total students (assuming class size of 25)	25,950
Total teachers	1,038
Teachers cut by seniority	72
Teachers cut by random	54
Difference in number of teachers	18
Difference (of total)	1.7%
Teachers left after seniority layoff	966
Class size after seniority layoff	26.86
Mean experience of those laid off (years)	13.63
Teachers left after random layoff	984
Class size after random layoff	26.37
Class size difference (benefit)	0.49
Mean experience of those laid off	1.80
Option 2: Lay off 50 teachers	
Money "saved" by laying off 50 least experienced teachers	2,631,191
Money "saved" by laying off 50 random teachers	3,530,365
Difference in money saved (benefit)	899,174
% of total salaries	1.2%

Source: 2009–10 NJDOE Fall Staffing Report, obtained by request.
Note: Includes only Job Code 1001, or K–8 classroom teachers.

received lower performance ratings, according to recent studies relating test-score-based effectiveness measures with experience.[18] That is, even the seniority-based layoff policy is likely to lead to disproportionate dismissal of teachers receiving lower quality ratings. The average experience of those laid off is 1.8 years. We end up laying off 72 teachers. Quality-based layoffs, using noisy test-score-based measures, are somewhat better at capturing teacher "effectiveness" (in terms of test score production), but only marginally so. To simplify this comparison, I assume that quality measures aren't associated with experience and, rather, are random by experience. If we use a random number generator to determine "quality based" layoffs (assuming the random numbers to represent experience-neutral quality ratings), we end up laying off only 54 teachers instead of 72. We save 18 teachers, or 1.7 percent of our elementary classroom teacher workforce.

Under the seniority-based layoff policy, class size rises from 25 to 26.86. Under the random layoff policy, class size rises from 25 to 26.37. That is, class size is affected by about half a student per class. This may be important, but it still seems like a relatively small effect for a big policy change—one which may come with other costs not considered here. This option necessarily assumes no downside to the random loss of experienced teachers based on imprecise measures of effectiveness. The bottom portion of the table shows the dollar advantage of laying off a fixed proportion of teachers rather than cutting a fixed proportion of spending.

The assumption that quality-based layoffs will be more cost-effective in the long run hinges on a larger share of children having exposure to "good" teachers, since the good teachers have been retained and the bad ones dismissed. Thus, if, as a result, there is a positive effect on student outcomes, for the same spending reduction there is also a possible win on cost-effectiveness. But hasty adoption of such policies under budgetary stress increases the likelihood that even less-precise, less-accurate metrics will be used, thereby decreasing the likelihood of a net gain in outcomes. Developing more thoughtful and thorough evaluation systems has associated costs but still may only marginally reduce the error rate in classifying "good" versus "bad" teachers. In addition, there exists a significant likelihood that imprecise and inaccurate ratings leading to employment consequences will lead to costly legal challenges, whereas seniority-based layoffs have already been vetted by courts.[19] So this becomes an entirely separate cost-benefit calculation, a question of how much more we must spend to reduce classification error, increase transparency and fairness, and yield a legally defensible system.

But perhaps the most important questions are: How does this new policy affect the future teacher workforce in Newark?[20] How does that trade-off balance with a net difference of about half a student per classroom? Quality-based layoffs as an alternative to seniority-based layoffs may yield a small win in terms of cost-benefit, assuming sufficient evaluation systems are already in place and depending on outcomes of legal challenges. But under most practical conditions, the margin of benefit is likely small. Cost-effectiveness depends largely on the accuracy of rating systems in determining future effectiveness of those retained, versus dismissed. It also assumes no downside or possible upside to future recruitment and retention, which depends on uncertain additional costs, including litigation. So when even the most seemingly obvious policy proposals are subjected to the most minimal scrutiny, as in this example, they may not yield substantive improvements over the status quo.

INSTITUTIONAL EFFICIENCY ANALYSIS

Efficiency analyses use large data sets on large numbers of institutions (schools or districts) over multiple years and estimating statistical models to discern which institutions are actually doing more with less, all else being equal. While debate persists on the best statistical approaches for estimating cost-efficiency or technical efficiency of production, the common goal of the available approaches is to determine which organizational units are more and less efficient producers of education outcomes.

Once schools or districts are identified as more (or less) efficient, the next step is to figure out why. Accordingly, researchers explore what variables across these institutions might make some more efficient than others, or what changes have been implemented that might have led to improvements in efficiency. They typically ask: Do districts or schools that do x tend to be more cost efficient than those doing y? Or, Did the schools or districts that changed their practices from x to y improve in their relative efficiency compared to districts that did not make similar changes? The researchers identify and evaluate variations across institutions, looking for insights in those estimated to be more efficient or evaluating changes to efficiency in districts that have altered practices or resource allocation in some way. The latter approach is generally considered more relevant, since it speaks directly to changing practices and resulting changes in efficiency.[21]

While statistically complex, efficiency analyses have been used to address a variety of practical questions about the management and organization of local public school districts:

- Can school district consolidation cut costs, and what is the most cost-efficient school district size?[22]
- Will allocating state aid to subsidize property tax exemptions to affluent suburban school districts compromise relative efficiency?[23]
- Is the allocation of larger shares of school district spending to instructional categories a more efficient way to produce better education outcomes?[24]
- Does decentralized governance of high schools improve efficiency?[25]

These analyses have not always produced the results that policy makers like to hear. Further, like many studies using rigorous scholarly methods, these analyses have limitations. They are necessarily constrained by the availability of data, they are sensitive to the quality of data, and they can produce different results when applied in different settings.[26]

There exists a relatively large body of empirical literature on applied efficiency analysis in education, the very kind of methods and models that might be used to distill whether one institution, organization, or jurisdiction more efficiently produces education outcomes than another.[27] The same basic principles and methods apply whether evaluating individual schools, public school districts, state school systems, or national education systems. The main difference is that in moving to increasingly geographically, economically, and culturally distant and distinct systems, constructing consistent measures of schooling inputs and outcomes (while considering confounding factors) becomes far more difficult—but also far more important.

Efficiency analysis may be framed from a cost perspective or a production perspective. These are flip sides of the same education spending coin. Each involves identifying outcomes, spending toward achieving those outcomes, and identifying various observable conditions, or cost factors, that affect the spending-outcome relationship. However, each perspective seeks to answer different questions. Cost efficiency asks, Given the outcomes School A currently achieves, compared to the lowest-spending school achieving the same (all else equal), how much does School A spend? Production efficiency asks, Given the current spending levels (and other factors), how do the outcomes of School A compare to the maximum outcomes achieved with comparable spending (and other factors)?

Figure 8.1 presents a view of cost efficiency across schools of varied scale or enrollment size. The "cost" of producing a given level of outcomes varies by the scale of the school, where very small schools face much higher costs to achieve the same outcomes as scale-efficient schools. A subset of schools may fall along the lower boundary, the underlying "cost frontier," or minimum expense, at a given school size at which the desired outcomes can be produced. Most schools will fall somewhere above that frontier, or are spending somewhat more than the minimum to achieve the same outcomes. Some of those differences may be attributed to factors missed in data and models because they weren't measured or were measured poorly (which is partly why we shouldn't live by the data and models alone). Some of those

FIGURE 8.1   Cost efficiency framework

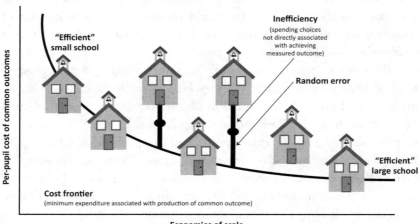

differences may also include expenditures deemed valuable by constituents but that don't contribute directly to the outcome measures in question. Valuable lessons may be learned from exploring both the schools that fall along the cost frontier and those that deviate from it. In figure 8.2, which presents the production efficiency perspective, it is assumed that for each additional dollar spent on schooling, there is a commensurate gain in student outcomes, with diminishing returns. Some schools will fall along—or define—the frontier or maximum output for any given level of expense, and others will fall below that frontier for the same reasons that schools deviate from the cost frontier.

These visuals are stylized for simplicity, reducing efficiency analysis to two dimensions. No credible scholar or analyst would consider a simple, unconditional cross-sectional analysis of the relationship between nominal per-pupil spending and average/aggregate test score levels as a legitimate basis for making efficiency comparisons. In contrast, figure 8.3 summarizes factors that affect education costs from one school to the next, one district or state to the next, one nation or continent to the next. Student outcomes in the cost model are an input: the amount a school system spends is determined, among other factors, by the education outcomes that system seeks to achieve. Once we step outside comparisons of schools operating within a single labor market

FIGURE 8.2   Production efficiency framework

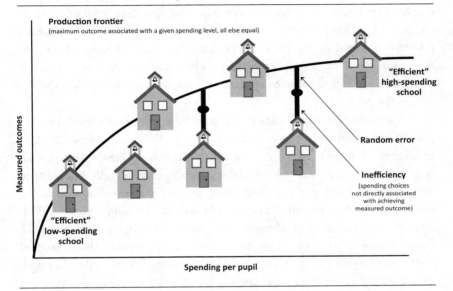

FIGURE 8.3   Factors affecting education costs

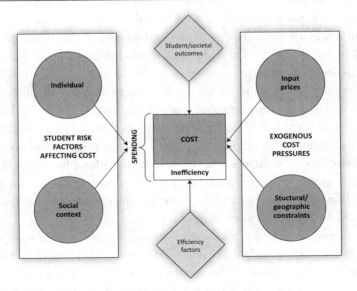

Source: Adapted from Baker and Levin, "Estimating the Real Cost of Community College."

of consistent geography (no huge swings in population density, no major geographic barriers, etc.), comparisons of education spending from one unit to the next are no longer simple. The value of the education dollar varies toward purchasing even the same quality and quantity of education inputs, where the key inputs to education are teachers and where the wage required to recruit and retain teachers of specific qualifications varies from one location and setting to the next.

One of the most significant factors affecting the cost of providing comparable education services across schools and districts is economies of scale, or average school size, which may be constrained by geography and population density.[28] Very small schools for which it's geographically infeasible to consolidate with other schools necessarily operate with much lower staffing ratios and have to maintain a basic level of overhead (buildings, grounds, utilities, administration), thus elevating per-pupil operating costs substantially. Public school districts in remote rural areas, serving around three hundred pupils, tend to operate at nearly double the per-pupil costs of districts with two thousand or more pupils in more population-dense areas, all else being equal. Further, when comparing education outcomes, we must consider various attributes of the student populations being served, to the extent that those attributes correlate with outcomes. Credible models comparing school or district efficiency across US schools and districts also typically consider student disability status (total numbers and severity levels), language proficiency status, indicators of child/family income and poverty, and sometimes race/ethnicity of student population.[29]

A separate body of literature has addressed attributes of public jurisdictions (those with control over public budgets, taxing, and spending) that may be associated with inefficiency.[30] In particular, measures of interjurisdictional competition and "public monitoring" (often measured by extent of proximal/local involvement in finance and decision making) have been identified as leading to greater efficiency. Inefficiency, however, is more likely to be associated with greater fiscal capacity: those who can spend more (even for constant measured outcomes) are more likely to do so.[31]

A thorough applied production efficiency analysis in education would estimate the gains in student outcomes—the value added over what students enter with—as a function of: the resources expended on comparable relevant services, the geographic factors affecting structural costs and input prices, and the student characteristics that might have exerted exogenous influence on achievement gains, including disability status, language proficiency, and child poverty.[32]

By contrast, cost modeling predicts the spending levels (as the dependent variable) associated with achieving given levels of student outcomes, controlling for factors that affect the value of the education dollar toward contributing to outcomes and also correcting for factors that may explain differences in inefficiency across institutions or jurisdictions. Typically, the models used would be estimated to schools or districts as units using multiple years of annual data to ensure stable, reliable estimates. Even then, our ability to precisely, consistently identify more- and less-efficient schools, districts, states, or even countries is suspect due to the imprecision of the data used to create the models and the many omitted variables that might bias those models.[33]

Studies of Charter School Efficiency

The motivation for studying charter school efficiency relative to district schools should be to discern whether specific charter schools have used their regulatory flexibility to adopt innovations that permit them to achieve common outcomes at lower cost or higher outcomes at comparable cost—that is, with greater efficiency. In fact, applying a single model across traditional public schools and charter schools, using equated spending measures and common outcome measures, we should be able to identify charter and/or district schools that deviate substantively from the cost or production frontier and then seek answers about how they got there. Analyses need not focus on sectoral differences but may include consideration of those differences.

A handful of studies have attempted to explore the relative efficiency of charter versus district schooling, applying methods that largely comport with the technical specifications I've laid out. Perhaps the strongest evidence of charter school efficiency advantages comes from the work of Timothy Gronberg, Dennis Jansen, and Lori Taylor on Texas charter schools, who find that, generally, Texas "charter schools are able to produce educational outcomes at lower cost than traditional public schools—probably because they face fewer regulations—but are not systematically more efficient relative to their frontier than are traditional public schools."[34] Evidence from related work by these authors reveals that the lower overall expenses are largely a function of lower salaries and inexperienced staff, which means that maintaining efficiency may require ongoing reliance on inexperienced staff.[35]

Frequently cited studies touting the relative effectiveness of charter schools operated by major CMOs have typically measured poorly or not at all the resources available in these schools, which are identified as often spending substantially more than nearby district schools.[36] Most charter schools, and large CMO charters in particular, operate under a similar human resource intensive model as traditional district schools.[37] Specifically, well-endowed CMOs allocate their additional resources to competitive wages (higher than expected for relatively inexperienced teachers), small classes, and longer school days and years.[38]

ALIGNING SERVICES WITH EXPENDITURES

Texas charter school efficiency analyses have the advantage of the Texas data system, which for years has collected reasonably accurate and precise school site (campus-level) expenditure data, and the Texas policy context, which includes a mix of both fiscally independent charter operators (charter schools directly financed by the state) and fiscally independent (district operated and financed) charters. Arriving at comparable expenditure figures in the case of fiscally dependent charters is more complicated but remains a prerequisite for accurate and precise efficiency comparisons.

Ideally, a well-aligned efficiency analysis involves a set of institutions striving to achieve common goals. There is precise information on the expenditures of those institutions that are dedicated toward those outcome goals and precise measurements of those outcome goals and all mitigating or intervening conditions. For example, if one school or set of schools has in its budget additional expenditures for evening community-based programs, we may decide that these expenditures should be excluded from our analysis. Alternatively, if another school receives in-kind or donated support specifically for core academic offerings from an outside source, we likely should include the value of those contributions as an expense.

However, it can be especially difficult to arrive at comparable spending figures for schools (as units of analysis) embedded within districts when those schools operate under different financial and governance models, as is the case with fiscally dependent charter schools. If the input measurement is wrong, any attempt to determine the input-outcome relationship will also be wrong. It is especially problematic if we upwardly or downwardly bias the spending figures for one set of schools versus another—if the point of our analyses is to compare the relative efficiency of those sets.

In public finance literature it is assumed that government entities like local public school districts have as their primary purpose the delivery of a defined set of services directly to constituents. In the case of public schooling, that is the provision of educational programs and services to children, as well as the potential delivery of community and other services. Service delivery agencies can be organized into "mission centers" and "service centers" (see figure 8.4). Mission centers are those cost centers that provide direct services flowing from the overall institutional mission. Commonly, in public school finance, individual school sites are the primary mission centers. Service centers provide services internal to the institution, including administrative services (payroll management, enrollment management, professional development, etc.) to mission centers.

This structural understanding guides institutional cost analysis. Presuming that the services of service centers are necessary for carrying out the institutional mission, it is necessary to determine how to allocate the expenses associated with those services out to mission centers. But it remains important to understand and to delineate those resources that are actually attributed directly to (spent directly at) mission centers versus those resources spent at higher levels on services to those mission centers and can only be estimated by some formula.

FIGURE 8.4   Allocation of resources between district and charter schools

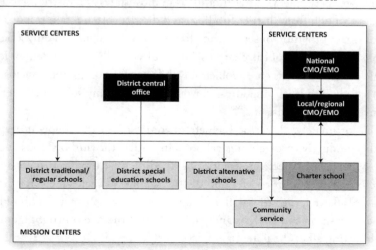

To compare the relative efficiency of charter and district schools in achieving common outcome goals, we must first identify the mission centers, those providing services associated with the measured outcomes. If our interest is in commonly assessed academic outcomes, we should focus on district traditional schools and charter schools, excluding special education and other kinds of alternative schools (though we must be careful not to attribute centralized expenses of the excluded schools to our included schools). We must also find some way to measure the value of centralized services provided to both district schools and charter schools while also capturing any additional supports provided to charters from their management organizations above the value of fees paid. So yes, it's a complicated process. But it can be done.

One especially egregious example of getting the input comparisons wrong appears in a set of recurring reports from the University of Arkansas.[39] In the first report, the authors compare what they refer to as "all revenues" for charter and district schools, which results in substantial inflation of district resources and deflation of charter resources. As I explain in a critique of this report, there are many ways the report errs in comparing charter and district school inputs. Most significantly, the authors convey a "complete lack of understanding of intergovernmental fiscal relationships, which results in the blatantly erroneous assignment of 'revenues' between charters and district schools." A significant problem with the report's logic is that one entity's expenditure is another's revenue. More specifically, a district's expenditure can be a charter's revenue. Charter funding is in most states and districts received by pass-through from district funding, and districts often retain responsibility for direct provision of services to charter school students. In only a handful of states are most of the charter schools fully fiscally independent of local public districts—"This core problem invalidates all findings and conclusions of the study, and if left unaddressed would invalidate any subsequent 'return on investment' comparisons."[40]

Unfortunately, the error was left unaddressed in the follow-up report on the productivity of charter schools, in which the authors constructed state-by-state cost-effectiveness ratios by dividing their input measures by average NAEP scores for charter and district schools in each state.[41] If the numerator is flawed, the ratios will be wrong. This is a simple matter of building worse analysis on bad analysis and paying short shrift to or outright ignoring and omitting all of the potential intervening factors.[42]

DISSECTING THE NEW ORLEANS MIRACLE

There has been much reporting on the successes of the New Orleans (NOLA) portfolio managed, charter-dominant school choice model, which emerged after Hurricane Katrina. Until recently, studies of the NOLA model reported exclusively on the outcome side of the productivity equation. For example, Doug Harris and Matthew Larsen explain that "the results suggest that, over time, as the reforms yielded a new system of schools, they had large positive cumulative effects on achievement of 0.2–0.4 standard deviations."[43]

However, little attention had been paid to the fact that this new system shuffled a smaller number of students throughout the same geographic area that had been served by the pre-Katrina public school district. Those students were reshuffled through a centralized enrollment management system, providing choices among schools and providers based largely on individual preferences. The dispersed choice model led to increased numbers of small, start-up schools in an otherwise population-dense area. Having multiple autonomously managed schools in the single context led to administrative redundancies. And since no "counterfactual" (traditional system) was left behind, no reasonable cost-effectiveness or relative efficiency comparisons can be made. So we don't know how children attending an otherwise similarly funded traditional public system would have performed.

Recent reports on NOLA schools reveal the extent of resource infusion that accompanied the shift to this loosely governed charter choice system. Harris, director of the Education Research Alliance for New Orleans, explains that "New Orleans' publicly funded schools spent 13% ($1,358 per student) more per pupil on operating expenditures than the comparison group after the reforms, even though the comparison group had nearly identical spending before the reforms." Further, spending on administration increased substantially (66 percent, or nearly $700 per pupil) relative to other similar schools statewide, more than half of which was attributable to administrative salaries. Instructional expenditures per pupil declined by a margin similar to the increase in administrative spending. About half of that decline was related to reduced staff benefits, with the next largest decline being in staffing salaries, consistent with prior studies showing charter school staffing dominated by less-experienced and lower-paid staff.[44] Finally, Harris notes that "transportation spending and other expenditures, which typically include contracts to outside firms, each increased by 33%."[45]

Indeed, the New Orleans reforms do appear to show measurable positive effects. But those effects were accompanied by a significant infusion of funds, much of which went toward transportation, administration, and consulting contracts. It remains unknown whether these substantively different resource allocation strategies lead to a more or less efficient system, whether, for example, spending more on administration and transportation and less on instruction have adversely affected the efficiency of NOLA schools. At face value, these resource allocation shifts would seem to introduce inefficiencies that may have been avoided by strategic reinvestment in a more traditional public system. Unfortunately, we are left with few options for reasonably judging the cost-effectiveness or relative efficiency of these concurrent changes, whether the measured effects themselves are a function of the resources or the reforms or whether the reforms would have succeeded absent the resources.

PARSING INSTITUTIONS:
ONLINE SCHOOLING AND COURSES

A comparison of online and traditional brick-and-mortar schooling introduces additional complexities in aligning services provided with measured outcomes and determining all relevant expenditures associated with the provision of those services. The usual oversimplified argument focuses only on the rate at which the student is subsidized to take online courses versus the expense associated with providing that same child a brick-and-mortar education. This is somewhat like comparing private school tuition rates, or even partial tuition subsidies (vouchers), with public district total expenditures, where tuition and subsidies fail to capture the full costs of providing the service.

Table 8.2 illustrates the relationship between subsidies, spending, outcomes, and efficiency to consider at what rate to subsidize online education/virtual schooling (OE/VS) alternatives relative to brick-and-mortar schooling and comparing alternatives that provide exactly the same breadth of services (only the core academic curriculum). If both types of school receive the same per-pupil annual subsidy (and neither receives additional funding), both have equal spending, and both produce the same quality of outcomes, then their efficiency is considered equal. Financially, it's a break-even scenario. The underlying assumption in such a system is that the cost of producing the same outcomes is the same for each alternative, that the same outcomes can be produced with the same level of efficiency and with the same level of spending.

TABLE 8.2 Framework for evaluating cost-effectiveness of online education/virtual schooling subsidies compared to brick-and-mortar schooling

OE/VS subsidy compared to brick-and-mortar schools	Supplement	Relative spending	Outcome	Efficiency
Constant/Equal	None	Equal	Equal	Equal
Constant/Equal	Supplement	Higher	Equal	Reduced
Constant/Equal	Supplement	Higher	Increased	Equal
Reduced	None	Lower	Equal	Increased
Reduced	Supplement/Offset	Equal	Equal	Equal

However, consider the possibility that one or the other alternative schools relies more heavily on additional sources of funding. Perhaps the online option requires substantial additional parent supervision, costly high-speed home internet service, and high-quality hardware at parent expense. When factored in, these additional contributions yield a higher total spending for the OE/VS alternative. So if outcomes were still equal, then efficiency would be reduced, since the same outcome had a higher overall cost for the online option. However, it's also possible that the increased total spending might lead to higher average outcomes. Importantly, though, this would still be a break-even on efficiency: higher cost producing better outcomes. Still, we might decide that the gain in outcome is worth the extra cost, particularly if that additional cost is not paid out of public tax monies. The obvious point here is that efficiency is properly calculated based not simply on government subsidy; calculations must take into account whether a program receives supplemental income from other sources, whether services provided are equal, and how outcomes compare.

In the current policy context, it seems likely that the emphasis will be on reducing the subsidy rate for one option or the other. Some argue that funding cuts, or subsidy reductions, can be effectively used to squeeze schools into producing the same outcomes more efficiently.[46] Let's assume that there were some unnecessary inefficiencies embedded in our online provider's model. If we reduce the subsidy rate, and no one picks up the difference, spending will be lower. If the provider can continue to produce the same outcomes while spending less, it will have increased its efficiency.

However, there exists little, if any, evidence that cuts can induce such efficiencies.[47] If $500 per pupil were cut from the state subsidy, but private philanthropists stepped in to replace that $500 per pupil, spending per pupil would remain constant. So would the efficiency. The baseline efficiency consideration for policy makers when subsidizing OE/VS alternatives is to avoid paying the same or more for options that provide fewer services or lower outcomes.

Two approaches to providing cost estimates of the relevant, comparable services between brick-and-mortar schools and OE/VS alternatives are to use detailed expenditure data, peeling back layers of expenditures (exclusion method) to isolate those expenditures associated with the provision of the comparable service set, or use a bottom-up, ingredients-summing approach, identifying the resources and related expenses associated with the provision of each essential unit of the service set.

Figure 8.5 lays out the complexities of sorting through the top-down approach. For example, if a student in online schooling is receiving from the online provider curricular content and assessment in five core academic

FIGURE 8.5 Comparing the delivery of online versus brick-and-mortar schooling

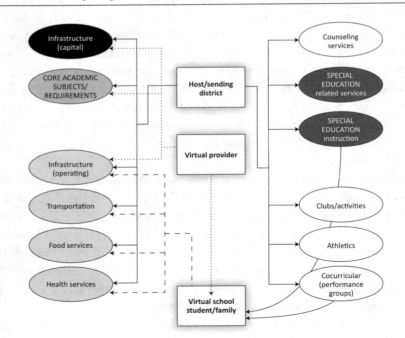

courses, we must attempt to identify the brick-and-mortar costs for offering that child those five core academic courses. If it is assumed that the child provides her own space, adult supervision, computing hardware, software, and Internet access, we must find some way to estimate the value of those resources. The same applies to food and transportation provided to students by the brick-and-mortar school, if costs are passed along to parents in online schooling (including, for example, costs of field trips to support course work, and parents' opportunity costs to supervise those field trips). We must also be sure to include any distributed overhead expenses of the online provider.

Figure 8.6 presents the bottom-up, unit-cost-based approach, which is particularly useful when considering secondary and postsecondary, departmentally organized and delivered course "units." If the student in the OE/VS setting is taking one or more courses for which there are equivalent offerings in the brick-and-mortar setting, we can attempt to identify the costs (per pupil) associated with providing that unit of instruction (course, credit hour, etc.). While tedious, this approach works whether we are comparing the delivery of a single course or the full complement of academic requirements. It can be used for generating cost estimates for full packages of services across institutions, for use in efficiency analyses, or for cost-effectiveness analyses with smaller sets of institutions, programs, and services.

FIGURE 8.6 Summing up the costs of delivering instructional units

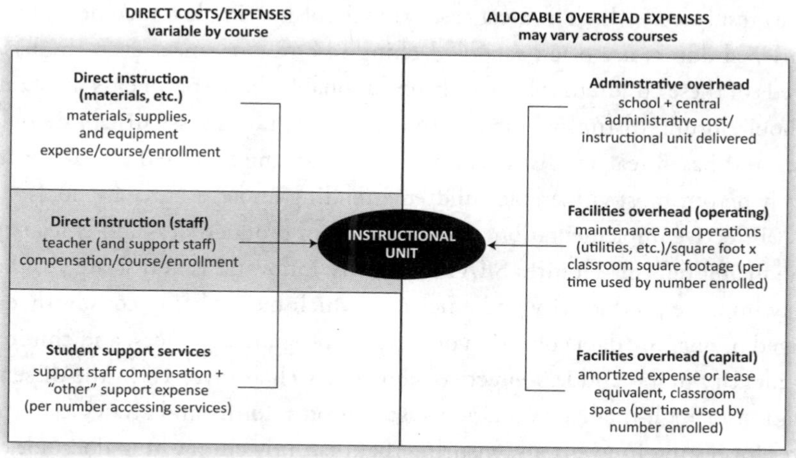

LESSONS LEARNED AND LOOKING FORWARD

There was a time not so long ago when it at least seemed that state education agencies (SEAs) and the US Department of Education were more involved in advancing understanding of educational productivity and efficiency. There are some guiding principles for testing, evaluating, and improving educational productivity and efficiency.

First, innovations require investment. Any new technology—be it new evaluation systems, curricular modules, or assistive technologies— requires expertise and training to implement it. Schools and districts facing tight budgets are poorly positioned to make the necessary investments for effective adoption.

Second, changes don't always improve productivity. It's possible to do worse than the status quo. It's possible to do harm, reducing productivity and efficiency, by implementing ineffective strategies and/or implementing any strategy poorly.

Third, evaluation, formative and summative, of any substantive reform is essential. Without thorough evaluation of costs, benefits, and effects, we have little to go on for replicating and scaling up reforms.

Fourth, the possibility of doing harm raises important ethical concerns. Which students should be subjected to "experiments" with innovations that are, in many cases, as likely to do harm as they are to do good, especially if lacking appropriate investment? Under recent federal policies, states have been encouraged to experiment on schools with the lowest (bottom 5 percent) test scores, which in most cases are schools serving low income and minority children, are often schools lacking resources to meet even the basic needs of these children. It is morally objectionable that experiments involving school closure, disruptive turnaround strategies, no-excuses discipline policies, test-based teacher dismissal, or virtual learning be tested almost exclusively on our most vulnerable children attending underresourced schools.

Effective implementation and evaluation of productivity- and efficiency-enhancing reforms requires SEAs to identify innovations and strategies that may improve productivity and efficiency, which means being constantly engaged in ongoing data collection on schools, programs, services, and children to identify more- and less-effective schools as well as involved in the dissemination of high-quality evaluation research on reforms and strategies select sites for testing innovations, ensuring that disruptive innovation does not repeatedly, disproportionately fall on our most disadvantaged children, based on sound research principles with ethical boundaries commonly applied in university settings. SEAs should also provide guidance on initial implementation of innovations under evaluation and for the scaling up of effective innovations to additional settings beyond the original test sites, as well as play an ongoing role in the development, collection, and management of relevant measures related to costs and expenditures, programs and services, and a variety of student outcomes as well as in the ongoing use of those measures and data for evaluation of innovations. SEAs also must endeavor to mitigate harm that might be caused by educational experimentation, even being willing to acknowledge that it is indeed possible to do worse than the status quo.

The federal role should embrace similar priorities and employ similar strategies. As Kevin Welner and I explain in *Educational Researcher*, if the US Department of Education really wants to play a substantive role in helping states and local school districts improve productivity and efficiency, then they should seek guidance from leading published scholars in the areas of understanding and measuring education costs, productivity and efficiency. The Department of Education should collaborate, as it has in past decades, to advance high-quality research and develop an agenda focused on a balance of five key factors: improving empirical methods and related data; evaluating major education reform models, programs, and strategies; disseminating the results of those evaluations; expanding and improving stakeholder understanding of cost-effectiveness, cost-benefit, and relative-efficiency analyses; and supporting the training of future scholars in these methods.[48]

CHAPTER 9

APPLYING HIGH-QUALITY COST ANALYSIS TO SCHOOL FINANCE POLICY

The postrecession political environment marked the end of the empirical era of school finance and roughly coincided with the shift away from rigor and toward political expedience in state and federally supported research related to school funding, productivity, and efficiency. During the empirical era, the mid-1990s through 2007, state school finance systems became more grounded in both conceptions of equity and adequacy and in empirical analyses linking desired outcome objectives with estimates of the costs of achieving those outcomes. In some cases, these changes resulted from judicial pressure, but in other cases changes resulted from legislative initiative. Unfortunately, many of these "cost" studies, some of which informed directly state school finance policies, were vulnerable to straightforward and not highly technical criticism.[1]

Studies of education cost, performed as consultancies to state legislatures and advocacy organizations, were often less rigorous than the academic research being conducted during that same period, including research supported by state or federal agencies. School finance specialists, including John Augenblick and John Meyers, consulted with several states to determine costs associated with achieving state-mandated or court-ordered outcome goals. The accounting firm Standard & Poors, on behalf of New York governor George Pataki, assisted the Zarb Commission in estimating expenditures of schools meeting state standards. Findings of these consultancies rarely found their way into academic outlets, other than in summary and critique of academic research. In a seemingly parallel universe, several academics were advancing the development of cost modeling methods and publishing their findings in academic journals but had little direct impact on policy. Over time, however, methods, researchers, and consultants began to intersect.

In the context of litigation over the adequacy of funding for schools, advocates frequently provided analyses on behalf of the plaintiffs asserting that all or most local public school districts required substantially more funding to achieve desired outcomes. Yet, it could often be shown that many schools and districts, at current funding levels, already exceeded the desired outcomes, making it relatively easy for states to refute claims of inadequate funding and to further posit that the total cost of achieving the desired outcomes was no higher than the level of funding that was provided across all districts. In other cases, cost analyses were built on unrealistic, if not outright mythical, outcome goals, including estimating the costs of achieving 100 percent proficiency on state assessments by 2014, a remnant of the Federal No Child Left Behind Act that required 100 percent proficiency as an end goal. Equally suspect were assertions that school funding adequacy deficits might be resolvable by imposing a single best whole-school model constructed by summing up the research on effective school practices and reforms and applying it across varied state contexts.

Unfortunately, the conceptual and empirical gaps in the large body of studies conducted during the empirical era complicate attempts to reinvigorate the conversations around the costs of achieving desired outcome levels and the extent to which empirical evidence on costs might guide state school finance formulas through the funding challenges created by the recession. For this reason, some guidance is needed on the development of conceptually grounded, empirically rigorous evidence for informing the design of equitable and adequate state school finance systems.

USING EMPIRICAL EVIDENCE TO INFLUENCE STATE SCHOOL FINANCE POLICIES

In order to design a state school finance system that achieves equal opportunity or educational adequacy, we must be able to generate reasonable estimates of the costs of achieving equal or adequate outcomes at any given level of student outcomes, including current average outcomes across a state education system. Where adequacy is concerned, it is necessary to attempt, by extrapolation, to predict the costs of achieving adequate education outcomes, which might be higher or lower than current averages. State systems vary widely both in terms of their current average outcomes and what their current accountability systems demand.

Since the mid-1990s, numerous state legislatures, boards of education, and advocacy groups have attempted to estimate the cost of meeting specific state legislative and constitutional standards, including how those costs vary from one location to the next and one child to the next.[2] While efforts to link such cost estimates to constitutional, statutory, and regulatory standards were popularized in the era following the 1989 *Rose v. Council for Better Education* decision, one of the first major cases in which a state court had laid out specific guidance on outcomes and standards that constitute an adequate or thorough and efficient education, empirical methods for estimating education costs, including costs of specific standards, predate this era. In fact, these methods gained initial popularity in application to public school finance in 1970s and 1980s.

Modern efforts to cost out state constitutional obligations can be reclassified into two straightforward categories: input-oriented analyses and outcome-oriented analyses. Input-oriented analyses identify the human resources/staffing; materials, supplies, and equipment; physical space; and other elements required to provide specific educational programs and services. These programs and services may be identified as typically yielding certain outcomes for certain student populations when applied in certain settings. Outcome-oriented analyses start with measured student outcomes of institutions or specific programs and services and can then explore either the aggregate spending on those programs and services yielding specific outcomes or, in greater depth, the allocation of spending on specific inputs. One approach works forward, toward actual or desired outcomes, starting with inputs; the other works backward from outcomes achieved. Ideally, both work in concert, providing iterative feedback to one another. Regardless of the approach, any measure of cost must consider the outcomes to be achieved through any given level of expenditure and resource allocation.[3]

Input-Oriented Methods

Setting aside for the moment the modern proprietary jargon of "costing out" studies, there really exists one basic method for input-oriented analysis, called either the ingredients method or the resource cost model (RCM).[4] This method involves three basic steps:

1. identifying the various resources, or ingredients, necessary to implement a set of educational programs and services (where an entire school or district or statewide system would be a comprehensive package of programs and services);
2. determining the input price for those ingredients or resources (competitive wages, other market prices); and
3. combining the necessary resource quantities with their corresponding prices to calculate a total cost estimate (resource quantities × price = cost).

RCM was applied by Jay Chambers and colleagues in the early 1980s to determine statewide costs of providing the desired level (implicitly "adequate") of programs and services; this was over a decade before the use of such methods in the context of school finance adequacy litigation in Wyoming in 1995.[5]

A distinction between the studies conducted prior to and after *Rose v. Council for Better Education* is that the pre-*Rose* studies in Alaska and Illinois focused on tallying the resource needs of education systems designed to provide a set of curricular requirements, programs, and services intended to be available to all children. Modern analyses instead begin with stating the outcomes the system intends to achieve and then requiring consultants and/or expert panels to identify the inputs needed to achieve those goals. Even then, the empirical method is still one of tallying inputs, attaching prices, and summing costs.

RCM can be used to evaluate resources currently allocated to actual programs and services (geared toward or measurably achieving specific outcomes); resources needed for providing specific programs and services where they are not currently being provided; and resources hypothetically needed to achieve some specific set of outcome goals—both depth and breadth.

Where actual existing resources are involved, we must thoroughly quantify those inputs, determine their prices, and sum their costs. In order to ensure the findings are generalizable, we must explore how input prices for both personnel (e.g., teacher compensation) and nonpersonnel (e.g., materials and supplies) vary across other sites where the programs and services might be implemented and consider whether context (economies of scale, grade ranges) affects how inputs are organized in ways consequential to cost estimates. RCM is also the primary costing out tool of cost-effectiveness or cost-benefit analyses.

Where hypothetical outcome goals are involved, a number of approaches can be taken to imagine, in effect, the resource requirements for achieving desired outcomes with specific populations of children educated in particular settings. Competing consultants have attached names to the methods they prefer for identifying the quantities of resources or ingredients. Professional judgment involves convening focus groups to propose resource quantities for hypothetical schools to achieve specific outcomes. Evidence-based methods involve compiling published research into model schools presumed adequate regardless of context because of their reliance on published research. A well-designed input-oriented resource cost analysis should engage informed constituents in a context-specific process that also makes available sufficient information (e.g., through prompts and advanced reading) on related "evidence."

These two approaches should not be applied in isolation from one another. Arguably, the delineation between professional judgment (PJ) and evidence-based approaches for input identification came about from consultants' desire to sell competing services and their interest in laying claim to using multiple methods for determining costs.

The assertion is that PJ analysis draws on judgments of informed professionals (teachers, administrators, state education officials), usually in a focus group format, to hypothesize the resources needed for achieving outcome goals, while evidence-based analysis aggregates the best available empirical research into a whole-school model for achieving those same outcome goals. Evidence-based models are generally proposed by consultants alone, independent of any focus group activities. It is difficult to conceive, however, that in professional judgment analyses informed professionals engaged in focus groups would bring no "research" evidence to bear on their proposals, or that a researcher overseeing such methods would exclude entirely research evidence that might inform focus group recommendations. In contrast, with an evidence-based approach, where specific state outcome goals are of interest, it makes little sense to rely exclusively on a consultants' aggregation of published studies on specific interventions implemented with specific populations toward outcomes objectives that differ substantially from the outcomes of interest. States have their own specific standards and accountability guidelines, and state courts have applied them to constitutional requirements differently from one state to the next. Whole-school reform models (e.g., *Success for All*) and specific interventions researched in certain contexts and states may not align well with other states' standards or accountability goals. As Lori Taylor, Arnie Vedlitz, and I explain: "While proponents of Evidence-Based analysis infer a strong connection between specific comprehensive school reforms and improved outcomes, research evidence regarding the effectiveness and more specifically the cost effectiveness of these reforms is mixed at best and may not apply in all contexts. Furthermore, there may be little connection between the outcomes such reform models are 'proven' to accomplish and the outcomes policymakers hope to achieve."[6]

The presumption that evidence-based strategies are superior to professional recommendations because they are based on researched interventions is also problematic because those interventions are not easily aggregated into whole-school models. It is difficult, if not entirely implausible, to use existing research on specific effective interventions to cobble together an entire, comprehensive school and all the resources it takes to run that school effectively and efficiently. Consultant assertions regarding the expected outcome effects of discrete interventions compiled into whole-school models are often overstated and built on dubious summation of effects.[7] After all, we cannot simply take the positive effects of multiple specific interventions and add them up to an overall effectiveness estimate of a school model combining "all of the above" interventions. Even under the best application, the result of this process is a hypothetical depiction of the resources necessary to achieve the desired outcome goals. Where RCM is applied to programs and services already associated with certain actual, measured outcomes, that hypothesis is certainly more informed.

Outcome-Oriented Methods

The primary tool of outcome-based cost analysis is the education cost function (ECF). Attempts to statistically model education costs with respect to outcomes across varied student populations date back to the 1970s but reemerged in academic literature in the 1990s.[8] Cost functions typically focus on the outcome-producing organizational unit, or the decision-making unit, as a whole to evaluate relationships between aggregate spending and outcomes given the conditions under which the outcomes are produced. These conditions regularly include economies of scale (higher unit production costs of very small organizational units), variations in labor costs, and, in the case of education, characteristics of the student populations that may require greater or fewer resources to achieve common outcome goals.

Identifying statistical relationships between resources and outcomes under varied conditions requires high-quality and sufficiently broad measures of desired outcomes, inputs, and conditions and sufficient numbers of organizational units to evaluate that exhibit sufficient variation in the conditions under which they operate. Much can be learned from the variation that presently exists across our local public, charter, and private schools regarding the production of student outcomes, aggregate spending, and specific programs and services associated with those outcomes.

Some critics of education cost analysis in general, and cost function modeling in particular, assert that all local public school districts are grossly inefficient because teacher pay, the largest single component of school spending, is tied to degree levels and years of service, which are not clearly and directly associated with improved student outcomes. A common version of this argument goes: if teachers were paid based on their direct influence on student test scores, and schools/districts systematically dismissed ineffective teachers, productivity would increase dramatically, spending would decline, and educational adequacy could be achieved at much lower cost. By this logic, estimating costs based on current (inefficient) conditions/practices is a meaningless endeavor, one that can only serve to reinforce current inefficiencies.

However, the most significant problem with this logic is that there exists little, if any, empirical evidence to support it. It is entirely speculative and is frequently based on the assertion that teacher workforce quality can be improved with no increase to average wages simply by firing the bottom 5 percent of teachers each year and paying the rest based on the student test scores they produce. One way to test this assertion would be to permit or encourage some schools/districts to experiment with alternative compensation strategies and other "reforms" and to include these schools/districts among those employing other more common strategies (production technologies) in a cost function model and see where they land along the cost curve. Are schools/districts that adopt these alternative strategies observed in different locations along the cost curve compared to their counterparts employing "status quo" compensation schemes? Do they get the same outcomes with the same kids at much lower spending?

In addition to estimating spending or cost targets, cost functions can be useful for exploring how otherwise similar schools or districts achieve different outcomes with the same level of spending, or the same outcomes with different levels of spending. Researchers have come to learn that inefficiency found in an ECF context is not exclusively a function of mismanagement and waste and is often statistically explainable. Inefficient "spending" in a cost function is that portion of spending variation across schools or districts that is not associated with variation in children's outcomes, after controlling for other factors. The appearance of inefficiency might simply reflect the fact that there have been investments made that, while improving the quality of educational offerings, may not have a measurable impact on the limited outcomes under investigation. It might, for example, have been spent to expand the school's music program, which may be desirable to local constituents. These programs and services may affect other important student outcomes, including persistence and completion and college access, and may even indirectly affect the measured outcomes.

Factors that influence this type of measured "inefficiency" are also increasingly well understood and include three general categories: *fiscal capacity* factors, *public monitoring* factors, and *competition* to attract individuals, families, or households. Local public school districts with greater fiscal capacity, or greater ability to raise and spend more, are more likely to do so and may spend more in ways that do not directly affect measured student outcomes. But that is not to suggest that all additional spending is frivolous, especially where outcome measurement is usually limited to basic reading and math achievement. Public monitoring factors often include such measures as the share of school funding coming from state or federal sources, where higher shares of intergovernmental aid (e.g., federal Title I aid or state categorical aid) may lead to reduced local public involvement, and thus an increased likelihood of inefficient spending. Increased competition, including more competing districts within a geographic space and other available schooling options, is presumed to increase efficiency (decrease inefficiency). But, competition to attract households may also lead to expenditures that are not revealed as "efficient" with respect to measured outcomes, such as providing a high-quality orchestra program or a state-champion lacrosse team.

A thorough ECF model considers spending as a function of measured outcomes, student population characteristics, characteristics of the educational setting (economies of scale, population sparsity, etc.), regional variation in the prices of inputs (such as teacher wages), factors affecting spending that are unassociated with outcomes ("inefficiency"), and interactions among all of the above (figure 9.1). Note that these are the same factors that are important for making efficiency comparisons across schools and districts, because it's the same model of costs associated with the production of certain outcomes.

This illustration of the cost function raises a thorny issue regarding the consultant cottage industry of education cost analysis. Referred to as the Successful Schools analysis for determining the "costs" of educational adequacy, this method is popular among state policy makers for its simplicity and malleability in producing desired, predetermined results.[9] In its simplest and usual form, Successful Schools (or districts) analysis simply involves taking the average expenditure of those schools or districts which currently achieve average outcomes that meet or exceed desired, perhaps adequate, levels. In some cases, consultants arbitrarily prune the sample of successful districts to include those spending the least to achieve those outcomes, claiming this screening to be a control for "inefficiency."[10] The method is little more than a cost function without any controls for student characteristics, context, or input price variation and devoid of any sufficient controls for inefficiency or missing these controls altogether. Thus, in its usual application, Successful Schools analysis is of negligible use for determining costs.

FIGURE 9.1   Factors affecting education costs and efficiency

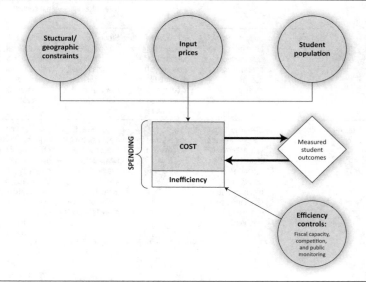

Table 9.1 summarizes methods of education cost analysis, organizing the methods into input-oriented and outcome-oriented methods, which are subsequently applied to hypothetical or actual spending and outcomes, and addressing the method by which information is commonly gathered (e.g., focus groups or consultant synthesis of literature) and the unit of analysis, which also includes the issue of sampling density. Most focus group activities can only practically address the needs of a limited number of prototypical schools and student populations, whereas cost modeling involves all schools and districts, potentially over multiple years (to capture time dynamics of the system

TABLE 9.1 Summary of cost analysis methods in education

General method	Outcome/ Goal basis	Information gathering	Unit of application	Strengths	Weaknesses
Input-oriented (ingredients method or resource cost model)	*Hypothetical*	Focus groups (professional judgment)	Prototypes (limited set)	Requires stakeholder involvement; is context sensitive	Has only hypothetical connection to outcomes; addresses only limited conditions/ settings
	Hypothetical	Consultant synthesis (evidence based)	Single model (transposed across settings)	Requires limited effort; able to use and apply boilerplate to any situation; built on empirically validated strategies	Aggregation of "strategies" to whole school is suspect; transferability of "strategies" is limited; is not context sensitive
	Actual	State data systems (personnel data, annual financial reports, outcome measures)	Schools/Districts sampled from outcome-based modeling (efficient producers of outcomes under varied conditions)	Grounded in reality (what various schools/ districts actually accomplish and how they organize resources)	Requires rich personnel, fiscal, and outcome data; potentially infeasible where outcome goal far exceeds any reality
Outcome-oriented (cost function)	*Actual*	State fiscal data systems that provide accurate district- or school-level spending estimates that account for district spending on overhead	All districts/ schools over multiple years	Based on estimated statistical relationship between actual outcomes and actual spending; evaluates distribution across all districts/schools	Requires rich, high-quality personnel, fiscal, and outcome data; is potentially infeasible where outcome goal far exceeds any reality; focuses on limited measured outcomes; offers limited insights into internal resource use/allocation underlying cost estimate

in addition to cross-sectional variation). It can be difficult to capture fully the nuanced differences in cost factors affecting schools and districts across a large diverse state through only four to six (or even forty) prototypes. Alternatively, traditional professional judgment approaches might be hybridized with survey techniques to gather information across a wider array of settings (increase sampling density).

Certainly, all methods have their strengths and weaknesses—but some weaknesses are critical flaws. I exclude the Successful Schools approach from this table because it is not a credible method of cost analysis. It could be argued that a pure evidence-based approach is also unreliable, since it makes no attempt to estimate the costs of the state's own outcome goals and further and because it fails to consider how needs vary across settings and children in the state-specific context.

The greatest shortcoming of the arguably more robust RCM process used in the professional judgment approach is that the link between resources and outcomes is hypothetical (based solely on professional opinion). The greatest weaknesses of the ECF approach are that predictions may understate true costs of comprehensive adequacy where outcome measures are too narrow and, like any costing out method, when desired goals far exceed those presently achieved, extrapolations may be suspect.

UNDERSTANDING THE DYNAMICS OF EDUCATION COSTS

Identifying education costs at a given point in time is a useful and necessary endeavor for calibrating state school finance systems—for setting foundation levels to achieve desired outcomes and for determining how costs vary from one child to the next, one school to the next, one geographic region to the next. But we must also pay sufficient attention to how education costs change over time and the factors that influence those costs so that state school finance systems can be sufficiently adaptive, and thus maintaining equitable and adequate resources to achieve desired outcomes.

The Labor Market for Quality Teachers

If we want to maintain constant quality education over time, the first thing we must do is maintain a constant quality workforce in the schools (mainly a teacher workforce, but administrators and other education system employees as well), with everything else in the system remaining constant.

The quality of the teacher workforce is influenced much more by the competitiveness of the wages for teachers, compared to other professions, than to changes in the price of a loaf of bread or gallon of gas, as reflected in the more commonly used consumer price index (CPI). If we want to get good teachers, teaching must be perceived as a desirable profession with a competitive wage. To maintain teacher quality we must maintain the competitiveness of teacher wages (which we have not over time), and to improve teacher quality we must make teacher wages (or working conditions) more competitive. On average, nonteacher wage growth has outpaced the CPI over time, and teacher wages have lagged behind nonteacher wages.[11] If we allow for a decline in the quality of the key input—teachers—we can expect a decline in the outcomes, however we choose to measure them.

Higher Standards Cost More

If we want to achieve higher outcomes, a broader array of outcomes, or a higher outcomes in key areas without sacrificing the broader array of outcomes (e.g., improving math and science without cutting music or art), costs will rise. A substantial body of rigorous peer-reviewed empirical literature supports this contention.[12] If we expect our children to compete in a twenty-first-century economy, to develop technology skills and still have access to physical education and arts, it will likely cost more, not less, than achieving the skills of 1980. But we must also make sure we are adequately measuring the full range of outcomes we expect schools to accomplish. If we are expecting schools to produce engaged civic participants, we may or may not see the measured effects in elementary reading and math test scores.

Changing Demography Affects Costs

An additional factor that affects the costs of achieving education outcomes is the student inputs—who is showing up at the schoolhouse door or logging in to the virtual school. Again, a substantial body of research addresses how child poverty, limited English proficiency, unplanned family mobility, and school racial composition may influence the costs of achieving any given level of student outcomes. The various ways children are sorted across districts and schools create large differences in the costs of achieving comparable outcomes, as do changes in the overall demography of the student population over time. Rises in poverty, mobility due to housing disruptions, and the numbers of children not speaking English proficiently all lead to increases in the cost of achieving even the same level of outcomes achieved in prior years. This is not an excuse. It's reality. It costs more to achieve the same outcomes with some students than with others. These differences exist both across school settings and over time as student population demographics shift.

Interactions Among Cost Factors

Costs also change as a function of the interaction of all three of these factors. For example, changing student populations make teaching more difficult (a working condition), which means that a higher wage might be required to simply maintain constant teacher quality (to offset the increased likelihood of teacher attrition or difficulty in recruitment). Also, increasing the complexity of outcome goals might require a more skilled teaching workforce, also requiring higher wages.

The combination of these forces often leads to an increase in education spending that far outpaces the CPI, and it should. Costs rise as we ask more of our schools, as we ask them to produce a citizenry that can compete in the future rather than the past. Costs rise as the student population inputs to our public schooling system change over time. Increased poverty, language barriers, and other factors make even the current outcomes more costly to achieve. And costs of maintaining the quality of the teacher workforce change as competitive wages in other occupations and industries change, which they have.

TRANSLATING COST ANALYSIS INTO POLICY IN NEW JERSEY, KANSAS, AND PENNSYLVANIA

Estimates of education costs have been used to guide development and eventual adoption of new state school finance formulas, namely in New Jersey, Kansas, and Pennsylvania (table 9.2). These three cases provide useful insights regarding the role of empirical estimates of costs in influencing state school finance policy, including cases where state courts may rely on that evidence to push legislatures toward more equitable and adequate remedies.

In the early 2000s, New Jersey state officials contracted the firm of Augenblick, Palaich and Associates to estimate education costs using both professional judgment and Successful Schools analyses. A notable result of the professional judgment analysis was that, instead of requiring panels to recommend resource configurations on their own, state Department of Education officials provided panels with a recommended set of resources to all the prototypical schools and permitted them to make adjustments. The Department of Education used this report to provide guidance for a new school funding formula that would account for differences in student needs and regional costs, the School Funding Reform Act (SFRA), stating: "After years of a court-driven, ad-hoc approach to school funding, the New Jersey Department of Education (Department) is proposing a new funding formula designed to ensure that all children in all communities have the opportunity to succeed. The proposal is a culmination of five years of work by the Department to develop an equitable and predictable way to distribute State aid for education."[13] The formula was adopted in 2008 and subsequently litigated in state court to determine whether the formula sufficiently complied with prior judicial mandates. In 2009 the act was found constitutional.[14] Within a few years after adoption, the formula was no longer fully funded and has not been since. Further, parameters have been altered to reduce aid to high-need districts, and aid for other districts has been frozen or cut.

Like New Jersey, Kansas has seen decades of litigation over the constitutionality of its school finance system. The empirical era in Kansas dates back to the late 1990s, when a task force convened by Governor Bill Graves recommended to the legislature that it contract consultants to determine the costs of meeting the state's constitutional mandate under Article 6, Section 6 of the Kansas Constitution to "make suitable provision for finance of the educational interests of the state." A legislative subcommittee contracted a study that they then released in 2002. No action was taken by the legislature in response to the study. The study was, however, used as evidence against the state in the case of *Montoy v. Kansas,* where a lower court in 2003 and a higher court in 2005 held that the current funding system was unconstitutional. Wanting a "redo" on their cost estimates, legislators contracted a new study that would be overseen by their independent research division and would include a combination of evidence-based methods and a cost function estimated by hired consultants. The end result was highly correlated with the original 2002 cost study but included some unique features, such as a poverty/density factor. In 2018 the Kansas legislature pursued yet another adequacy cost analysis, under pressure from the state's supreme court in *Gannon v. Kansas.*[15] This study by WestEd and Lori Taylor used a cost modeling method and yielded findings highly correlated with those of the 2006 study.[16]

Pennsylvania represents a unique case of advocacy groups, legislators, and the governor collaborating to pursue cost analysis and, subsequently, a redesign of state school finance policy without judicial pressure. The General

TABLE 9.2 From cost studies to aid formulas in three states

	New Jersey	Pennsylvania	Kansas
Context	Achieve dismissal of long-running judicial oversight	None	Comply with court mandate (and achieve dismissal)
Policy objective	Eliminate *Abbott* classification and achieve unified statewide formula (and spread aid across more districts)	Achieve unified, more equitable, and adequate formula	None
Analyses			
Cost studies	Augenblick, Palaich and Associates adapted by NJ Department of Education (2006)[a]	Augenblick, Palaich and Associates (2007)[b]	Augenblick and Myers (2002)[c] and Kansas Legislative Division of Post Audit (LDPA)[d], with William Duncombe (2006)[e]
Methods	Successful schools and professional judgment	Successful schools and professional judgment	Augenblick and Myers: successful schools and professional judgment; LDPA: ECF and evidence based
Methodological notes	NJDOE proposed initial resource configurations; panels provided opportunity to adjust; NJDOE produced summary report (three years after study completed).	Professional judgment estimates based on achieving 100 percent proficiency in 2014; included separate Philadelphia panel[b]	Hired consultants Duncombe & Yinger; explored relationship between poverty and population density, finding significant cost effect[g]
Translation to legislation			
Base figure	Adopted $9,649 for 2009; cost study yielded $8,016 (professional judgment) to $8,493 (successful schools) in 2005[b]	Adopted $8,355 for 2008–9; cost study yielded $8,003 (professional judgment) in 2006[i]	Adopted $4,257 for 2007; cost function minimum estimate was $4,565; general fund budget only[f]
Other base adjustments	Added grade-level weighting (study included cost differences by grade range served)		Backed out of federal funding and focused exclusively on general fund expenses
Wage adjustment	Estimated county-level "comparable wage" adjustment (claiming NCES ECWI as precedent); drives funds to high-income counties[j]	Location cost metric (largely based on cost study)[b,i]	Adopted special adjustment for 16 districts with highest housing prices. Provided additional taxing authority for wealthiest districts.[l]
Economies of scale adjustment	None	District size supplement[h]	Carryover of prior legislation[l]
Student need factors	Adopted sliding scale for poverty concentration factor (from 47% to 57%) and constant ELL weight at 50%; significantly reduced need weight by creating "combination" weight for children who are both low income and ELL (on basis of "redundant services")[e]	Adopted 43% low-income weight ($3,593/$8,355); adopted variable ELL multiplier, which varied with district enrollment 1.5–2.5 (smaller weight in larger districts, based largely on Augenblick, Palaich and Associates study)[b]	Adopted high-density poverty weight (applied to select locations); drives resources to high-need, more "urban" districts; adopted nonproficient non–low income weight (not in study); drives money to lower-need suburban districts[f]

Sources: [a]A. Dupree, J. Augenblick, and J. Silverstein, "Report on the Cost of Education," 2006, http://nj.gov/education/sff/archive/report.pdf; [b]Augenblick, Palaich and Associates, "Costing out the Resources Needed to Meet Pennsylvania's Public Education Goals," Pennsylvania State Board of Education, 2007, http://www.apaconsulting.net/uploads/reports/6.pdf; [c]J. Augenblick, J. Myers, J. Silverstein, and A. Barkas, "Calculation of the Cost of a Suitable Education in Kansas Using Two Different Analytic Approaches" (report, Kansas Legislature, Topeka, 2002), http://skyways.lib.ks.us/ksleg/KLRD/Publications/SchoolFinanceFinalReport.pdf; [d]Kansas Legislative Division of Post Audit, Cost Study Analysis. Elementary and Secondary Education in Kansas: Estimating the Costs of K–12 Education Using Two Approaches, 2006, http://skyways.lib.ks.us/kansas/ksleg/KLRD/Publications/Education_Cost_Study_Report.pdf (study by William Duncombe and John Yinger in Appendix C); [e]Bruce D. Baker, "Evaluating the 'Concrete Link' Between Professional Judgment Analysis, New Jersey's School Finance Reform Act and the Costs of Meeting State Standards in Abbott Districts" (report, Education Law Center of New Jersey, Newark, 2009), http://schoolfinance101.files.wordpress.com/2011/10/baker-pjp-sfra-report-web.pdf; [f]William Duncombe and John Yinger, "Estimating the Cost of Meeting Student Performance Outcomes Adopted by the Kansas State Board of Education" (report, Kansas Legislature, Topeka, 2006); [g]"A Formula for Success: All Children, All Communities," New Jersey Department of Education, December 18, 2007, http://nj.gov/education/sff/reports/AllChildrenAllCommunities.pdf; [h]Basic Education Funding worksheets, http://www.portal.state.pa.us/portal/http://www.portal.state.pa.us:80/portal/server.pt/gateway/PTARGS_0_123706_1342399_0_0_18/Finance%20BEF%202008-09%20May2013.xlsx; [i]Bruce D. Baker, "Still Wide of Any Reasonable Mark: A Reexamination of Kansas School Finance," Schools for Fair Funding, 2011, http://www.robblaw.com/PDFs/P384.pdf; [j]Bruce D. Baker, "Doing More Harm Than Good? A Commentary on the Politics of Cost Adjustments for Wage Variation in State School Finance Formulas," *Journal of Education Finance* 33, no. 4 (2008): 406–40.

Assembly called for the study in 2006 and the study, also by Augenblick, Palaich and Associates, which applied a combination of professional judgment and Successful Schools analysis was released in 2007. A notable, often-criticized aspect of the study is the charge given to professional judgment panels to determine the costs of achieving an arguably unrealistic "universal mastery of state standards in 12 academic areas for all students" and 100 percent proficiency on state assessments in reading and math by the year 2014.[17]

As these three examples make clear, we must consider the studies themselves in their political context. Such analyses are not, nor can they ever be, entirely apolitical. In New Jersey, there were questionable alterations of the usual professional judgment methodology, which led to a lower base cost (and the only occasion where the professional judgment base cost came in lower than the Successful Schools estimate). In Kansas, what was an attempt under judicial pressure to yield a more favorable result by calling for a reexamination of costs that originally required evaluating only the resources needed to achieve bare-bones inputs. The parameters of that do-over were subsequently modified and strengthened under court pressure.[18] Political influence on the cost analysis itself is less apparent (in public records) in Pennsylvania.

In New Jersey, several substantive changes were made in the translation of the cost study to school finance legislation. Some of these changes were made out of convenience, including providing a weight on the grade level children attended rather than providing a cost differential for districts serving different grade ranges. Other changes were made using arguments of transparency or familiarity, including the choice to adjust labor costs for county level rather than labor market wages (though neither was mentioned in the original study), and student need adjustments were adapted and altered. Professional judgment studies often produce varied weights on poverty or ELL status based on context. New Jersey officials chose to approach poverty weighting differently, scaling up the weights with concentration based on subsequent convening with external consultants, and they also chose to provide a reduced combination weight for children who would otherwise qualify for both the ELL and low-income weighting.

In Kansas, policy makers also adopted piecemeal components of the cost studies, but then counterbalanced them, as they had on many previous occasions, with their own "cost adjustments" that drove resources back to lower-need districts—including maintaining the weight on children attending new facilities, adding a weight for non–low income nonproficient students, and adding a special taxing authority for the seventeen districts with the highest-priced houses—asserting that adjustment was necessary for accounting for labor cost variation.[19] None of these adjustments was validated by the cost studies.

Pennsylvania's school finance statute adopted in 2008 represents perhaps the closest adherence to a cost study. Notably, valid or not, the legislation went so far as to include the weightings for ELL status that varied with respect to (the natural logarithm of) enrollment and to similarly adopt the district size weighting along a smooth economies of scale curve. That said, the formula was never close to being fully phased in and was abandoned entirely.

LESSONS LEARNED AND LOOKING FORWARD

State school finance policies can be reasonably guided by high-quality research and analysis—which means putting effort and resources into the development of high-quality research and analysis, and the translation of that research into useable policy guidance. To do so, we must consider that

- reasonable empirical evidence can and should guide policy;
- there is much to be learned from the diversity of existing US public schools and systems;
- reconciling and/or triangulating top-down (modeling from ten-thousand feet) and bottom-up insights (a deep dive into resources) can inform policy and practice at all levels;
- the path from empirical evidence to policy design is not a straight one
- informed policy (conceptually and empirically) is likely better than uninformed policy; and
- empirical evidence and conceptual frameworks can "bend" school finance systems toward a better state than might otherwise have occurred.

State school finance policies will always be a product of political deliberation among state legislators and governors and will always depend on state tax and spending choices. And state school finance systems will always be subject to the economic and political pressures of the context in which they exist, including the fluctuating economic conditions, political preferences, and vast array of other programs and services provided by state and local governments. While these pressures many limit or modify the influence of empirical evidence, they need not necessarily negate it entirely. The goal is a modest one: to render state school finance systems better than they might have been in the absence of high-quality, conceptually grounded empirical evidence.

CHAPTER 10

EQUITABLE, ADEQUATE, AND SUSTAINABLE SCHOOL FUNDING

To conclude this volume, I lay out a framework for the provision of a nationwide equitable, adequate, and sustainable system of public schools. The basic design elements of state school finance systems can be applied to achieve more appropriately targeted federal aid based on need, cost, and states' own fiscal capacity and effort. And with equitable and adequate resources, states, local districts, and schools, including charters, may then tend to the business of adopting those educational strategies and interventions that best serve their unique student populations, keeping in mind common outcome goals. State and federal education agencies can then refocus their efforts on the development and dissemination of technical assistance to advance the efficient and productive use of financial resources.

The plan involves five steps:

1. applying the best available methods and data to estimate "costs" of providing equal educational opportunity across children, settings, and states;
2. designing an equitable and adequate financing system around empirically based targets of the costs and needs of providing equal educational opportunity;
3. financing that system with balanced, stable, and equitable revenue sources;
4. leveraging federal financial resources to counterbalance interstate inequality, while requiring equitable effort on the part of states; and

5. charging state education agencies and the US Department of Education with the primary responsibility of developing technical guidance for education systems through the support and development of both basic and applied high-quality research.

IDENTIFYING THE GAPS AND SETTING TARGETS

The process begins with high-quality analysis and data—more specifically, with the estimation of a national education cost model using outcome-based methods. For decades, school finance researchers have explored the impact of inequities across local public school districts on children's opportunities to meet state student achievement accountability standards. Such analyses usually rely on several (five or more) years of annual data on student outcomes (across all districts), district expenditure data, and data on the characteristics of the student populations served and the settings in which they are served. The goals of these analyses have been to determine the per-pupil costs of achieving state-mandated student outcome goals across children, schools, and districts and to evaluate whether existing resources allocated to local public school districts are sufficient for meeting these goals.

In the past few years, the release of two new national data panels of local public school district data has increased the feasibility of conducting such analyses across all local public school districts in all states and the District of Columbia. First, the *School Funding Fairness Data System* has released a twenty-two-year panel of district-level data on school expenditures, student population characteristics, and various district organizational, structural, and economic characteristics.[1] Second, the *Stanford Education Data Archive* has released nationally equated estimates of district-level state assessments of reading and math for the years 2009 to 2015. Third, in 2013 Lori Taylor and colleagues developed a method for better equating poverty measurement from one US region to another and across rural and urban settings within states.[2] And finally, Taylor has continued to produce an annual, district-level geographic competitive wage adjustment to aid in accounting for cost differences across regions and across local districts within states.[3]

The goal of education cost modeling, whether for evaluating equal educational opportunity or for producing adequacy cost estimates, is to establish reasonable marks to provide guidance in developing more rational state school finance systems.[4] Historically, funding levels for state school finance systems have been determined by taking the total revenue generated for schooling as a function of statewide tastes for taxation and dividing that funding by the number of students in the system. Thus, the budget constraint, or total available revenue, and total student enrollment have been the key determinants of the foundation level or basic allotment. To some degree, this will always be true. But reasonable estimates of the "cost" of producing desired outcomes, given current technologies of production, may influence additional taxes by revealing that the preferences regarding taxation and the preferences regarding desired quality of public education are misaligned, meaning that one or the other should be adjusted. It's like the individual who wants to buy a Cadillac Escalade but wants to spend only $25,000. After a little research, he finds that he can either buy a Ford F-150 for $25,000 or an Escalade for $65,000; he must then decide to go with the Ford or increase his spending to enable the purchase of the Escalade (or choose a different car priced somewhere in the middle).

That's where the research comes in—to identify the gap between uninformed assumptions and reasonably informed ones. Reasonable estimates of cost may assist legislators in setting spending levels consistent with outcome demands and in setting outcome demands attainable at desired spending levels. Reasonable estimates of cost may also assist courts in determining whether current funding levels and distributions are wide of a reasonable mark or substantially misaligned with constitutional standards.

Further, cost model estimates cannot predict what student outcomes will necessarily occur next year if we suddenly adopt a school finance system based on them. Cost models provide guidance regarding the general levels of funding increases that would be required to produce measured outcomes at a certain level, assuming that districts are able to absorb the additional resources without efficiency loss. Studies of school finance reform also suggest that the key to successful school finance reform is that it is both substantive and sustained.[5] Moreover, the immediacy of outcome changes due to funding increases depends on what is being funded. If additional dollars to high-need districts are best leveraged toward high-quality preschool programs and/or early grades class size reduction, we are unlikely to see changes in college readiness outcomes the following year (or even in the following five years). If the additional dollars are best leveraged toward increasing salaries for teachers in their optimal years of experience, allowing districts to recruit and retain more skilled teachers over time, we are also unlikely to see immediate returns in student test scores.

When estimating a cost model linking existing spending to outcome measures, with consideration for various district and student population characteristics—there are certain expectations of what will or can be identified by that model, including the idea that higher spending is associated with higher outcomes and that the cost of achieving common outcomes is higher in areas where competitive wages for recruiting and retaining a teacher workforce is higher, in remote rural areas with sparse populations and schools and districts that cannot achieve economies of scale, and in areas serving higher-poverty student populations (and/or other indicators of student need).

Once a model is estimated, costs of common outcomes can be predicted and gaps between current spending and costs can be identified. Certain basic patterns should be observable. For example, if we set out to conservatively estimate the costs associated with achieving national average outcomes, at average efficiency, we would not expect that most districts fall short of these cost targets. Rather, if we're aiming for current average outcomes, a target many districts and children already exceed, we should expect that only about half of districts, and/or the children who attend districts and schools, have resources insufficient to achieve these outcomes. Further, there should exist a relatively clear, albeit imperfect, relationship between the size of the spending gap relative to what's needed and the actual outcomes achieved. We should expect that if our model is reasonable, districts estimated to have too little funding to achieve the desired outcome generally fall short of that outcome, and districts estimated to have more than enough generally exceed that outcome.

Figure 10.1 illustrates this. At the midpoint of the horizontal axis are the predicted resources needed to achieve average outcomes. School districts (or states) falling to the left of that point have resources estimated to be insufficient to achieve average outcomes (at average efficiency), and districts (or states) to the right of that line have more than enough resources to achieve average outcomes. On the vertical axis are actual outcomes, with the average marked by the solid horizontal line at midpoint. We would expect that, on average, districts with more than enough resources to achieve average outcomes would achieve or exceed average outcomes, and vice versa. At the intersection of the two lines is the point of equal opportunity, where the district with average resources achieves average outcomes. Notably, if we set an "adequacy" target higher than current averages, more districts will fall below that target. Raising the target raises the cost of achieving it.

FIGURE 10.1 Linking resources, outcomes, and adequacy targets

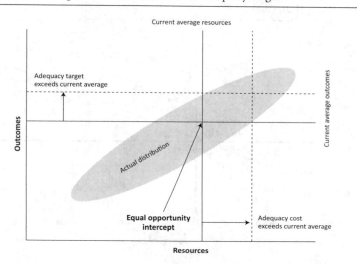

My focus is on the national average outcomes, because it is a level of outcomes commonly achieved by American schoolchildren. Thus, I am not trying to craft estimates for costs of outcomes well beyond current realities. That said, current average outcomes may be entirely insufficient as a national policy goal. Our current averages lie somewhere between well-funded, high-performing states like New Jersey and Massachusetts and poorly funded, low-performing states like Mississippi and Arizona. Large swaths of our nation have, for decades, thrown their public school systems under the bus, providing substandard education systems yielding substandard outcomes (see appendix). In the longer term, our national goal should be to move more states in the direction of our top-performing states, but at this point just getting to average may seem overwhelming.

COST MODEL FINDINGS: GAPS ACROSS STATES

Figure 10.2 shows the state average funding gaps (deficits and surpluses) to achieve national average outcomes for school districts falling in the middle quintile of child poverty in each state. Middle-poverty quintile districts in Connecticut, Massachusetts, and New Jersey spend between $5,000 and $10,000 more per pupil than they would need to produce merely average

FIGURE 10.2   Funding and outcomes relative to national average (middle-poverty quintile)

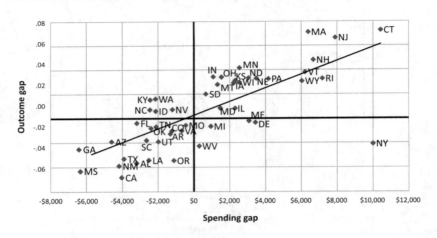

Source: Data from Baker et al., *The Real Shame of the Nation.*

outcomes. And they do produce much-higher-than-average outcomes. In all likelihood, the residents of these states would not prefer to lower their spending to achieve merely national average outcomes. New York is somewhat of an outlier; it spends as much as these other states per pupil but falls short of national average outcomes. The implication here is that New York State school districts, for some reason, on average, leverage their resources less efficiently, or that the model has missed some unique features of the districts that drive their costs higher than expected. At the other end of the distribution gap are states like Mississippi, Georgia, California, Louisiana, New Mexico, and Alabama, each of which spends much less than needed on middle-poverty quintile districts to achieve average outcomes and currently yields much-less-than-average outcomes. Of course, these averages mask huge disparities within states. On average, Illinois and Pennsylvania spend enough in middle-poverty districts to marginally exceed national average outcomes. But these two states are also among the least equitable in the nation in disadvantaging high-poverty districts.

Figure 10.3 shows that for the lowest-poverty quintile districts in most states, resources are sufficient to achieve national average outcomes. This is unsurprising given that the costs of achieving national average outcomes are

FIGURE 10.3   Funding and outcomes relative to national average (lowest-poverty quintile)

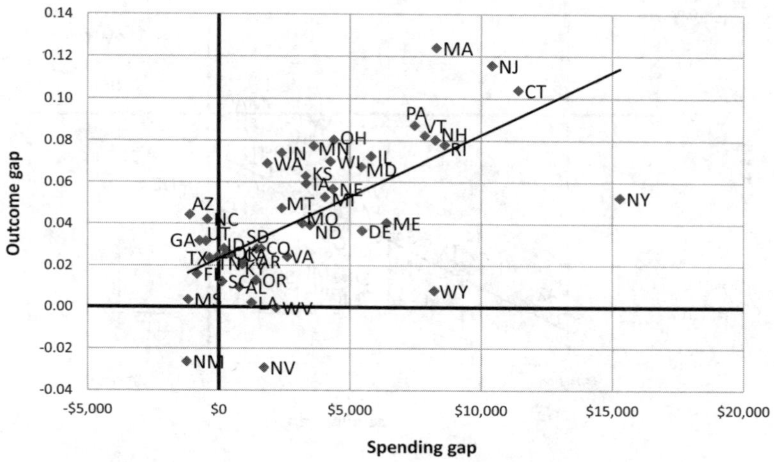

Source: Data from Baker et al., *The Real Shame of the Nation*.

necessarily much lower in low-poverty districts. However, in New Mexico and Mississippi, where the lowest-poverty quintile district is relatively high in poverty and where spending is low across the board, even the lowest-poverty districts have spending levels insufficient to achieve the modest goal of national average outcomes.

Figure 10.4 shows the distribution for the highest-poverty quintile of districts within each state. In only a few states do the highest-poverty districts have sufficient funding to achieve national average outcomes. The highest-poverty quintile of districts in Mississippi, Arizona, and California have funding gaps of greater than $10,000 per pupil, along with the largest outcome gaps among states. Nebraska appears to have sufficient funding to achieve national average outcomes in high-poverty districts but falls short on actual outcomes, raising the possibility of inefficiencies or, alternatively, a failure of the model to capture additional costs facing high-poverty Nebraska school districts.

Figure 10.5 compares a state at the high end, New Jersey, and one at the low end, Mississippi, across all poverty quintiles. In New Jersey, all but the

FIGURE 10.4 Funding and outcomes relative to national average (highest-poverty quintile)

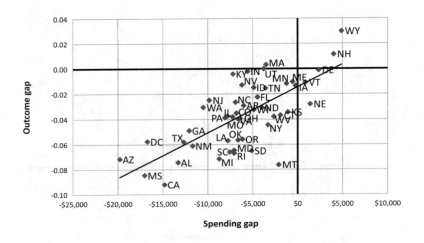

Source: Data from Baker et al., *The Real Shame of the Nation*.

FIGURE 10.5 Comparing cost of national average outcomes to current spending in Mississippi and New Jersey

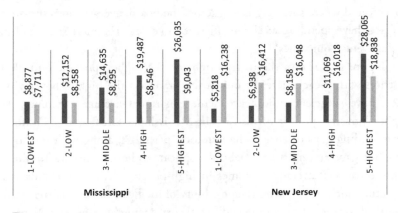

Source: Data from Baker et al., *The Real Shame of the Nation*.

highest-poverty quintile of districts has current (2013–15) average spending per pupil higher than spending needed to achieve average outcomes. While per-pupil spending is higher in higher-poverty districts in New Jersey, the margin of spending difference is insufficient to cover the margin of cost difference. By contrast, across all poverty quintiles, cost targets (for average outcomes) exceed current spending in Mississippi districts. While the gap is small for the lowest-poverty districts, the gap is seemingly astronomical for the highest-poverty Mississippi districts. These are among the highest-poverty districts in the nation (even after adjusting the income thresholds for regional wage variation to correct poverty measurements), and they have among the lowest current outcomes in the nation and provide very little funding per pupil.[6] The hole we must dig ourselves out of as a nation is huge in states like Mississippi and many other southern and southwestern states that have either neglected their public education systems for decades or simply lack the fiscal capacity to support adequate public schools.

While estimates of education costs at the individual district level may be imprecise, they are nonetheless useful in the absence of any other rigorously derived guidance. Some findings for individual districts and even for entire quintiles of districts within states suggest extreme disparities resulting in very costly remedies. The models included here suggest that, in some states, the highest-poverty quintile of districts fall as much as $14,000 to $16,000 per pupil below necessary spending levels. While these models may overestimate these needs, we can safely assume that very-high-poverty districts in, for example, some parts of California or in the lower Mississippi Delta, do require a huge infusion of additional funding to achieve more adequate and equitable student outcomes.

ESTABLISHING SUSTAINABLE, ADEQUATE REVENUE STREAMS

The framework for a more equitable national system can be built on the basic design elements of state school finance systems: accounting for differences in the costs of achieving equal educational opportunity in reaching desired outcomes across schools, districts, and the children they serve and for differences in the ability of local public school districts to cover those costs. In state school finance formulas, first cost targets are set as foundation levels, including student need factors and other cost factors. Next, the appropriate, fair local contribution is determined and state aid is calculated to make up the difference between that local contribution and the cost target. A similar approach can be taken for determining the distribution of federal aid.

ALLOCATING EXISTING STATE AID MORE EQUITABLY

Equity, equal opportunity, and adequacy of resources delivered under state school finance systems depend less on the split between state and local shares and more on the sufficient targeting of state resources where they are needed most. First and foremost, states must identify those features of their aid systems, including the "within the formula" and "outside the formula" allocations that create stealth inequalities. Pressure to eliminate stealth inequalities and redistribute equitably the resources recaptured might be induced by annual federal reporting and analyses on these inequalities.

Second, state aid must be allocated in sufficient amounts to not only offset variations in local capacity to raise revenue but also to address differences in needs and cost. The addition of state aid to local systems should lead to an overall progressive distribution of resources, as measured by a model similar to the one used in "Is School Funding Fair?"[7] Again, regular federal reporting and analysis can play a role in guiding states toward more progressive state school finance systems by offering ongoing research support and guidance.

BALANCING STATE REVENUE PORTFOLIOS

States must also figure out how to best organize their tax systems to provide for sustained, stable financing of adequate levels of funding. The best approach involves a balanced portfolio of state and local revenue sources and considers both the equity in tax treatment and revenue and the volatility of revenue. Organizations such as the Tax Foundation make a big deal about interstate competition around business and household mobility, focusing on state taxes as the exclusive determinant of desirability.[8] This assertion that high taxes, regardless of public service quality, drive families and business away is simply incorrect and inconsistent with how market theories are applied to public goods.[9] While the prices paid in taxes matter, so do the quality and breadth of services available as a result of those tax dollars. It's about the entire package—and the quality of public schooling, which depends on sufficient taxation and financing, is a central element of that package (along with health-care access, parks, roads, police and fire protection, etc.).

While property taxes have the potential to be inequitable to taxpayers and to raise vastly inequitable revenue across districts and/or other local jurisdictions, they still have the virtue of stability, which is necessary for the provision of local public services like schooling. Further, if and when they do fluctuate, those fluctuations tend to lag and be off-cycle with more volatile income tax revenue fluctuations, thus playing an important counterbalancing and stabilizing role (table 10.1). The best way to ensure equitable property taxation for taxpayers across jurisdictions of varied wealth is to ensure that state aid is allocated in sufficient proportions to low-wealth communities. Further, if state aid calculations depend on measures of local property wealth, the state must ensure accurate and up-to-date measurement of property wealth and must control the extent to which local jurisdictions are permitted to adjust assessments or grant abatements or incentives. Such decisions have implications for the distribution and available levels of state aid. States may choose to include circuit breakers or exemptions in cases where property taxes exceed a certain share of income or for senior citizens on fixed income, but absolute thresholds can create perverse incentives at their margins.

While state income tax systems can be implemented progressively across taxpayers and can provide substantial revenue for state general funds, they face the increasing problem of volatility. State income tax revenue increase or decline quickly with economic ups and downs, but public services like education require stable and predictable budgets. Volatility varies dramatically by state due to the composition of income. While increased taxes on nonwage income can increase revenue generated in "good times" and tend to be more progressive, the revenue generated by these taxes are also more volatile. A 2014 report

TABLE 10.1   Evaluating state and local tax policy options

		EQUITY		VOLATILITY/SUSTAINABILITY	
		Status	Options	Status	Options
Local property tax	Taxpayer treatment	Potentially inequitable	Sufficient "equalization"; statewide uniform assessment (data system); exemptions/circuit breakers		
	Revenue	Highly inequitable	Statewide taxation of nonresidential property	Stable (and lags)	
State income tax	Taxpayer treatment	Equitable/ Progressive			
	Revenue	Equitable		Volatile	
State sales tax	Taxpayer treatment	Potentially regressive	Exemptions for necessities; luxury taxes		
	Revenue			Less volatile	Broaden tax base (services, transactions, etc.)

from the Pew Charitable Trust argues that states should use revenue volatility to their advantage by depositing revenue windfalls from natural resources, capital gains, and corporate income taxes into rainy day funds to protect against eventual downturns and smooth out state budgets over the long term.[10]

Sales tax revenue tends to be somewhat less volatile than income tax revenue, and balancing state revenue portfolios between the two is necessary, though some states can clearly lean more heavily on one than the other. Regressiveness of sales taxes on taxpayers can be reduced by exempting necessities, and progressiveness can be achieved by differentially taxing luxuries. Most importantly, as Rob Tannenwald notes, broadening the sales tax base to be inclusive of services might stabilize and rebalance the sales tax revenue portfolio.[11]

One of the more clever state and local tax reforms from academic literature that has never taken hold in state policy conversations involves the statewide taxation of nonresidential properties for raising state revenue to be distributed specifically for equalizing school funding. In 1976 Helen (Sunny) Ladd proposed statewide taxation of nonresidential properties to equalize school funding, and in 1999 Brian Brent modeled Ladd's policy proposal applied to regions within New York State to evaluate the effectiveness of the approach for resolving school funding disparities.[12] In many states the most substantial disparities in property wealth from one jurisdiction to the next are not a result of differences in housing prices but a result of the location of high-value nonresidential facilities (corporate parks and headquarters, utilities, commercial shopping districts, etc.), or "ratables," as the locals call them. The values of these properties are not contingent on the consumer behavior of those residing in their immediate school district, even if those locals may incur some of costs associated with their presence. So it makes little sense that locals alone—those owning taxable residential properties in the same district—would reap the tax benefits of the presence of the ratables. It is also the case that when ratables lose their value due to closure or reassessment, host districts are disproportionately and substantially affected.

If, however, we separate commercial, industrial, utility, and oil/gas/mineral properties from residential properties, the extent of disparity in local revenue-raising capacity can be reduced dramatically. Not only that, if we then apply a statewide uniform tax to the nonresidential properties, we can generate a relatively stable revenue source that can be distributed in accordance with capacity, need, and costs.

By way of example, figure 10.6 shows Texas local district property value data separated along these lines for the year 2010. The figure presents the "bell curves" (distributions of total property values and residential property values) as bar charts for Texas school districts. The bars in the chart are weighted by district enrollment. Residential (single and multifamily) property districts tend to fall between 100,000 and 400,000, with most clustered around 200,000. But when commercial, industrial, utility, and oil/gas/mineral properties are added, the distribution spreads substantially, as does the revenue raised at any constant tax rate that might be used in a foundation aid formula.

Table 10.2 shows the average, minimum, and maximum property wealth per pupil for combined property types, residential only property, and nonresidential property for Texas school districts in 2010. The table also shows the yield produced by a constant tax rate. The coefficient of variation indicates

FIGURE 10.6   Distribution of total versus residential property value per pupil in Texas

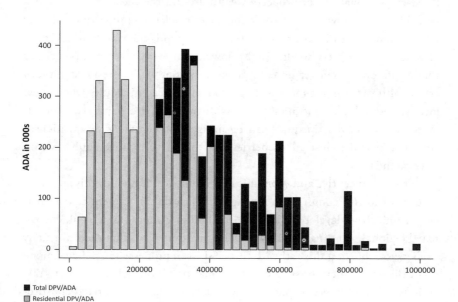

■ Total DPV/ADA
□ Residential DPV/ADA

Source: Texas Comptroller, "Property Values by Category Tax Year 2004 to 2010."

TABLE 10.2   Texas districts' property wealth value (DPV) per pupil in average daily attendance (ADA), 2010

Variable	DPV/ADA	Residential/ADA	Nonresidential*/ADA
Districts	1024	1024	1024
Students	4501883	4501883	4501883
Average DPV	$371,204	$226,377	$117,094
Standard deviation	$277,755	$149,399	$227,736
Minimum	$30,720	$0	$813
Maximum	$13,900,000	$3,907,666	$11,800,000
Coefficient of variation	74.8%	66.0%	194.5%
Yield from 1.5% tax			
Mean	$5,568	$3,396	$1,756
Standard deviation	$4,166	$2,241	$3,416

Note: *Commercial, industrial, utilities, and oil/gas/mineral.

Source: "Property Values by Category: Tax Year 2004 to 2010," Office of the Comptroller, https://comptroller.texas.gov/transparency/open -data/search-datasets/.

the average deviations of property wealth around the mean, expressed as a percent, which shows us that while the mean residential property wealth per pupil is lower than total property wealth per pupil, the standard deviation of residential property wealth is also lower, and even lower as a percent of that mean (66 percent versus 74.8 percent). By contrast, nonresidential property wealth varies much more widely, producing greater inequity when taxed locally, and is highly inequitable across districts in Texas and elsewhere. If taxed statewide, that inequity can be mitigated. But statewide taxation of commercial and industrial properties only helps to improve equity within state boundaries.

From an incentive and economic development standpoint, this approach reduces distortive competition among local jurisdictions to entice commercial or industrial developers, and it also allows for more thoughtful, coordinated regional planning. The downside to the approach is that there are many barriers to achieving this rather dramatic shift in property tax policy, among them the amendment of state constitutional provisions where property taxation is either addressed explicitly or where courts have interpreted constitutions as prohibiting statewide property taxation. Even so, the benefits of this singular shift in state tax policy, where attainable, would be substantial.

A NEW FEDERAL ROLE IN FINANCE

Even with relatively high effort, some states simply lack the capacity to close the gaps I identify here. These interstate variations in revenue-raising capacity speak to the need for a new and different federal role in improving interstate inequality to advance our national interest in improved education outcomes across states. Federal funding for schools has been insufficient for improving interstate inequality. Arguably, the gaps are at the core of our national interest, and substantial portions of K–12 federal education funds should be pooled and targeted to resolve these disparities, with particular emphasis on raising spending levels in states with large spending gaps and little fiscal capacity of their own to close them (e.g., Mississippi, New Mexico). The federal government should also use its bully pulpit and financial incentives to encourage low-effort, higher-capacity states with large school funding shortfalls and inequities (e.g., Arizona, Texas, California) to take appropriate steps to resolve them. In short, the federal government must act to reduce inequality both within and between states to further the national interest.

The new federal approach to distributing aid should resemble that of a nationwide need-and-cost-adjusted foundation formula, thereby pooling existing federal funding sources. We should begin by adopting the funding targets as foundation targets, then determine the state and local effort that should be put forth toward meeting those targets, and, finally, pool existing federal aid sources and allocate aid to fill remaining gaps, assuming constant effort. Figure 10.7 shows the current "effort" of states measured as total state and local revenue for elementary and secondary schools as a percent of state GDP in relation to funding gaps (for national average outcomes) for median poverty districts. For example, Arizona has among the lowest effort rates in the nation, 2.5–3 percent GDP, and its highest-poverty districts face per-pupil funding gaps of more than $15,000. From a national policy perspective, this should be entirely inexcusable. Mississippi's high-poverty districts have similarly large gaps, but its contribution as a share of its GDP is much higher and above average nationally.

Median-poverty districts in these states face sizeable gaps as well. But in some states wealthy districts easily exceed state adequacy targets with well-below-average effort. For example, Delaware, a small state that is home to a large segment of the financial industry, can levy low effort and still raise resources more than sufficient to achieve national average outcomes. Even

FIGURE 10.7   Effort versus funding gaps, 2013–15

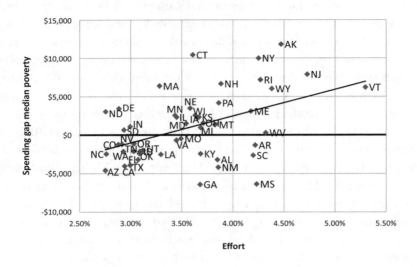

Source: Data from Baker et al., *The Real Shame of the Nation*.

Kansas, a relatively average state in nearly every regard, can raise relatively average resources with average effort and achieve average or better outcomes. The nations' highest-effort state, Vermont, raises nearly enough for its highest-poverty districts at current effort, but under a reasonable federal foundation formula it might actually be able to reduce its effort.

Figure 10.8 simulates two local effort scenarios to evaluate gap closure by requiring states to raise and spend 4–5 percent of their GDP on elementary and secondary education. The focus is on the median gaps within states, not the extremes for high-poverty districts. So while Arizona's high-poverty 2013–15 spending gaps are greater than $15,000 per pupil, the average gap is just under $5,000 per pupil, which is still very large. But if Arizona spent 4 percent of its GDP on schools, a level many other states spend, the gap would be reduced to under $2,000 per pupil. That's a substantial gap reduction achieved by simply requiring Arizona to put forth more effort for its schools *in the national interest*. If Arizona moved all the way to 5 percent of its GDP, the average spending gap would be eliminated altogether. The case is similar for many other states, including California, Nevada, and Tennessee.

FIGURE 10.8   Changes in funding gaps at varied required effort thresholds

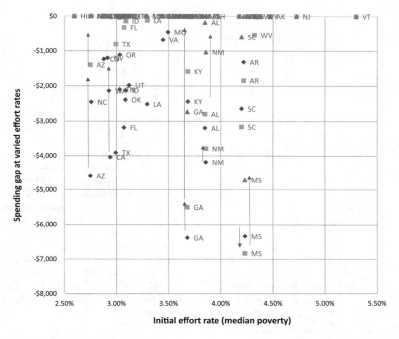

♦ Spending gap (average outcomes) median poverty
▲ Spending gap at 5% Gross State Product effort
■ Spending gap at 4% Gross State Product effort

Source: Data from Baker et al., *The Real Shame of the Nation.*

Other states, however, like Mississippi, are simply unable to close their own spending gaps, even with a 5 percent GDP contribution. Moving to a 4 percent contribution would actually lower Mississippi's contribution and increase its average spending gap, while moving to a 5 percent contribution of its GDP would reduce the per-pupil spending gap from over $6,000 to just under $5,000.

Figure 10.9 presents this from another angle, showing that with a 4 percent effort requirement, about ten states require federal funding to close their spending gaps. At existing (2013–15) effort, the total spending gap across all states and children exceeds $1 trillion. But raising the effort requirement to 4 percent narrows that gap by about one-third, to about $365 billion. And at

FIGURE 10.9   Reduction of funding gaps at varied required effort thresholds, 2013–15

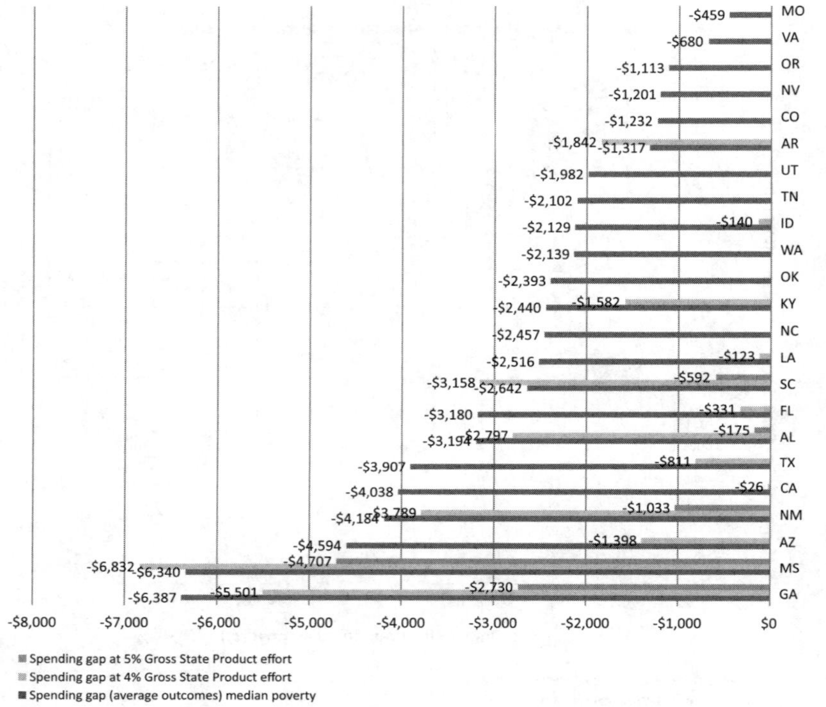

Spending gap at 5% Gross State Product effort
Spending gap at 4% Gross State Product effort
Spending gap (average outcomes) median poverty

Source: Data from Baker et al., *The Real Shame of the Nation.*

a 5 percent requirement, only five states have spending gaps in achieving national average outcomes, namely Georgia, Mississippi, New Mexico, South Carolina, and Alabama. Raising the effort requirement to this level also cuts the total remaining gaps to about $9 billion. Total federal allocations to Title I in 2015 were about $14.4 billion. Thus, with a high imposed state and local effort requirement, it would be plausible to close the funding gap to average outcomes across states. Of course, because we are operating with a normative adequacy goal here (existing averages), this policy would likely shift future averages upward, and with it the cost of chasing those averages.

Indeed, this proposal is somewhat of a pipe dream. States have not only chosen in recent years to put low effort toward financing their schools, but they lower that effort further year after year. In the most egregious cases, states like Arizona or Michigan have chosen to lower their state and local effort while shifting large shares of children to private schools (through tax credits in Arizona) and/or privately governed and managed charter schools. Their emphasis has largely been on the dismantling of public education systems, not reinvigorating those systems. Further, federal policy has endorsed these state efforts, allocating federal funds through competitive grant programs that encourage choice expansion rather than focus on equity and adequacy. And even equity-oriented requirements associated with Title I funding have focused on within-district budget allocations to schools (with insufficient regard for factors that affect those allocations) and given little or no attention to equity between districts under state school finance policies. Moving forward on this policy framework will require a major shift in thinking among both state and federal policy makers.

THE ROLE OF FEDERAL
AND STATE EDUCATION AGENCIES

One role of the US Department of Education should be the continued collection of data on and monitoring of the equity and adequacy of state school finance systems. While much of the data collection has already been in place for decades, this work should be continued by the Department of Education and made publicly available in a timely manner.[13] This data should include an annual reestimation of national wage adjustment indices and adjustments to income thresholds for poverty measures, as well as a compilation of common outcome measures like those provided in the Stanford Education Data Archive.

Equally important, the Department of Education should conduct ongoing analyses of the equity and adequacy of state schools, using appropriate, widely accepted measures, including the model used for evaluating progressiveness of state school finance systems in "Is School Funding Fair?"[14] The federal agency should also provide annual reporting on the condition—specifically, the equity and adequacy—of state school finance systems to provide guidance to states on improving those systems and to inform the allocation of federal aid. In addition, it should be tasked with producing annual reports on estimates of the costs of achieving specific national outcome targets and also with providing periodic (five-year) reviews of state school finance programs to determine, for example, the extent to which states are allocating aid in ways that perpetuate regressive school funding systems or other inequities and irregularities.

Finally, the US Department of Education should play a more significant role in reinvigorating high-quality research to advance understanding of the productivity and efficiency of schools, school systems, and potential interventions. These efforts should be accompanied by sufficient resources to develop and test interventions across varied contexts in collaboration with state education agencies.

GOVERNING AND MANAGING MIXED PROVIDER SYSTEMS

Mixed-delivery systems are an entrenched part of our American model of schooling. Public schooling systems serve only about 88 percent of children nationwide, inclusive of charter schooling. This share has been constant for decades. States have increased tax credit subsidies in an effort to shift more students to private and home schooling, and many states have increased substantially the share of children attending charter schools. It is difficult to achieve equitable education systems when student sorting based on individual choices drives substantial demographic sorting across schools, when funding systems are insufficiently sensitive to resultant student sorting patterns, and when private operators of quasi-public charter schools have widely varied access to private, often unaccounted-for and poorly measured, resources. Fixing disparities we can neither control nor measure accurately is an untenable task.

Therefore, federal policy makers must be willing to provide guidance on and state policy makers must be willing to act on the following:

- managing student sorting across schools to mitigate the extent to which individual choices, based on limited available options, lead to further resegregation of schools by race, ethnicity, and student needs;
- developing and managing school-based funding models that sufficiently address differences in needs across schools and settings, while appropriately addressing the role of privately managed charter operators within district geographic contexts to ensure maintenance of equity and efficiency;
- optimizing transportation systems and the delivery and organization of centralized services to schools;
- optimizing the use and financing of public space;
- maintaining public stewardship of public resources; and
- preserving student, employee, and taxpayer rights.

On the issue of student sorting and resource targeting, I remain skeptical that equity can be sufficiently managed even with tight controls over student sorting and resource allocation. Liberty of choice itself is not a substitute for equity. And whatever efficiency benefits might arise from competitive pressure, those benefits might easily be offset by costs associated with inefficient transportation systems, including lost time for travel, increased congestion and reduced air quality, and inefficient financing of capital, such as use of public dollars to access high-interest revenue bonds to acquire land and buildings for private operators.

State and federal policy makers must be proactive in equally protecting the rights of all children and school employees, where those rights are not presently clear under hybrid delivery systems across states and where those most likely to face deprivation of rights are the most vulnerable low-income and minority children.[15] Students' constitutional rights to free speech and due process, for example, are protected from interference by government (both branches and agents), including public district-operated schools. But increased reliance on private providers means increased numbers of children may not have these protections. Children in low-income, predominantly minority neighborhoods are more likely than children in predominantly White suburbs to have their district schools replaced with private charter operators, and thus their rights compromised.

CONSIDERATIONS FOR THE FUTURE

Strengthening our national education system requires both immediate and ongoing attention. The framework and targets provided here should not be static; as such, these data and modeled targets (from 2009 to 2015) should be updated. But perhaps even more important than merely applying data updates for the maintenance of an equitable and adequate system is thinking forward toward broader and bolder outcomes that take us beyond our current (or historical) averages, which many education "reformers" and critics have argued are woefully insufficient, if not disgraceful. While I differ with this characterization—for many schools, districts, and states are already performing quite well and can provide guidance on setting a higher national bar for the future—it is certainly reasonable to decry the state of schooling and student outcomes in many US states.

The next frontier in expanding equity and adequacy of educational opportunities in the United States will likely include postsecondary education, beginning with the provision of more equitable and adequate public two-year, community college systems. Tammy Kolbe and I found that just as with elementary and secondary education systems, state community college systems are often regressively funded. That is, community colleges in counties with the most advantaged student populations tend to have the most resources, and vice versa. Clearly, equalizing elementary and secondary educational opportunities is prerequisite to equalizing longer-term outcomes, but it's insufficient when our public higher education systems remain inequitable and inadequate.

LESSONS LEARNED AND LOOKING FORWARD

Significant progress toward improving the equity of public education systems occurred from the 1970s through the 1980s, a period during which significant progress was also made in the reduction of racial achievement gaps.[16] Emphasis in policy making and in judicial review of state school finance systems shifted toward the provision of adequate funding to achieve desired outcome goals in the 1990s through the mid-2000s, with many states experiencing substantial infusions of funding during this period, leading to increased staffing and smaller classes. But as economic inequality grew, progress on closing achievement gaps stagnated. Further, the competitiveness of teacher wages stagnated, despite increased funding, as compensation in other professions grew more rapidly.

Though much progress was made from the 1970s through the mid-2000s, that progress came to a grinding halt with the economic collapse of 2007 and years of recession that followed. Resources declined and inequities re-emerged. More disconcertingly, a reinvigorated bipartisan rhetoric emerged that schools should be required to do more with less and that the days of flush budgets, elaborate spending, and gold-plated pensions for teachers were over. This rhetoric continued to strengthen even as the economy began to rebound, with three major persisting consequences:

- a continued disregard for the importance of equitable and adequate funding as a prerequisite condition for quality public (or any) education systems;
- a heightened emphasis in public policy on empirically weak, politically motivated "research" advancing preferred policies of choice, market competition, and disruptive innovation as substitutes for additional resources (purported solutions for equity, adequacy,

productivity, and efficiency of our public schools but without regard for conceptions or definitions of these terms or the vast body of rigorous empirical literature on these topics); and

- a continued full-speed-ahead approach to the preferred policies without regard for or careful measurement of the consequences of those policies.

At the outset of this book, I emphasized that there exist relevant, well-established frameworks, definitions, and empirical methods that must be considered when evaluating whether policy changes will lead to improved equity, adequacy, productivity, and efficiency. We must continue to apply these frameworks as we move forward out of this dark period for US public schools.

Further, rigorous analyses have been applied to the copious data on public school finance that have accumulated over the decades, validating the importance of equitable and adequate funding for improving both short-term student academic outcomes and longer-term life outcomes. This research has also shown us that traditional investments in public schooling still matter and that schooling remains a human resource–intensive industry. And that's not a bad thing. Human resources—more teachers, more qualified teachers, and smaller classes—matter. And more competitive compensation can lead to a stronger teacher workforce.

Past decades have provided useful experience and guidance on the role of academic research and applied policy analysis for informing the design and implementation of state school finance systems. Specifically, the empirical era of the mid-1990s through mid-2000s provided guidance on methods for estimating the costs associated with achieving desired outcome goals, whether under court order to meet state constitutional obligations or by proactive legislation to align state school finance formulas with state standards and accountability systems. The move toward common standards across states and the availability of new data for comparing outcomes across states provide opportunities to measure inequality across the states and to take initial steps toward mitigating it and thereby improving the overall adequacy of our public schools.

APPENDIX

COST ESTIMATES BY POVERTY QUINTILE FOR ALL STATES

State	Poverty quintile	Cost index mean	Cost of national average outcomes	Current spending per pupil	Gap between current outcomes & national mean (SD)	Gap between current spending & cost of average outcomes	Current spending adjusted for cost of average outcomes
Alabama	1 Lowest	0.69	$7,991	$8,767	0.010	$776	$13,072
Alabama	2 Low	0.90	$10,649	$8,888	−0.020	−$1,762	$10,005
Alabama	3 Middle	1.04	$12,102	$8,907	−0.037	−$3,194	$8,673
Alabama	4 High	1.29	$15,220	$8,926	−0.047	−$6,294	$7,081
Alabama	5 Highest	1.95	$22,898	$9,573	−0.074	−$13,325	$5,198
Alaska	1 Lowest	0.74	$8,338	$16,685	0.004	$8,347	$22,544
Alaska	2 Low	0.87	$10,192	$17,388	0.008	$7,196	$20,101
Alaska	3 Middle	1.51	$17,900	$29,714	−0.069	$11,814	$20,357
Alaska	4 High	1.90	$22,293	$30,799	−0.139	$8,506	$16,316
Alaska	5 Highest	2.63	$30,384	$29,229	−0.149	−$1,552	$11,419
Arizona	1 Lowest	0.67	$7,810	$6,712	0.044	−$1,098	$10,296
Arizona	2 Low	0.88	$10,200	$6,885	−0.004	−$3,315	$7,886
Arizona	3 Middle	1.07	$12,282	$7,688	−0.019	−$4,594	$7,281
Arizona	4 High	1.37	$16,132	$7,728	−0.041	−$8,404	$5,807
Arizona	5 Highest	2.36	$27,371	$7,756	−0.072	−$19,798	$3,611
Arkansas	1 Lowest	0.68	$7,940	$8,900	0.022	$960	$13,291
Arkansas	2 Low	0.83	$9,741	$9,354	−0.005	−$387	$11,461
Arkansas	3 Middle	0.94	$10,794	$9,477	−0.013	−$1,317	$10,258
Arkansas	4 High	1.05	$12,396	$9,879	−0.018	−$2,518	$9,450
Arkansas	5 Highest	1.34	$15,751	$9,737	−0.029	−$6,014	$7,630
California	1 Lowest	0.72	$8,387	$8,833	0.025	$447	$12,855
California	2 Low	0.97	$11,159	$8,899	−0.024	−$2,260	$9,561
California	3 Middle	1.14	$13,122	$9,084	−0.048	−$4,038	$8,280
California	4 High	1.65	$19,459	$10,150	−0.087	−$9,309	$6,251
California	5 Highest	2.21	$24,548	$9,918	−0.092	−$14,815	$4,663
Colorado	1 Lowest	0.60	$7,017	$8,628	0.028	$1,611	$14,620
Colorado	2 Low	0.72	$8,169	$8,702	0.009	$533	$12,217
Colorado	3 Middle	0.84	$9,782	$8,550	−0.010	−$1,232	$10,329

State	Poverty quintile	Cost index mean	Cost of national average outcomes	Current spending per pupil	Gap between current outcomes & national mean (SD)	Gap between current spending & cost of average outcomes	Current spending adjusted for cost of average outcomes
Colorado	4 High	1.16	$13,605	$9,582	−0.068	−$4,023	$8,351
Colorado	5 Highest	1.42	$16,200	$9,373	−0.035	−$6,827	$6,688
Connecticut	1 Lowest	0.53	$6,089	$17,504	0.104	$11,416	$34,129
Connecticut	2 Low	0.58	$6,783	$17,858	0.085	$11,076	$31,607
Connecticut	3 Middle	0.59	$6,721	$17,147	0.073	$10,426	$29,607
Connecticut	4 High	0.70	$8,033	$17,822	0.037	$9,789	$26,311
Connecticut	5 Highest	1.64	$18,916	$17,009	−0.037	−$1,907	$12,683
Delaware	1 Lowest	0.65	$7,573	$13,035	0.037	$5,463	$20,228
Delaware	2 Low	0.82	$9,782	$13,565	0.022	$3,783	$16,886
Delaware	3 Middle	0.96	$11,224	$14,657	−0.003	$3,433	$15,407
Delaware	4 High	1.00	$11,906	$14,907	0.001	$3,002	$15,047
Delaware	5 Highest	0.95	$11,141	$13,476	−0.001	$2,336	$14,295
District of Columbia	5 Highest	3.02	$35,340	$18,622	−0.058	−$16,718	$6,184
Florida	1 Lowest	0.82	$9,449	$8,632	0.016	−$817	$10,740
Florida	2 Low	0.90	$10,604	$8,806	0.002	−$1,799	$9,800
Florida	3 Middle	1.02	$11,856	$8,676	−0.004	−$3,180	$8,588
Florida	4 High	1.10	$13,100	$8,906	−0.011	−$4,194	$8,181
Florida	5 Highest	1.16	$13,585	$9,096	−0.023	−$4,489	$8,131
Georgia	1 Lowest	0.82	$9,626	$8,895	0.032	−$732	$11,034
Georgia	2 Low	1.16	$13,745	$9,174	−0.011	−$4,571	$8,326
Georgia	3 Middle	1.33	$15,478	$9,091	−0.025	−$6,387	$7,098
Georgia	4 High	1.66	$19,421	$9,742	−0.042	−$9,679	$6,101
Georgia	5 Highest	1.89	$21,832	$9,771	−0.049	−$12,086	$5,408
Idaho	1 Lowest	0.58	$6,719	$6,922	0.028	$203	$12,110
Idaho	2 Low	0.66	$7,491	$7,008	0.019	−$483	$10,722
Idaho	3 Middle	0.74	$8,519	$6,390	0.006	−$2,129	$8,658
Idaho	4 High	0.84	$9,892	$6,942	−0.002	−$2,950	$8,338
Idaho	5 Highest	1.03	$11,565	$6,655	−0.015	−$4,910	$6,493
Illinois	1 Lowest	0.53	$6,240	$12,053	0.073	$5,813	$23,196
Illinois	2 Low	0.66	$7,729	$12,094	0.043	$4,365	$18,781
Illinois	3 Middle	0.81	$9,496	$11,801	0.008	$2,305	$14,757
Illinois	4 High	0.92	$10,717	$11,073	−0.014	$356	$12,302
Illinois	5 Highest	1.74	$20,009	$12,228	−0.038	−$7,820	$7,560
Indiana	1 Lowest	0.51	$6,030	$8,437	0.074	$2,408	$16,612

State	Poverty quintile	Cost index mean	Cost of national average outcomes	Current spending per pupil	Gap between current outcomes & national mean (SD)	Gap between current spending & cost of average outcomes	Current spending adjusted for cost of average outcomes
Indiana	2 Low	0.63	$7,367	$8,744	0.049	$1,377	$13,983
Indiana	3 Middle	0.72	$8,340	$9,423	0.034	$1,083	$13,195
Indiana	4 High	0.84	$9,813	$9,587	0.026	−$226	$11,609
Indiana	5 Highest	1.38	$16,156	$10,587	−0.002	−$5,569	$8,622
Iowa	1 Lowest	0.54	$6,326	$9,667	0.059	$3,341	$18,183
Iowa	2 Low	0.61	$7,153	$9,986	0.045	$2,833	$16,780
Iowa	3 Middle	0.68	$7,910	$10,128	0.029	$2,218	$15,277
Iowa	4 High	0.73	$8,502	$10,180	0.014	$1,678	$14,361
Iowa	5 Highest	0.90	$10,501	$10,259	−0.014	−$242	$11,684
Kansas	1 Lowest	0.50	$5,796	$9,126	0.063	$3,330	$18,490
Kansas	2 Low	0.63	$7,233	$10,003	0.034	$2,769	$16,110
Kansas	3 Middle	0.66	$7,619	$9,924	0.031	$2,305	$15,241
Kansas	4 High	0.73	$8,521	$10,234	−0.001	$1,713	$14,151
Kansas	5 Highest	1.02	$11,646	$10,560	−0.034	−$1,086	$11,172
Kentucky	1 Lowest	0.76	$8,625	$9,528	0.020	$903	$12,722
Kentucky	2 Low	0.89	$10,594	$10,013	0.011	−$582	$11,335
Kentucky	3 Middle	0.99	$11,468	$9,028	0.015	−$2,440	$9,395
Kentucky	4 High	1.13	$13,190	$9,306	0.008	−$3,884	$8,494
Kentucky	5 Highest	1.45	$17,006	$9,810	−0.004	−$7,196	$7,205
Louisiana	1 Lowest	0.81	$9,390	$10,642	0.002	$1,252	$13,257
Louisiana	2 Low	1.04	$12,392	$10,518	−0.025	−$1,873	$10,160
Louisiana	3 Middle	1.15	$13,311	$10,795	−0.034	−$2,516	$9,430
Louisiana	4 High	1.29	$15,173	$10,659	−0.047	−$4,513	$8,421
Louisiana	5 Highest	1.64	$19,115	$11,351	−0.057	−$7,764	$7,182
Maine	1 Lowest	0.55	$6,353	$12,746	0.040	$6,393	$23,928
Maine	2 Low	0.68	$7,891	$12,560	0.009	$4,669	$18,821
Maine	3 Middle	0.78	$9,186	$12,259	−0.002	$3,073	$15,898
Maine	4 High	0.89	$10,497	$12,970	−0.021	$2,472	$14,731
Maine	5 Highest	1.10	$12,826	$12,255	−0.010	−$571	$11,317
Maryland	1 Lowest	0.70	$8,228	$13,671	0.067	$5,444	$20,135
Maryland	2 Low	0.83	$9,775	$13,932	0.061	$4,157	$17,066
Maryland	3 Middle	1.03	$12,049	$13,525	0.008	$1,476	$13,818
Maryland	4 High	0.81	$9,563	$13,620	0.023	$4,057	$16,917
Maryland	5 Highest	1.87	$21,919	$14,853	−0.065	−$7,066	$8,889
Massachusetts	1 Lowest	0.52	$6,145	$14,454	0.124	$8,310	$28,662

State	Poverty quintile	Cost index mean	Cost of national average outcomes	Current spending per pupil	Gap between current outcomes & national mean (SD)	Gap between current spending & cost of average outcomes	Current spending adjusted for cost of average outcomes
Massachusetts	2 Low	0.57	$6,593	$13,811	0.101	$7,218	$25,022
Massachusetts	3 Middle	0.64	$7,534	$13,914	0.071	$6,381	$22,506
Massachusetts	4 High	0.77	$8,944	$15,212	0.052	$6,268	$20,202
Massachusetts	5 Highest	1.66	$19,319	$15,833	0.003	−$3,507	$11,130
Michigan	1 Lowest	0.50	$5,803	$9,870	0.053	$4,066	$20,205
Michigan	2 Low	0.61	$7,153	$9,323	0.014	$2,170	$15,410
Michigan	3 Middle	0.73	$8,567	$9,516	−0.007	$948	$13,088
Michigan	4 High	0.89	$10,366	$9,621	−0.026	−$745	$11,021
Michigan	5 Highest	1.71	$19,644	$11,275	−0.071	−$8,733	$7,691
Minnesota	1 Lowest	0.54	$6,303	$9,937	0.077	$3,634	$18,681
Minnesota	2 Low	0.64	$7,418	$10,327	0.049	$2,909	$16,391
Minnesota	3 Middle	0.70	$8,227	$10,772	0.042	$2,545	$15,505
Minnesota	4 High	0.77	$9,021	$10,706	0.025	$1,685	$13,962
Minnesota	5 Highest	1.20	$13,987	$12,754	−0.012	−$1,233	$11,132
Mississippi	1 Lowest	0.76	$8,877	$7,711	0.004	−$1,166	$10,365
Mississippi	2 Low	1.03	$12,152	$8,358	−0.020	−$3,793	$8,169
Mississippi	3 Middle	1.26	$14,635	$8,295	−0.043	−$6,340	$6,623
Mississippi	4 High	1.66	$19,487	$8,546	−0.066	−$10,941	$5,258
Mississippi	5 Highest	2.28	$26,035	$9,043	−0.085	−$17,010	$4,098
Missouri	1 Lowest	0.56	$6,590	$9,777	0.040	$3,187	$17,943
Missouri	2 Low	0.70	$8,174	$9,312	0.008	$1,138	$13,624
Missouri	3 Middle	0.80	$9,420	$8,961	−0.006	−$459	$11,385
Missouri	4 High	0.90	$10,441	$8,932	−0.007	−$1,509	$10,172
Missouri	5 Highest	1.46	$16,982	$9,739	−0.038	−$7,243	$7,206
Montana	1 Lowest	0.63	$6,860	$9,272	0.048	$2,413	$15,140
Montana	2 Low	0.61	$6,625	$9,183	0.040	$2,558	$15,318
Montana	3 Middle	0.71	$7,711	$9,034	0.028	$1,324	$12,813
Montana	4 High	0.81	$8,778	$9,365	0.034	$587	$11,769
Montana	5 Highest	1.35	$14,665	$12,563	−0.076	−$2,103	$9,583
Nebraska	1 Lowest	0.50	$5,947	$10,307	0.057	$4,360	$20,523
Nebraska	2 Low	0.61	$7,068	$11,600	0.030	$4,532	$19,249
Nebraska	3 Middle	0.66	$7,593	$11,077	0.033	$3,484	$16,847
Nebraska	4 High	0.69	$8,146	$11,130	0.027	$2,984	$16,257
Nebraska	5 Highest	0.89	$10,462	$11,848	−0.028	$1,386	$13,590
Nevada	1 Lowest	0.78	$8,464	$10,186	−0.029	$1,721	$12,919

State	Poverty quintile	Cost index mean	Cost of national average outcomes	Current spending per pupil	Gap between current outcomes & national mean (SD)	Gap between current spending & cost of average outcomes	Current spending adjusted for cost of average outcomes
Nevada	2 Low	0.79	$8,599	$9,691	0.003	$1,092	$12,329
Nevada	3 Middle	0.90	$9,808	$8,608	0.007	−$1,201	$9,536
Nevada	4 High	0.92	$10,064	$10,084	−0.002	$20	$10,999
Nevada	5 Highest	1.31	$14,287	$8,085	−0.013	−$6,202	$6,159
New Hampshire	1 Lowest	0.49	$5,685	$13,954	0.080	$8,268	$31,804
New Hampshire	2 Low	0.55	$6,446	$13,702	0.057	$7,256	$26,356
New Hampshire	3 Middle	0.64	$7,425	$14,093	0.048	$6,668	$22,763
New Hampshire	4 High	0.72	$8,483	$15,308	0.043	$6,824	$21,639
New Hampshire	5 Highest	0.92	$10,654	$14,691	0.011	$4,036	$16,516
New Jersey	1 Lowest	0.51	$5,818	$16,238	0.116	$10,419	$32,393
New Jersey	2 Low	0.60	$6,938	$16,412	0.092	$9,474	$28,310
New Jersey	3 Middle	0.71	$8,158	$16,048	0.067	$7,890	$23,297
New Jersey	4 High	0.96	$11,069	$16,018	0.029	$4,949	$17,232
New Jersey	5 Highest	2.50	$28,065	$18,838	−0.025	−$9,834	$8,791
New Mexico	1 Lowest	0.87	$10,099	$8,882	−0.026	−$1,217	$10,553
New Mexico	2 Low	1.02	$11,880	$8,851	−0.036	−$3,029	$8,776
New Mexico	3 Middle	1.16	$13,374	$9,190	−0.039	−$4,184	$7,985
New Mexico	4 High	1.36	$15,903	$9,953	−0.044	−$5,950	$7,414
New Mexico	5 Highest	1.90	$22,130	$10,430	−0.061	−$11,701	$5,685
New York	1 Lowest	0.55	$6,171	$21,464	0.053	$15,292	$39,637
New York	2 Low	0.61	$6,932	$19,379	0.017	$12,447	$31,941
New York	3 Middle	0.79	$8,986	$18,988	−0.021	$10,002	$24,662
New York	4 High	1.02	$11,677	$19,161	−0.050	$7,483	$19,627
New York	5 Highest	2.06	$23,548	$20,248	−0.044	−$3,300	$10,311
North Carolina	1 Lowest	0.74	$8,659	$8,232	0.042	−$427	$11,300
North Carolina	2 Low	0.87	$10,126	$8,581	0.012	−$1,545	$10,004
North Carolina	3 Middle	0.95	$11,011	$8,554	0.007	−$2,457	$9,160
North Carolina	4 High	1.04	$12,139	$8,926	−0.008	−$3,213	$8,737
North Carolina	5 Highest	1.36	$16,011	$9,074	−0.027	−$6,936	$6,869
North Dakota	1 Lowest	0.64	$7,640	$11,125	0.039	$3,485	$17,407
North Dakota	2 Low	0.66	$7,769	$11,219	0.055	$3,450	$17,235
North Dakota	3 Middle	0.72	$8,251	$11,294	0.033	$3,043	$15,894
North Dakota	4 High	0.85	$9,766	$12,413	0.022	$2,648	$15,349
North Dakota	5 Highest	1.51	$17,625	$13,659	−0.031	−$3,966	$10,351
Ohio	1 Lowest	0.51	$5,937	$10,335	0.080	$4,398	$20,680

State	Poverty quintile	Cost index mean	Cost of national average outcomes	Current spending per pupil	Gap between current outcomes & national mean (SD)	Gap between current spending & cost of average outcomes	Current spending adjusted for cost of average outcomes
Ohio	2 Low	0.62	$7,191	$9,578	0.049	$2,388	$15,758
Ohio	3 Middle	0.69	$8,095	$9,640	0.034	$1,545	$14,039
Ohio	4 High	0.83	$9,640	$9,798	0.018	$158	$12,035
Ohio	5 Highest	1.52	$17,798	$11,374	−0.039	−$6,424	$8,053
Oklahoma	1 Lowest	0.59	$6,936	$7,228	0.026	$299	$12,357
Oklahoma	2 Low	0.75	$8,810	$7,789	0.003	−$1,020	$10,478
Oklahoma	3 Middle	0.87	$10,201	$7,809	−0.008	−$2,393	$9,003
Oklahoma	4 High	1.03	$12,087	$8,175	−0.027	−$3,913	$8,014
Oklahoma	5 Highest	1.30	$15,130	$8,476	−0.056	−$6,654	$6,624
Oregon	1 Lowest	0.64	$7,485	$8,897	0.013	$1,412	$13,905
Oregon	2 Low	0.77	$9,062	$9,535	−0.012	$472	$12,376
Oregon	3 Middle	0.88	$10,448	$9,334	−0.035	−$1,113	$10,598
Oregon	4 High	1.03	$11,868	$9,238	−0.029	−$2,631	$9,045
Oregon	5 Highest	1.39	$16,061	$9,916	−0.056	−$6,145	$7,371
Pennsylvania	1 Lowest	0.52	$6,140	$13,617	0.087	$7,476	$26,162
Pennsylvania	2 Low	0.61	$7,123	$12,430	0.052	$5,307	$20,681
Pennsylvania	3 Middle	0.72	$8,355	$12,522	0.033	$4,167	$17,664
Pennsylvania	4 High	0.83	$9,789	$12,689	0.018	$2,901	$15,536
Pennsylvania	5 Highest	1.73	$20,304	$12,226	−0.039	−$8,085	$8,718
Rhode Island	1 Lowest	0.51	$5,825	$14,450	0.078	$8,626	$29,478
Rhode Island	2 Low	0.60	$7,079	$14,900	0.049	$7,821	$24,770
Rhode Island	3 Middle	0.69	$8,039	$15,211	0.033	$7,172	$22,602
Rhode Island	4 High	0.82	$9,576	$14,292	0.008	$4,716	$17,679
Rhode Island	5 Highest	1.83	$21,374	$14,298	−0.067	−$7,076	$9,583
South Carolina	1 Lowest	0.77	$9,070	$9,200	0.012	$130	$12,239
South Carolina	2 Low	0.99	$11,559	$9,589	−0.008	−$1,971	$9,809
South Carolina	3 Middle	1.08	$12,622	$9,980	−0.018	−$2,642	$9,294
South Carolina	4 High	1.28	$14,946	$10,060	−0.042	−$4,886	$7,923
South Carolina	5 Highest	1.54	$17,742	$10,177	−0.066	−$7,565	$6,697
South Dakota	1 Lowest	0.56	$6,475	$7,921	0.028	$1,446	$14,331
South Dakota	2 Low	0.61	$7,041	$8,062	0.027	$1,021	$13,461
South Dakota	3 Middle	0.65	$7,497	$8,165	0.020	$668	$12,594
South Dakota	4 High	0.76	$8,738	$8,590	−0.002	−$147	$11,344
South Dakota	5 Highest	1.41	$16,282	$11,163	−0.065	−$5,120	$8,810
Tennessee	1 Lowest	0.70	$8,216	$8,168	0.024	−$48	$11,980

State	Poverty quintile	Cost index mean	Cost of national average outcomes	Current spending per pupil	Gap between current outcomes & national mean (SD)	Gap between current spending & cost of average outcomes	Current spending adjusted for cost of average outcomes
Tennessee	2 Low	0.79	$9,271	$8,317	0.005	−$954	$10,709
Tennessee	3 Middle	0.92	$10,986	$8,884	−0.007	−$2,102	$9,766
Tennessee	4 High	1.00	$11,674	$8,734	−0.021	−$2,940	$8,868
Tennessee	5 Highest	1.01	$11,673	$8,096	−0.016	−$3,577	$8,190
Texas	1 Lowest	0.72	$8,400	$8,052	0.024	−$348	$11,496
Texas	2 Low	0.87	$10,153	$8,343	−0.013	−$1,810	$9,842
Texas	3 Middle	1.07	$12,437	$8,530	−0.033	−$3,907	$8,205
Texas	4 High	1.22	$14,362	$8,747	−0.040	−$5,615	$7,465
Texas	5 Highest	1.85	$21,578	$8,896	−0.058	−$12,682	$5,216
Utah	1 Lowest	0.56	$6,508	$6,027	0.032	−$482	$10,892
Utah	2 Low	0.63	$7,516	$6,135	0.022	−$1,381	$9,763
Utah	3 Middle	0.74	$8,870	$6,888	−0.019	−$1,982	$9,365
Utah	4 High	0.81	$9,408	$6,893	−0.002	−$2,516	$8,533
Utah	5 Highest	0.99	$11,533	$7,780	0.000	−$3,753	$7,914
Vermont	1 Lowest	0.53	$6,125	$13,983	0.082	$7,859	$30,127
Vermont	2 Low	0.66	$7,551	$14,838	0.057	$7,288	$26,947
Vermont	3 Middle	0.82	$9,263	$15,474	0.038	$6,210	$21,743
Vermont	4 High	0.95	$10,947	$15,807	0.027	$4,859	$18,399
Vermont	5 Highest	1.29	$14,936	$15,798	−0.011	$862	$14,750
Virginia	1 Lowest	0.76	$8,867	$11,495	0.024	$2,629	$15,455
Virginia	2 Low	0.78	$9,267	$10,395	0.005	$1,129	$13,694
Virginia	3 Middle	0.96	$11,201	$10,520	−0.010	−$680	$11,198
Virginia	4 High	1.06	$12,637	$10,245	−0.016	−$2,392	$9,847
Virginia	5 Highest	1.50	$17,384	$10,762	−0.040	−$6,623	$7,665
Washington	1 Lowest	0.67	$7,278	$9,125	0.069	$1,848	$13,814
Washington	2 Low	0.90	$9,774	$9,650	0.041	−$124	$10,835
Washington	3 Middle	1.06	$11,534	$9,395	0.016	−$2,139	$9,118
Washington	4 High	1.23	$13,345	$9,781	0.002	−$3,563	$8,166
Washington	5 Highest	1.91	$19,808	$10,257	−0.031	−$10,516	$5,765
West Virginia	1 Lowest	0.77	$8,844	$11,034	0.000	$2,190	$14,575
West Virginia	2 Low	0.85	$9,862	$11,266	−0.016	$1,404	$13,371
West Virginia	3 Middle	0.90	$10,675	$10,970	−0.023	$296	$12,294
West Virginia	4 High	0.97	$11,340	$11,250	−0.033	−$90	$11,677
West Virginia	5 Highest	1.19	$13,815	$11,162	−0.038	−$2,653	$9,591
Wisconsin	1 Lowest	0.53	$6,172	$10,437	0.070	$4,265	$20,086

State	Poverty quintile	Cost index mean	Cost of national average outcomes	Current spending per pupil	Gap between current outcomes & national mean (SD)	Gap between current spending & cost of average outcomes	Current spending adjusted for cost of average outcomes
Wisconsin	2 Low	0.62	$7,217	$10,704	0.044	$3,487	$17,367
Wisconsin	3 Middle	0.72	$8,441	$10,978	0.030	$2,537	$15,334
Wisconsin	4 High	0.86	$9,903	$11,363	0.018	$1,460	$13,313
Wisconsin	5 Highest	1.44	$16,908	$12,012	−0.032	−$4,896	$9,441
Wyoming	1 Lowest	0.68	$7,734	$15,950	0.008	$8,216	$23,573
Wyoming	2 Low	0.73	$8,546	$16,452	0.037	$7,906	$22,772
Wyoming	3 Middle	0.78	$9,232	$15,264	0.031	$6,032	$19,549
Wyoming	4 High	0.81	$9,374	$15,643	0.023	$6,268	$19,555
Wyoming	5 Highest	1.04	$12,235	$17,122	0.030	$4,887	$16,936

Source: Bruce D. Baker, Bob Kim, Mark Weber, Ajay Srikanth, and Michael Atzbi, *The Real Shame of the Nation: The Causes and Consequences of Interstate Inequity in Public School Investments* (Newark, NJ: Education Law Center; New Brunswick, NJ: Rutgers Graduate School of Education, 2018).

NOTES

CHAPTER 1

1. This project was undertaken in collaboration with Rutgers Graduate School of Education and with support from the William T. Grant Foundation.
2. Bill Gates, "How Teacher Development Could Revolutionize Our Schools," *Washington Post,* February 28, 2011, http://www.washingtonpost.com/wp-dyn/content /article/2011/02/27/AR2011022702876.html.
3. Bill Gates, "Flip the Curve: Student Achievemeent vs. School Budgets," *Huffington Post,* March 1, 2011, http://www.huffingtonpost.com/bill-gates/bill-gates-school -performance_b_829771.html. The graph Gates includes, which purports to show that the US has increased education spending dramatically with little improvement in test scores, was critiqued in "Bill Gates Should Hire a Statistical Advisor," *Junk Charts,* April 2011, http://junkcharts.typepad.com/junk_charts/2011/04/bill-gates -should-hire-a-statistical-advisor.html.
4. Dmitri Mehlhorn, "The United States Spends More on Schools Than Any Society in Human History," *Higher Education Revolution,* November 9, 2015, https:// higheredrevolution.com/the-united-states-spends-more-on-schools-than-any -society-in-human-history-d5988649d73e#.1jk6bfskq.
5. Benjamin Scafidi, *The School Staffing Surge: Decades of Employment Growth in America's Public Schools* (Indianapolis: Friedman Foundation for Educational Choice, 2012).
6. Paul Hill and Marguerite Roza, *Curing Baumol's Disease: In Search of Productivity Gains in K–12 Schooling* (Seattle: Center on Reinventing Public Education, 2010).
7. Lucy Dadayan and Donald J. Boyd, "State Revenue Report #107" (Rockefeller Institute of Government, Albany, NY, 2017), http://www.rockinst.org/pdf/government _finance/state_revenue_report/2017-06-13-srr_107.pdf.
8. David Brooks, "The New Normal," *New York Times,* February 28, 2011, http://www .nytimes.com/2011/03/01/opinion/01brooks.html.
9. *Framing Educational Productivity,* US Department of Education, http://www.ed.gov /oii-news/resources-framing-educational-productivity.
10. Bruce D. Baker, *Does Money Matter in Education?* (Washington, DC: Albert Shanker Institute, 2016), 1.
11. Michael Leachman, "State K–12 Funding Still Lagging in Many States" (blog post), Center on Budget and Policy Priorities, October 20, 2016, https://www.cbpp.org /blog/state-k-12-funding-still-lagging-in-many-states.

12. Bruce Baker, Mark Weber, and Ajay Srikanth, *School Funding Fairness Data System* (New Brunswick, NJ: Rutgers Graduate School of Education; Newark, NJ: Education Law Center, 2017), http://www.schoolfundingfairness.org/data-download; Bruce D. Baker, David G. Sciarra, and Danielle Farrie, "Is School Funding Fair? A National Report Card" (report, Education Law Center, Newark, NJ, 2014).

13. Sam Brownback, "Tax Cuts Needed to Grow Economy," *Wichita Eagle,* July 29, 2012, http://www.kansas.com/opinion/opn-columns-blogs/article1096336.html #storylink=cpy.

14. Michael Leachman, "Timeline: 5 Years of Kansas' Tax-Cut Disaster," Center on Budget and Policy Priorities, May 24, 2017, https://www.cbpp.org/blog/timeline-5 -years-of-kansas-tax-cut-disaster.

15. Michael Leachman. "Kansas' K–12 Funding Just One Casualty of Unaffordable Tax Cuts," Center on Budget and Policy Priorities, March 2, 2017, https://www.cbpp.org /blog/kansas-k-12-funding-just-one-casualty-of-unaffordable-tax-cuts.

16. Leachman, "Timeline."

17. Thomas Frank, *What's the Matter with Kansas? How Conservatives Won the Heart of America* (New York: Metropolitan Books, 2007).

18. Kirabo Jackson, "Could the Disappointing 2017 NAEP Scores Be Due to the Great Recession?" *Education Next,* April 10, 2018, http://educationnext.org/could-be -disappointing-2017-naep-scores-due-to-great-recession/.

19. Bruce D. Baker, "Corporate Reform or Failed Desperate Corporate Management," *School Finance 101,* July 26, 2013, https://schoolfinance101.wordpress.com/2013/07 /26/corporate-reform-or-failed-desperate-corporate-management/.

20. Richard Rothstein, "Fact-Challenged Policy" (Policy Memorandum No. 182, Economic Policy Institute, Washington, DC, 2011).

21. Martin Carnoy and Richard Rothstein, *What Do International Tests Really Show About US Student Performance?* (Washington, DC: Economic Policy Institute, 2013), 32–33.

22. Paul E. Barton and Richard J. Coley, "The Black-White Achievement Gap: When Progress Stopped" (Policy Information Report, Educational Testing Service, Princeton, NJ, 2010).

23. On these exams, American students have improved substantially, in some cases phenomenally. In general, the improvements have been greatest for African American students, and for the most disadvantaged among them. The improvements have been greatest for both Black and White fourth and eighth graders in mathematics. Improvements have been less great but still substantial for Black fourth and eighth graders in reading and for Black twelfth graders in both mathematics and reading. Improvements have been modest for Whites in twelfth-grade mathematics and at all three grade levels in reading. Rothstein, "Fact-Challenged Policy."

24. Joydeep Roy, "Review of *The School Staffing Surge: Decades of Employment Growth in America's Public Schools,*" National Education Policy Center, December 4, 2012, 3, https://nepc.colorado.edu/thinktank/review-school-staffing.

25. See ANOVA blogger Frederik DeBoer, "Study of the Week: What Actually Helps Poor Students? Human Beings!" May 16, 2017, https://fredrikdeboer.com/2017/05 /16/study-of-the-week-what-actually-helps-poor-students-human-beings/; and Jens Dietrichson, Martin Bøg, Trine Filges, and Anne-Marie Klint Jørgensen, "Academic Interventions for Elementary and Middle School Students with Low Socio-

economic Status: A Systematic Review and Meta-Analysis," *Review of Educational Research* 87, no. 2 (2017): 243–82, https://search-ebscohost-com.proxy.libraries.rutgers .edu/login.aspx?direct=true&db=eric&AN=EJ1133345&site=eds-live.

26. An example of this claim can be found at "Employer Contributions for Retirement," Center for Education Reform, University of Arkansas, April 4, 2017, http://www.uaed reform.org/downloads/2017/04/employer-contributions-for-retirement-4-4-17.pdf.

27. Teacher weekly wage in 2015 = $1,092 x 1.20 = $1,311; nonteacher college graduate weekly wage in 2015 = $1,416 x 1.10 = $1,557; adjusted share = 84% ("Employer Contributions for Retirement").

28. Sean F. Reardon, Demetra Kalogrides, Andrew Ho, Ben Shear, Kenneth Shores, and Erin Fahle, *Stanford Education Data Archive*, http://purl.stanford.edu/db586ns4974.

CHAPTER 2

1. Alexis de Tocqueville, *Democracy in America*, trans. Henry Reeve (Auckland, New Zealand): Floating Press, 1840).

2. Scott Sweetland, "Human Capital Theory: Foundations of a Field of Inquiry," *Review of Educational Research* 66, no. 3 (1996): 341–59, http://www.jstor.org.proxy .libraries.rutgers.edu/stable/1170527.

3. Charles M. Tiebout, "A Pure Theory of Local Expenditures," *Journal of Political Economy* 64, no. 5 (1956): 416–24, http://www.jstor.org.proxy.libraries.rutgers.edu /stable/1826343.

4. William A. Fischel, *The Homevoter Hypothesis* (Cambridge, MA: Harvard University Press, 2009).

5. "'Troost Wall' the Product of Kansas City's Long-Running Racial Plight," *University News,* University of Missouri at Kansas City, March 5, 2013, http://info.umkc .edu/unews/troost-wall-the-product-of-kansas-citys-long-running-racial-plight/; Whet Moser, "How Redlining Segregated Chicago, and America," *Chicago Magazine*, August 22, 2017, http://www.chicagomag.com/city-life/August-2017/How -Redlining-Segregated-Chicago-and-America/; John Yinger, *Closed Doors, Opportunities Lost: The Continuing Costs of Housing Discrimination* (New York: Russell Sage Foundation, 1995); Richard Rothstein, *The Color of Law: A Forgotten History of How Our Government Segregated America* (New York: Liveright, 2017).

6. *Brown v. Board of Education of Topeka* (1), www.oyez.org/cases/1940-1955/347us483.

7. *Brown v. Board of Education of Topeka* (2), www.oyez.org/ cases/1940-1955/349us294.

8. Ibid.; *Swann v. Charlotte-Mecklenburg Board of Education*, www.oyez.org/cases /1970/281.

9. *Milliken v. Bradley*, www.oyez.org/cases/1976/76-447.

10. *Board of Education of Oklahoma City Public Schools v. Dowell*, www.oyez.org/cases/1990 /89-1080; *Missouri v. Jenkins*, www.oyez.org/cases/1994/93-1823; *Meredith v. Jefferson County Board of Education*, www.oyez.org/cases/2006/05-915; *Parents Involved in Community Schools v. Seattle School District No. 1*, www.oyez.org/cases/2006/05-908.

11. "Fractured: The Breakdown of America's School Districts," EdBuild, June 2017, https://edbuild.org/content/fractured.

12. Preston C. Green III and Bruce D. Baker, "Urban Legends, Desegregation and School Finance: Did Kansas City Really Prove That Money Doesn't Matter?" *Michigan Journal of Race & Law* 12 (2006): 57.

13. This section draws on collaborative work with Preston Green of the University of Connecticut.

14. Robert Berne and Leanna Stiefel, "The Equity of School Finance Systems Over Time: The Value Judgments Inherent in Evaluation," *Educational Administration Quarterly* 15, no. 2 (1979): 14–34, doi:10.1177/0013161X7901500205; Robert Berne and Leanna Stiefel, *The Measurement of Equity in School Finance: Conceptual, Methodological and Empirical Dimensions* (Baltimore: Johns Hopkins University Press, 1984); Robert Berne and Leanna Stiefel, "Concepts of School Finance Equity: 1970 to the Present," in *Equity and Adequacy in Education Finance: Issues and Perspectives*, ed. Helen Ladd, Rosemary Chalk, and Janet Hansen (Washington, DC: National Research Council, 1999), 7–33.

15. Berne and Stiefel, *The Measurement of Equity in School Finance.*

16. Regarding children with disabilities, see *Endrew F. v. Douglas County School District Re-1*, 137 S. Ct. 29 (U.S. 2016). Regarding children with limited English language proficiency, see *Issa v. School District of Lancaster*, no. 16-3528 (3d Cir. Jan. 30, 2017).

17. Bruce D. Baker and Preston Green, "Conceptions of Equity and Adequacy in School Finance," in *Handbook of Research in Education Finance and Policy*, ed. Helen Ladd and Edward Fiske (New York: Routledge, 2008), 203–21; Bruce D. Baker and Preston C. Green III, "Conceptions, Measurement, and Application of Educational Adequacy and Equal Educational Opportunity," in *The Handbook of Education Policy Research*, ed. Gary Sykes, Barbara Schneider, and David Plank (New York: Routledge, 2009), 438–52.

18. William H. Clune, "The Shift from Equity to Adequacy in School Finance," *Educational Policy* 8, no. 4 (1994): 376–94.

19. William S. Koski and Rob Reich, "When Adequate Isn't: The Retreat from Equity in Educational Law and Policy and Why It Matters," *Emory Law Journal* 56 (2006): 545.

20. For example, Kansas's constitution requires that the legislature "shall make suitable provision for finance of the educational interests of the state." Those educational interests are articulated in standards adopted by the state board of education, which holds independent constitutional authority for the "general supervision of public schools." Kansas courts have repeatedly held that the legislature's obligation is to provide financing that grants all children equal opportunity to achieve those standards. See *Gannon v. State*, 368 P.3d 1024, 303 Kan. 682 (2016); *Gannon v. State*, No. 113,267 (Kan. June 28, 2016); *Montoy v. State*, 279 Kan. 817, 112 P.3d 923 (2005); and *USD NO. 229 v. State*, 256 Kan. 232, 885 P.2d 1170 (1994).

21. Avidan Y. Cover, "Is Adequacy a More Political Question Than Equality? The Effect of Standards-Based Education on Judicial Standards for Education Finance," *Cornell Journal of Law & Public Policy* 11 (2001): 403.

22. Michael A. Rebell, "Safeguarding the Right to a Sound Basic Education in Times of Fiscal Constraint," *Albany Law Review* 75 (2011): 1855.

23. Baker and Green, "Conceptions of Equity and Adequacy in School Finance"; Baker and Green, "Conceptions, Measurement, and Application."

24. Bruce D. Baker and Kevin G. Welner, "Evidence and Rigor: Scrutinizing the Rhetorical Embrace of Evidence-Based Decision Making," *Educational Researcher* 41, no. 3 (2012): 98–101; Bruce D. Baker and K. G. Welner, *Productivity Research, the US Department of Education, and High-Quality Evidence* (Boulder, CO: National

Education Policy Center, 2011), http://nepc.colorado.edu/publication/productivity -research.

25. Henry M. Levin, *Cost-Effectiveness: A Primer,* vol. 4 (Thousand Oaks, CA: Sage, 1983); Henry M. Levin and Patrick J. McEwan, *Cost-Effectiveness Analysis: Methods and Applications* (Thousand Oaks, CA: Sage, 2001); Henry M. Levin, "A Cost-Effectiveness Analysis of Teacher Selection," *Journal of Human Resources* 5 (1970): 24–33; Henry M. Levin, *Cost-Effectiveness of Four Educational Interventions* (Palo Alto: California Institute for Research on Educational Finance and Governance, Stanford University, 1984); Henry M. Levin, "Cost-Effectiveness and Educational Policy," *Educational Evaluation and Policy Analysis* 10, no. 1 (1988): 51–69; Henry M. Levin, "Waiting for Godot: Cost-Effectiveness Analysis in Education," *New Directions for Evaluation* 2001, no. 90 (2001): 55–68.

26. de Tocqueville, *Democracy in America.*

27. Henry M. Levin, *Privatizing Education: Can the School Marketplace Deliver Freedom of Choice, Efficiency, Equity, and Social Cohesion?* (New York: Routledge/Westview Press, 2001); Ann Matear, "Equity in Education in Chile: The Tensions Between Policy and Practice," *International Journal of Educational Development* 27, no. 1 (2007): 101–13, doi:10.1016/j.ijedudev.2006.06.015.

28. Eric Brunner, Jon Sonstelie, and Mark Thayer, "Capitalization and the Voucher: An Analysis of Precinct Returns from California's Proposition 174," *Journal of Urban Economics* 50, no. 3 (2001): 517–36, doi:www.sciencedirect.com/science/journal /00941190.

29. Preston C. Green III, Bruce D. Baker, and Jospeh O. Oluwole, "Having It Both Ways: How Charter Schools Try to Obtain Funding of Public Schools and the Autonomy of Private Schools," *Emory Law Journal* 63 (2013): 303; Preston C. Green III, Bruce D. Baker, and Joseph Oluwole, "The Legal Status of Charter Schools in State Statutory Law," *University of Massachusetts Law Review* 10 (2015): 240.

30. Bruce D. Baker, Ken Libby, and Kathryn Wiley, "Charter School Expansion and Within-District Equity: Confluence or Conflict?" *Education Finance and Policy* 10, no. 3 (2015): 423–65; Bruce D. Baker, "Exploring the Consequences of Charter School Expansion in US Cities" (white paper, Economic Policy Institute, Washington, DC, November 30, 2016).

31. Baker et al., "Charter School Expansion and Within-District Equity."

32. Education, or public schooling in particular, is not typically considered a "public good," as the provision of public schooling does not comply with the definition of a "pure public good," which can be equally accessed by all without reduction in benefits to any. The intent here is to shed some light on the importance of understanding the role/position of these publicly financed education systems in society and to show that there's more to these systems than the year-to-year provision of "schooling" to those who happen to be school aged in a specific community at a specific point in time.

33. Andy Smarick, *The Urban School System of the Future: Applying the Principles and Lessons of Chartering* (New York: R&L Education, 2012).

34. See Neerav Kingsland's blog *Relinquishment,* https://relinquishment.org/; Neerav Kingsland, "An Open Letter to Urban Superintendents in the United States," *Education Week: Rick Hess Straight Up,* January 23, 2012, http://blogs.edweek.org /edweek/rick_hess_straight_up/2012/01/an_open_letter_to_urban_superintendents _in_the_united_states_of_america.html. For a critique of these arguments, see

Bruce D. Baker, "The Disturbing Language and Shallow Logic of Ed Reform," *School Finance 101*, April 8, 2013, https://schoolfinance101.wordpress.com/2013/04/08/the-disturbing-language-and-shallow-logic-of-ed-reform-comments-on-relinquishment-sector-agnosticism/.

CHAPTER 3

This chapter draws on my collaborations with Matthew DiCarlo of the Shanker Institute.

1. Also widely cited in the Social Science Citation Index is Eric A. Hanushek, "Assessing the Effects of School Resources on Student Performance: An Update," *Educational Evaluation and Policy Analysis* 19, no. 2 (1997): 141–64.

2. Eric A. Hanushek, "The Economics of Schooling: Production and Efficiency in Public Schools," *Journal of Economic Literature* 24, no. 3 (1986): 1162. A few years later Hanushek paraphrased this conclusion: "Variations in school expenditures are not systematically related to variations in student performance." See Eric A. Hanushek, "The Impact of Differential Expenditures on School Performance," *Educational Researcher* 18, no. 4 (1989): 45–62.

3. In a 2014 report he provided as an expert witness for New York State, Hanushek opined that "an enormous amount of scientific analysis has focused on how spending and resources of schools relates to student outcomes. It is now commonly believed that spending on schools is not systematically related to student outcomes." He also said that "there has been substantial econometric evidence that supports this lack of relationship." See Eric A. Hanushek, "Expert Report Submitted in the Case of *Maisto v. New York*, November 13, 2004," http://www.edlawcenter.org/assets/files/pdfs/maisto/masito%20trial%20documents/State's%20Expert%20Report%20-%20Dr.%20Eric%20Hanushek.pdf. In a 2015 opinion piece he made the same claim: "Considerable prior research has failed to find a consistent relationship between school spending and student performance, making skepticism about such a relationship the conventional wisdom." See Eric Hanushek, "Does Money Matter After All?" (opinion piece), Hoover Institution, Stanford University, July 7, 2015, http://hanushek.stanford.edu/opinions/does-money-matter-after-all. But the considerable research he cited to support this claim included only his own 2003 piece (hyperlinked to "prior research" in the online piece) on the "failure of input-based schooling policies," which largely rehashes his earlier work combined with a version of the international comparison addressed earlier in this chapter. See Eric A. Hanushek, "The Failure of Input-Based Schooling Policies," *The Economic Journal* 113, no. 485 (2003), http://hanushek.stanford.edu/sites/default/files/publications/Hanushek%202003%20EJ%20113%28485%29.pdf.

4. Rob Greenwald, Larry V. Hedges, and Richard D. Laine, "The Effect of School Resources on Student Achievement," *Review of Educational Research* 66, no. 3 (1996): 361–96.

5. Bruce D. Baker, *Does Money Matter in Education?* (Washington, DC: Albert Shanker Institute, 2016).

6. See ibid.

7. Greenwald et al., "The Effect of School Resources," 384, 361.

8. Harold Wenglinsky, "How Money Matters: The Effect of School District Spending on Academic Achievement," *Sociology of Education* 70, no. 3 (1997): 221, doi:10.2307/2673210.

9. Corrine Taylor, "Does Money Matter? An Empirical Study Introducing Resource Costs and Student Needs into Educational Production Function Analysis," in *Developments in School Finance, 1997*, ed. William Fowler (Washington, DC: NCES, 1998), 83, http://nces.ed.gov/pubs98/98212.pdf#page=83; Bruce D. Baker, "Can Flexible Non-Linear Modeling Tell Us Anything New About Educational Productivity?" *Economics of Education Review* 20, no. 1 (2001): 81–92, doi:10.1016/S0272 -7757(99)00051-5; David N. Figlio, "Functional Form and the Estimated Effects of School Resources," *Economics of Education Review* 18, no. 2 (1999): 241–52, doi:10.1016/S0272-7757(98)00047-8; James Dewey, Thomas A. Husted, and Lawrence W. Kenny, "The Ineffectiveness of School Inputs: A Product of Misspecification?" *Economics of Education Review* 19, no. 1 (2000): 27–45, doi:10.1016/S0272 -7757(99)00015-1.

10. Eric Hanushek, "Report Prepared on Behalf of State of Connecticut (Defendants) in *Connecticut Coalition for Justice in Education Funding et al. v. Rell et al.*," April 28, 2014.

11. Jeannette Catsoulis, "Children Left Behind," *New York Times*, April 15, 2010, http:// www.nytimes.com/2010/04/16/movies/16cartel.html; Amy Biancolli, "*The Cartel*: Attempt to Point Out Flaws of Public Schools Fails to Make the Grade," *Chron*, April 22, 2010, http://www.chron.com/entertainment/movies/article/The-Cartel -1701547.php; Stephen Whitty, "*The Cartel* Movie Review: Documentary on Jersey Schools Fails Debate Class," *NJ.com*, October 8, 2009, http://www.nj.com /entertainment/tv/index.ssf/2009/10/the_cartel_movie_review_docume.html.

12. Bill Gates, "How Teacher Development Could Revolutionize Our Schools," *Washington Post*, February 28, 2011, http://www.washingtonpost.com/wp-dyn/content /article/2011/02/27/AR2011022702876.html.

13. The graph used by Gates can be found at http://images.huffingtonpost.com/2011-03 -01-studentspendvsachievementblog.jpg. This version is similar to the Students First version, which can be found at https://schoolfinance101.files.wordpress.com/2011/04 /students-first-version.jpg. Even more misleading versions of this graph exist. See, for example, the Cato Institute's version at https://schoolfinance101.files.wordpress .com/2011/04/inflationadjustedcostk-12achievement.jpg.

14. "Bill Gates Should Hire a Statistical Advisor," *JunkCharts*, April 2011, http:// junkcharts.typepad.com/junk_charts/2011/04/bill-gates-should-hire-a-statistical -advisor.html.

15. Hanushek, "Expert Report."

16. C. Kirabo Jackson, Rucker Johnson, and Claudia L. Persico, "Money Does Matter After All," *Education Next*, July 17, 2015, http://educationnext.org/money-matter; C. Kirabo Jackson, Claudia Persico, and Rucker Johnson, "The Effects of School Spending on Educational and Economic Outcomes: Evidence from School Finance Reforms," *Quarterly Journal of Economics* 131, no. 1 (2016): 157–218, doi:10.1093/qje /qjv036.

17. Bill Gates, "Flip the Curve: Student Achievemeent vs. School Budgets," *Huffington Post*, March 1, 2011, http://www.huffingtonpost.com/bill-gates/bill-gates-school -performance_b_829771.html. The graph Gates includes with this piece, which purports to show the US has increased education spending dramatically with little improvement in test scores, was critiqued in "Bill Gates Should Hire a Statistical Advisor."

18. Bruce D. Baker and M. Weber, "Deconstructing the Myth of American Public Schooling Inefficiency" (report, Shanker Institute, Washington, DC, 2016), http://www.shankerinstitute.org/resource/publicschoolinginefficiency.

19. Dmitri Mehlhorn, "The United States Spends More on Schools Than Any Society in Human History," *The Higher Education Revolution*, November 9, 2015, https://higheredrevolution.com/the-united-states-spends-more-on-schools-than-any-society-in-human-history-d5988649d73e.

20. Baker and Weber, "Deconstructing the Myth."

21. Robert Bifulco and William Duncombe, "Evaluating School Performance: Are We Ready for Prime Time?" in *Developments in School Finance, 1999–2000*, ed. William Fowler (Washington, DC: NCES, 2002), 9.

22. Shanghai in particular has several mitigating factors that make comparing its scores to other nations highly suspect. See Tom Loveless, "PISA's China Problem" (Brown Center Chalkboard brief, Brookings Institution, Washington, DC, 2013).

23. "The Cash Street Kids," *The Economist*, August 28, 1993, 23–24.

24. Paul Ciotti, "Money and School Performance: Lessons from the Kansas City Desegregation Experiment" (white paper, Cato Institute, Washington, DC, 1998); Douglas Coate and James VanderHoff, "Public School Spending and Student Achievement: The Case of New Jersey," *Cato* 19 (1999): 85.

25. This is referred to as the so-called post-*Dowell* era. See Wendy Parker, "The Future of School Desegregation," *Northwestern University Law Review* 94 (1999): 1157.

26. Preston C. Green III and Bruce D. Baker, "Urban Legends, Desegregation and School Finance: Did Kansas City Really Prove That Money Doesn't Matter?" *Michigan Journal of Race and Law* 12 (2006): 57–83.

27. Eric A. Hanushek, "Have New York City Children Been Saved?" *Hoover Daily Report*, March 25, 2002, http://www.hoover.org/research/have-new-york-city-children-been-saved.

28. Eric A. Hanushek and Alfred A. Lindseth, *Schoolhouses, Courthouses, and Statehouses: Solving the Funding-Achievement Puzzle in America's Public Schools* (Princeton, NJ: Princeton University Press, 2009), 52, 53. Hanushek and Lindseth reiterate the New Jersey argument and add three new jurisdictions to the cast of purported failures: the states of Wyoming, Kentucky, and Massachusetts, though they admit that reforms in Massachusetts did in fact lead to some positive outcomes but attribute that success to reform efforts other than the court-ordered finance reform.

29. Green and Baker, "Urban Legends," 63.

30. Robert Bifulco, Casey D. Cobb, and Courtney Bell, "Can Interdistrict Choice Boost Student Achievement? The Case of Connecticut's Interdistrict Magnet School Program," *Educational Evaluation and Policy Analysis* 31, no. 4 (2009): 323–45, doi:10.3102/0162373709340917.

31. Green and Baker, "Urban Legends," 61.

32. Hanushek and Lindseth, *Schoolhouses, Courthouses, and Statehouses*, 159; Coate and VanderHoff, "Public School Spending," 85.

33. Coate and VanderHoff, "Public School Spending," 85. The article's statistical tests consist of cross-sectional estimates of the relationship between funding (across richer and poorer districts) and test scores, controlling for prior test scores and the district's socioeconomic characteristics. It offers separate models for 1988–89 and 1994–95 as well as separate models, including the average per-pupil spending from

1988–89 to 1994–95, presented in relation to test scores from 1994–95. That is, for any given year, the authors test whether higher-spending schools have higher test scores, controlling for prior scores and socioeconomic conditions. Finding no such cross-sectional relationships in any of their models, the authors "find no evidence of a positive effect of expenditures on student performance in New Jersey public high schools in urban school districts with smaller per capita tax bases" (98). Yet, the authors never test whether changes in the level or distribution of outcomes were associated with either of two other possible changes—in the distribution or the level of financial resources among some or all districts. Interestingly, this high-profile study was only published by *Cato*; it was not subsequently published in a peer-reviewed journal.

34. Bruce D. Baker, "Rebuttal Testimony in the Case of *Gannon v. Kansas*, March 9, 2012," http://www.robblaw.com/PDFs/989914GANNONvKSBakerRebuttalMarch 2012.pdf.

35. Hanushek, "Expert Report."

36. With no additional supporting evidence, Hanushek rehashed this claim in 2014 in his testimony in *Connecticut Coalition for Justice in Education Funding et al. v. Rell et al.*: "More than any other state, courts in New Jersey have had a dominant role in the determination of spending on schools. Up through today, with more than twenty N.J. Supreme Court rulings, a number of the largest and most impoverished school districts have been permitted to spend almost anything they requested, including expanded preschool and a variety of other specialized programs. It has, unfortunately, not showed up in student outcomes." And again in 2014 in his "Expert Report" for *Maisto v. New York*, he repeated the above, adding, "New Jersey is a useful comparison. It is geographically and demographically close to New York State. It has instituted very large spending increases because of court orders. And it has little to show for the added spending in terms of achievement of students."

37. As explained in Ludger Woessmann, Eric A. Hanushek, and Paul E. Peterson, "Is the US Catching Up? International and State Trends in Student Achievement" (white paper, Harvard University Program on Education Policy and Governance, Cambridge, MA, 2012), http://www.hks.harvard.edu/pepg/PDF/Papers/PEPG12 -03_CatchingUp.pdf: "We also examine changes in student performance in 41 states within the United States between 1992 and 2011, allowing us to compare these states with each other. Our findings come from assessments of performance in math, science, and reading of representative samples in particular political jurisdictions of students who at the time of testing were in 4th or 8th grade or were roughly ages 9–10 or 14–15."

38. Hanushek, "Expert Report."

39. Bruce D. Baker, "The Efficiency Smokescreen, Cuts Cause No Harm Argument and the 3 Kansas Judges Who Saw Right Through It," *School Finance 101*, January 12, 2013, https://schoolfinance101.wordpress.com/2013/01/12/the-efficiency-smokescreen -cuts-cause-no-harm-argument-the-3-kansas-judges-who-saw-right-through-it/.

40. Bruce D. Baker, *America's Most Financially Disadvantaged School Districts and How They Got That Way: How State and Local Governance Causes School Funding Disparities* (Washington, DC: Center for American Progress, 2014).

41. Jay P. Greene, "Does School Spending Matter After All?" *J. P. Greene's Blog.*, May 29, 2015, http://jaypgreene.com/2015/05/29/does-school-spending-matter-after-all;

David J. Armor, "The Impact of School Expenditures and Other Resources on Academic Achievement in New York: *Maisto v. New York*," Education Law Center, http://www.edlawcenter.org/assets/files/pdfs/maisto/masito%20trial%20documents/State's%20Expert%20Report%20-%20Dr.%20David%20Armor.pdf.

42. Richard J. Murnane, "Interpreting the Evidence on Does Money Matter," *Harvard Journal on Legislation* 28 (1991): 457.

43. "Memorandum Opinion and Entry of Judgment," *Gannon vs. State of Kansas*, 10C1569, January 11, 2013, http://www.shawneecourt.org/DocumentCenter/View/457.

CHAPTER 4

1. Tom Vander Ark, "The Rise of the Edupreneur," *Getting Smart*, September 15, 2013, http://www.gettingsmart.com/2013/09/rise-edupreneur/; Bruce D. Baker and Justin Bathon, *Financing Online Education and Virtual Schooling: A Guide for Policymakers and Advocates* (Boulder, CO: National Education Policy Center, 2013).

2. Mark Weber and Bruce Baker, "Do For-Profit Managers Spend Less on Schools and Instruction? A National Analysis of Charter School Staffing Expenditures," *Educational Policy* (2017), https://doi.org/10.1177/0895904816681525.

3. Anya Kamenetz, "High Test Scores at a Nationally Lauded Charter Network, but at What Cost?" *nprEd*, June 24, 2016, http://www.npr.org/sections/ed/2016/06/24/477345746/high-test-scores-at-a-nationally-lauded-charter-network-but-at-what-cost.

4. Per her CV, at the time Roza was serving as Senior Economic and Data Advisor to the Bill & Melinda Gates Foundation (http://www18.georgetown.edu/data/people/mr1170/cv.doc). The "Productivity Curve" slide deck is available at http://www.p12.nysed.gov/mgtserv/docs/SchoolFinanceForHighAchievement.pdf.

5. Note that the lines in the graph are actually drawn in by hand and not graphed from data. The hand-drawn lines imply that at $5,000 per-pupil expenditure, whether adopting the status quo, improved teacher effectiveness, or tech-based solutions, nothing can be accomplished. It is unclear whether the y axis represents an absolute standard or change or some other "relative" outcome standard.

6. Dennis Epple, Richard Romano, and Ron Zimmer, "Charter Schools: A Survey of Research on Their Characteristics and Effectiveness" (working paper no. w21256, National Bureau of Economic Research, Cambridge, MA, 2015), 55.

7. Jens Dietrichson, Martin Bøg, Trine Filges, and Anne-Marie Klint Jørgensen, "Academic Interventions for Elementary and Middle School Students with Low Socioeconomic Status: A Systematic Review and Meta-Analysis," *Review of Educational Research* 87, no. 2 (2017): 243–82. For a summary of the findings of this article, see Frederik DeBoer, "Study of the Week: What Actually Helps Poor Students? Human Beings" (blog post), May 16, 2017, https://fredrikdeboer.com/2017/05/16/study-of-the-week-what-actually-helps-poor-students-human-beings/.

8. Kenneth Shores and Matthew Steinberg, "The Impact of the Great Recession on Student Achievement: Evidence from Population Data" (report, Stanford University, Palo Alto, CA, 2017). These findings are consistent with those in C. Kirabo Jackson, Cora Wigger, and Heyu Xiong, "Do School Spending Cuts Matter? Evidence from the Great Recession" (working paper no. w24203, National Bureau of Economic Research, Cambridge, MA, 2018).

9. Bruce D. Baker, "School Finance and the Distribution of Equal Educational Opportunity in the Postrecession US," *Journal of Social Issues* 72, no. 4 (2016): 629–55, doi:10.1111/josi.12187.

10. Bruce D. Baker, *Does Money Matter in Education?* (Washington, DC: Albert Shanker Institute, 2016).

11. Bruce D. Baker, David G. Sciarra, and Danielle Farrie, "Is School Funding Fair? A National Report Card" (report, Education Law Center, Rutgers University, New Brunswick, NJ, 2014).

12. Bruce D. Baker, "Rearranging Deck Chairs in Dallas: Contextual Constraints and Within-District Resource Allocation in Urban Texas School Districts," *Journal of Education Finance* 37, no. 3 (2012): 287–315.

13. Bruce D. Baker, Ajay Srikanth, and Mark Weber, *The Incompatibility of Federal Policy Preferences for Charter School Expansion and Within District Equity* (New Brunswick, NJ: Rutgers Graduate School of Education, 2017).

14. Bruce D. Baker, "Unpacking the Consequences of Disparities in School District Financial Inputs: Evidence from Staffing Data in New York and Illinois" (paper, Association for Education Finance and Policy, Boston, 2012).

15. Courtney Preston, Ellen Goldring, Mark Berends, and Marisa Cannata, "School Innovation in District Context: Comparing Traditional Public Schools and Charter Schools," *Economics of Education Review* 31, no. 2 (2012): 318–30, doi:10.1016/j.econedurev.2011.07.016.

16. Michael Q. McShane and Jenn Hatfield, *Measuring Diversity in Charter School Offerings* (Washington, DC: American Enterprise Institute, 2015), 1, http://www.aei.org/wp-content/uploads/2015/07/Measuring-Diversity-in-Charter-School-Offerings.pdf.

17. Bruce D. Baker, Ken Libby, and Kathryn Wiley, *Spending by the Major Charter Management Organizations: Comparing Charter School and Local Public District Financial Resources in New York, Ohio, and Texas* (Boulder, CO: National Education Policy Center, 2012).

18. Epple et al., *Charter Schools*; Eugenia Toma and Ron Zimmer, "Two Decades of Charter Schools: Expectations, Reality, and the Future," *Economics of Education Review* 31, no. 2 (2012): 20912, doi:10.1016/j.econedurev.2011.10.001.

19. Philip M. Gleason, Christina Clark Tuttle, Brian Gill, Ira Nichols-Barrer, and Bing-ru Teh, "Do KIPP Schools Boost Student Achievement?" *Education Finance and Policy* 9, no. 1 (2014): 36–58; Joshua D. Angrist, Susan M. Dynarski, Thomas J. Kane, Parag A. Pathak, and Christopher R. Walters, "Who Benefits from KIPP?" *Journal of Policy Analysis and Management* 31, no. 4 (2012): 837–60; Will Dobbie, Roland G. Fryer, and G. Fryer Jr., "Are High-Quality Schools Enough to Increase Achievement Among the Poor? Evidence from the Harlem Children's Zone," *American Economic Journal: Applied Economics* 3, no. 3 (2011): 158–87; Will Dobbie and Roland G. Fryer Jr., "Getting Beneath the Veil of Effective Schools: Evidence from New York City," *American Economic Journal: Applied Economics* 5, no. 4 (2013): 28–60.

20. The data are from 2008–10 and are based on prior research. See Baker et al., *Spending by the Major Charter Management Organizations*; and Bruce D. Baker, Ken Libby, and Kathryn Wiley, "Charter School Expansion and Within-District Equity:

Confluence or Conflict?" *Education Finance and Policy* (2015), doi:10.1162/EDFP
_a_00169.

21. Baker et al., *Spending by the Major Charter Management Organizations.*

22. David Arsen and Yongmei Ni, "Is Administration Leaner in Charter Schools? Resource Allocation in Charter and Traditional Public Schools," *Education Policy
Analysis Archives/Archivos Analíticos de Políticas Educativas* 20 (2012): 1, 13.

23. Oded Izraeli and Kevin Murphy, "An Analysis of Michigan Charter Schools: Enrollment, Revenues, and Expenditures," *Journal of Education Finance* 37, no. 3
(2012): 265.

24. Robert Bifulco and Randall Reback, "Fiscal Impacts of Charter Schools: Lessons
from New York," *Education Finance and Policy* 9, no. 1 (2014): 86.

25. Dennis Epple, Richard Romano, and Ron Zimmer, "Charter Schools: A Survey of
Research on Their Characteristics and Effectiveness," in *Handbook of the Economics
of Education*, vol. 5, ed. Eric Hanushek, Stephen Machin, and Ludger Woessmann
(Amsterdam: Elsevier, 2016), 145.

26. Lori L. Taylor, Beverly L. Alford, Kayla B. Rollins, Danielle B. Brown, Jacqueline
R. Stillisano, and Hersh C. Waxman, *Evaluation of Texas Charter Schools* (College
Station, TX: Bush School of Government, 2011), ix.

27. Harmony Schools are actually subsumed under the Cosmos Foundation Inc., and
Harmony and Cosmos under the umbrella of the national network of Gulen charter
schools. See http://gulencharterschools.weebly.com/.

28. Timothy J. Gronberg, Dennis W. Jansen, and Lori L. Taylor, "The Relative Efficiency of Charter Schools: A Cost Frontier Approach," *Economics of Education Review* 31, no. 2 (2012): 302–17, doi:10.1016/j.econedurev.2011.07.001.

29. Bruce D. Baker, *Private Schooling in the US: Expenditures, Supply, and Policy Implications* (Boulder, CO: Education and the Public Interest Center and Education Policy Research, 2009).

30. Boarding schools were not part of the analysis.

31. For a video on the Harkness method and tables, see https://exeter.edu/exeter
-difference/how-youll-learn.

32. Bruce D. Baker and Gary Miron, *The Business of Charter Schooling: Understanding
the Policies That Charter Operators Use for Financial Benefit* (Boulder, CO: National
Education Policy Center, 2015).

33. Baker, *Private Schooling in the US.*

34. "Most Boston Charter Schools Reject Performance-Based Pay for Teachers," *Boston
Globe*, September 3, 2017, http://www.bostonglobe.com/metro/2017/09/03/most
-boston-charter-schools-reject-performance-based-pay-for-teachers/i64tLVRwL9
WqsRxzJ6Z7XJ/story.html?platform=hootsuite.

CHAPTER 5

This chapter draws on collaborations with Matthew DiCarlo of the Shanker Institute as well as, more recently, with leadership and staff at the Learning Policy Institute, including Linda Darling-Hammond, Titilayo Tinubu Ali, and Peter Cookson.

1. Bruce Baker and Kevin Welner, "School Finance and Courts: Does Reform Matter,
and How Can We Tell," *Teachers College Record* 113, no. 11 (2011): 2374–414.

2. Michael F. Addonizio, C. Philip Kearney, and Henry J. Prince, "Michigan's High
Wire Act," *Journal of Education Finance* 20, no. 3 (1995): 235–69; Charles Berger,

"Equity Without Adjudication: Kansas School Finance Reform and the 1992 School District Finance and Quality Performance Act," *Journal of Law & Education* 27 (1998): 1; Bruce D. Baker and Michael Imber, "Rational Educational Explanation or Politics as Usual? Evaluating the Outcome of Educational Finance Litigation in Kansas," *Journal of Education Finance* 25, no. 1 (1999): 121–39.

3. Jay P. Greene and Julie R. Trivitt, "Can Judges Improve Academic Achievement?" *Peabody Journal of Education* 83, no. 2 (2008): 224–37, doi:10.1080/01619560801997010.

4. Ibid., 224. The special journal issue featured published papers that were presented at the October 30, 2007, conference From Equity to Adequacy to Choice, hosted by the Show-Me Institute, a Missouri organization working to promote market-based policy solutions, and the Truman School of Public Affairs at the University of Missouri. The special issue consisted of a compilation of articles from witnesses who testified on behalf of the state in a challenge to the equity and adequacy of school funding in Missouri (*CEE v. State of Missouri*).

5. David Card and A. Abigail Payne, "School Finance Reform: The Distribution of School Spending, and the Distribution of Student Test Scores," *Journal of Public Economics* 83, no. 1 (2002): 49–82, doi:10.1016/S0047-2727(00)00177-8.

6. One publicly available longitudinal data set is Bruce Baker, Mark Weber, and Ajay Srikanth, *School Funding Fairness Data System* (New Brunswick, NJ: Rutgers Graduate School of Education; Newark, NJ: Education Law Center, 2017), http://www.schoolfundingfairness.org/data-download.

7. C. Kirabo Jackson, Rucker C. Johnson, and Claudia Persico, "The Effects of School Spending on Educational and Economic Outcomes: Evidence from School Finance Reforms," *Quarterly Journal of Economics* 131, no. 1 (2015): 157–218, doi:10.1093/qje/qjv036; C. Kirabo Jackson, Rucker C. Johnson, and Claudia Persico, "Boosting Educational Attainment and Adult Earnings," *Education Next* 15, no. 4 (2015): 69–76.

8. Jackson et al., "The Effects of School Spending."

9. The authors explain: "Our sample consists of PSID sample members born between 1955 and 1985 who have been followed from 1968 into adulthood through 2011. This corresponds to cohorts that both straddle the first set of court-mandated SFRs (the first of which was in 1972) and are old enough to have completed formal schooling by 2011. Two-thirds of those in these cohorts in the PSID grew up in a school district that was subject to a court-mandated school finance reform between 1972 and 2000" (ibid., 163–64).

10. Bruce D. Baker and Kevin Welner, "School Finance and Courts: Does Reform Matter, and How Can We Tell?" *Teachers College Record* 113, no. 11 (2011): 2374–414.

11. Jackson et al., "Boosting Educational Attainment," 72.

12. Jackson et al., "The Effects of School Spending," 157.

13. Ibid.; Jackson et al., "Boosting Educational Attainment."

14. Julien Lafortune, Jesse Rothstein, and Diane Whitmore Schanzenbach, "School Finance Reform and the Distribution of Student Achievement" (white paper no. w22011, National Bureau of Economic Research, Cambridge, MA, 2016), 1, www.nber.org/papers/w22011.pdf.

15. Bruce D. Baker and Mark Weber, "Beyond the Echo-Chamber: State Investments and Student Outcomes in US Elementary and Secondary Education," *Journal of Education Finance* 42, no. 1 (2016): 1–27; Bruce D. Baker, Danielle Farrie, and David G. Sciarra, "Mind the Gap: 20 Years of Progress and Retrenchment in

School Funding and Achievement Gaps," *ETS Research Report Series* 2016, no. 1 (2016): 1–37.

16. Christopher A. Candelaria and Kenneth A. Shores, "Court-Ordered Finance Reforms in the Adequacy Era: Heterogeneous Causal Effects and Sensitivity," *Education Finance and Policy* (2017): 1–91, https://doi.org/10.1162/EDFP_a_00236.

17. Kenneth Shores and Matthew Steinberg, "The Impact of the Great Recession on Student Achievement: Evidence from Population Data," Social Science Research Network (SSRN), August 28, 2017, 1, https://ssrn.com/abstract=3026151.

18. Sean F. Reardon, Demetra Kalogrides, Andrew Ho, Ben Shear, Kenneth Shores, and Erin Fahle, *Stanford Education Data Archive* (Version 1.1 File Title), 2016, http://purl.stanford.edu/db586ns4974.

19. Jackson, C. Kirabo, Cora Wigger, and Heyu Xiong, "Do School Spending Cuts Matter? Evidence from the Great Recession" (white paper no. w24203, National Bureau of Economic Research, Cambridge, MA, 2018).

20. Massachusetts's reform efforts have weakened, and Michigan's have largely collapsed. Bruce D. Baker, "School Finance and the Distribution of Equal Educational Opportunity in the Postrecession US," *Journal of Social Issues* 72, no. 4 (2016): 629–55, doi:10.1111/josi.12187. See also Bruce D. Baker, *Review of School Spending and Student Achievement in Michigan: What's the Relationship* (Boulder, CO: National Education Policy Center, 2016).

21. Eric A. Hanushek and Alfred A. Lindseth. *Schoolhouses, Courthouses, and Statehouses: Solving the Funding-Achievement Puzzle in America's Public Schools* (Princeton, NJ: Princeton University Press, 2009).

22. *McDuffy v. Secretary of the Executive Office of Education*, 415 Mass. 545 (1993); "The Massachusetts Foundation Budget," July 17, 2017, http://www.doe.mass.edu/finance /chapter70/chapter-cal.pdf.

23. "Demystifying the Chapter 70 Formula: How the Massachusetts Education Funding System Works" (report, Massachusetts Budget and Policy Center, Boston, December 7, 2010), http://www.massbudget.org/report_window.php?loc=Facts_10_22 _10.html.

24. Thomas A. Downes, Jeffrey Zabel, and Dana Elizabeth Ansel, *Incomplete Grade: Massachusetts Education Reform at 15* (Boston: MassINC, 2009), 5.

25. The magnitudes imply that a $1,000 increase in per-pupil spending leads to approximately a one-third to one-half standard deviation increase in average test scores. It is noted that the state aid driving the estimates is targeted to underfunded school districts, which may have atypical returns to additional expenditures. Jonathan Guryan, "Does Money Matter? Regression-Discontinuity Estimates from Education Finance Reform in Massachusetts" (white paper no. w8269, National Bureau of Economic Research, Cambridge, MA, 2001).

26. Phuong Nguyen-Hoang and John Yinger, "Education Finance Reform, Local Behavior, and Student Performance in Massachusetts," *Journal of Education Finance* 39, no. 4 (2014): 297.

27. "School Finance Reform in Michigan: Proposal A—A Retrospective" (report, Office of Revenue and Tax Analysis, Michigan Department of Treasury, Ann Arbor, December 2002), https://www.michigan.gov/documents/propa_3172_7.pdf.

28. Joydeep Roy studied the period 1995–2001; see "Impact of School Finance Reform on Resource Equalization and Academic Performance: Evidence from Michigan,"

Education Finance and Policy 6, no. 2 (2011): 137–67. Leslie Papke studied the period 1992–98; see "The Effects of Spending on Test Pass Rates: Evidence from Michigan," *Journal of Public Economics* 89, no. 5 (2005): 821–39, doi:10.1016/j.jpubeco .2004.05.008. Latika Chaudhary studied the period 1995–2000; see "Education Inputs, Student Performance and School Finance Reform in Michigan," *Economics of Education Review* 28, no. 1 (2009): 90–98, doi:10.1016/j.econedurev.2007.11.004. Joshua Hyman studied the period 1995–2010; see "Does Money Matter in the Long Run? Effects of School Spending on Educational Attainment," *American Economic Journal: Economic Policy* 9, no. 4 (2017): 256–80.

29. Chaudhary, "Education Inputs, Student Performance and School Finance Reform in Michigan," 90.
30. Jackson et al., "Boosting Educational Attainment."
31. Roy, "Impact of School Finance Reform," abstract.
32. Papke, "The Effects of Spending," 821. In a separate study, Leuven and colleagues attempted to isolate specific effects of increases to at-risk funding on at-risk pupil outcomes but did not find any positive effects. See Edwin Leuven, Mikael Lindahl, Hessel Oosterbeek, and Dinand Webbink, "The Effect of Extra Funding for Disadvantaged Pupils on Achievement," *Review of Economics and Statistics* 89, no. 4 (2007): 721–36.
33. Hyman, "Does Money Matter in the Long Run?" 1.
34. Baker, *Review of School Spending and Student Achievement in Michigan.*
35. Jackson et al., "The Effects of School Spending," 209, 211.
36. Shores and Steinberg, "The Impact of the Great Recession."
37. Jens Dietrichson, Martin Bøg, Trine Filges, and Anne-Marie Klint Jørgensen, "Academic Interventions for Elementary and Middle School Students with Low Socioeconomic Status: A Systematic Review and Meta-Analysis," *Review of Educational Research* 87, no. 2 (2017): 243–82.
38. Eric A. Hanushek, "Teacher Characteristics and Gains in Student Achievement: Estimation Using Micro Data," *American Economic Review* 61, no. 2 (1971): 280–88; Charles T. Clotfelter, Helen F. Ladd, and Jacob L. Vigdor, "Teacher Credentials and Student Achievement: Longitudinal Analysis with Student Fixed Effects," *Economics of Education Review* 26, no. 6 (2007): 673–82, doi:10.1016/j.econedurev.2007.10.002; Dan D. Goldhaber and Dominic J. Brewer, "Why Don't Schools and Teachers Seem to Matter? Assessing the Impact of Unobservables on Educational Productivity," *Journal of Human Resources* 32, no. 3 (1997): 505–23, doi:10.2307/146181; Ronald G. Ehrenberg and Dominic J. Brewer, "Do School and Teacher Characteristics Matter? Evidence from High School and Beyond," *Economics of Education Review* 13, no. 1 (1994): 1–17; Ronald G. Ehrenberg and Dominic J. Brewer, "Did Teachers' Verbal Ability and Race Matter in the 1960s? Coleman Revisited," *Economics of Education Review* 14, no. 1 (1995): 1–21; Christopher Jepsen, "Teacher Characteristics and Student Achievement: Evidence from Teacher Surveys," *Journal of Urban Economics* 57, no. 2 (2005): 302–19, doi:10.1016/j.jue.2004.11.001; Brian A. Jacob and Lars Lefgren, "The Impact of Teacher Training on Student Achievement Quasi-Experimental Evidence from School Reform Efforts in Chicago," *Journal of Human Resources* 39, no. 1 (2004): 50–79, doi:10.2307/3559005; Steven G. Rivkin, Eric A. Hanushek, and John F. Kain, "Teachers, Schools, and Academic Achievement," *Econometrica* 73, no. 2 (2005): 417–58; Andrew J. Wayne and Peter Youngs,

"Teacher Characteristics and Student Achievement Gains: A Review," *Review of Educational Research* 73, no. 1 (2003): 89–122. For a recent review of studies on the returns to teacher experience, see Jennifer King Rice, "The Impact of Teacher Experience: Examining the Evidence and Policy Implications" (Brief No. 11, National Center for Analysis of Longitudinal Data in Education Research, Washington, DC, 2010).

39. Some argue that half or more of teacher pay is allocated to "nonproductive" teacher attributes, and so it follows that the entire amount of funding could be reallocated toward making schools more productive. See, for example, the presentation by Stephen Frank of Education Resource Strategies to the New York State Board of Regents, September 13, 2011, www.p12.nysed.gov/mgtserv/docs/SchoolFinanceFor HighAchievement.pdf.

40. Hamilton Lankford, Susanna Loeb, and James Wyckoff, "Teacher Sorting and the Plight of Urban Schools: A Descriptive Analysis," *Educational Evaluation and Policy Analysis* 24, no. 1 (2002): 37–62.

41. Sylvia Allegretto, Sean Corcoran, and Lawrence Mishel, *The Teaching Penalty: Teacher Pay Losing Ground* (Washington, DC: Economic Policy Institute, 2008), https://www.epi.org/publication/book_teaching_penalty/.

42. Richard J. Murnane and Randall J. Olsen, "The Effects of Salaries and Opportunity Costs on Length of Stay in Teaching: Evidence from North Carolina," *Journal of Human Resources* 25, no. 1 (1990): 106–24, doi:10.2307/145729.

43. David N. Figlio, "Can Public Schools Buy Better-Qualified Teachers?" *ILR Review* 55, no. 4 (2002): 686–99; David N. Figlio, "Teacher Salaries and Teacher Quality," *Economics Letters* 55, no. 2 (1997): 267–71, doi:10.1016/S0165-1765(97)00070-0; Ronald F. Ferguson, "Paying for Public Education: New Evidence on How and Why Money Matters," *Harvard Journal on Legislation* 28 (1991): 465.

44. Susanna Loeb and Marianne E. Page, "Examining the Link Between Teacher Wages and Student Outcomes: The Importance of Alternative Labor Market Opportunities and Non-Pecuniary Variation," *Review of Economics and Statistics* 82, no. 3 (2000): 393–408.

45. David N. Figlio and Kim S. Rueben, "Tax Limits and the Qualifications of New Teachers," *Journal of Public Economics* 80, no. 1 (2001): 49–71, doi:10.1016/S0047 -2727(00)00116-X; Thomas A. Downes and David N. Figlio, "Do Tax and Expenditure Limits Provide a Free Lunch? Evidence on the Link Between Limits and Public Sector Service Quality," *National Tax Journal* 52, no. 1 (1999): 113–28.

46. Jan Ondrich, Emily Pas, and John Yinger, "The Determinants of Teacher Attrition in Upstate New York," *Public Finance Review* 36, no. 1 (2008): 112–44, doi:10.1177 /1091142106294716.

47. Eric A. Hanushek., John F. Kain, and Steven G. Rivkin, "Why Public Schools Lose Teachers," *Journal of Human Resources* 39, no. 2 (2004): 326–54, doi:10.2307 /3559017.

48. Charles T. Clotfelter, Helen F. Ladd, and Jacob L. Vigdor, "Teacher Mobility, School Segregation, and Pay-Based Policies to Level the Playing Field," *Education Finance and Policy* 6, no. 3 (2011): 399–438; Charles T. Clotfelter, Elizabeth Glennie, Helen Ladd, and Jacob Vigdor, "Would Higher Salaries Keep Teachers in High-Poverty Schools? Evidence from a Policy Intervention in North Carolina,"

Journal of Public Economics 92, no. 5 (2008): 1352–70, doi:10.1016/j.jpubeco.2007 .07.003.

49. For major studies on merit pay, each of which generally finds no positive effects of merit pay on student outcomes, see Steven Glazerman and Allison Seifullah, "An Evaluation of the Teacher Advancement Program (TAP) in Chicago: Year Two Impact Report" (report, Mathematica Policy Research, Princeton, NJ, May 17, 2010); Matthew G. Springer, Dale Ballou, Laura Hamilton, Vi-Nhuan Le, J. R. Lockwood, Daniel F. McCaffrey, Matthew Pepper, and Brian M. Stecher, "Teacher Pay for Performance: Experimental Evidence from the Project on Incentives in Teaching (POINT)" (working paper, Society for Research on Educational Effectiveness, Nashville, January 2011); Julie A. Marsh, Matthew G. Springer, Daniel F. McCaffrey, Kun Yuan, and Scott Epstein, "A Big Apple for Educators: New York City's Experiment with Schoolwide Performance Bonuses" (Final Evaluation Report, Rand Corporation, New York, 2011).

50. Kun Yuan, Vi-Nhuan Le, Daniel F. McCaffrey, Julie A. Marsh, Laura S. Hamilton, Brian M. Stecher, and Matthew G. Springer, "Incentive Pay Programs Do Not Affect Teacher Motivation or Reported Practices: Results from Three Randomized Studies," *Educational Evaluation and Policy Analysis* 35, no. 1 (2013): 3–22, doi:10.3102/0162373712462625; Springer et al., "Teacher Pay for Performance"; Matthew G. Springer, John F. Pane, Vi-Nhuan Le, Daniel F. McCaffrey, Susan Freeman Bus, Laura S. Hamilton, and Brian Stecher, "Team Pay for Performance: Experimental Evidence from the Round Rock Pilot Project on Team Incentives," *Educational Evaluation and Policy Analysis* 34, no. 4 (2012): 367–90.

51. Thomas S. Dee and James Wyckoff, "Incentives, Selection, and Teacher Performance: Evidence from IMPACT," *Journal of Policy Analysis and Management* 34, no. 2 (2015): 267–97.

52. Ryan Balch and Matthew G. Springer, "Performance Pay, Test Scores, and Student Learning Objectives," *Economics of Education Review* 44 (2015): 114–25, doi:10.1016/j.econedurev.2014.11.002.

53. Aaron J. Sojourner, Elton Mykerezi, and Kristine L. West, "Teacher Pay Reform and Productivity Panel Data Evidence from Adoptions of Q-Comp in Minnesota," *Journal of Human Resources* 49, no. 4 (2014): 945–81.

54. Roland G. Fryer Jr., Steven D. Levitt, John List, and Sally Sadoff, "Enhancing the Efficacy of Teacher Incentives Through Loss Aversion: A Field Experiment" (working paper no. 18237, National Bureau of Economic Research, Cambridge, MA, July 1, 2012).

55. Matthew D. Hendricks, "Public Schools Are Hemorrhaging Talented Teachers: Can Higher Salaries Function as a Tourniquet?" (paper, Tulsa, OK, March 24, 2015), http://papers.ssrn.com/sol3/papers.cfm?abstract_id=2564703.

56. Matthew D. Hendricks, "Towards an Optimal Teacher Salary Schedule: Designing Base Salary to Attract and Retain Effective Teachers," *Economics of Education Review* 47, no. 1 (2015): 143–67, doi:10.1016/j.econedurev.2015.05.008.

57. Matthew Wiswall, "The Dynamics of Teacher Quality," *Journal of Public Economics* 100 (2013): 61–78, doi:10.1016/j.jpubeco.2013.01.006.

58. John P. Papay and Matthew A. Kraft, "Productivity Returns to Experience in the Teacher Labor Market: Methodological Challenges and New Evidence on

Long-Term Career Improvement," *Journal of Public Economics* 130, no. 1 (2015): 105–19, doi:10.1016/j.jpubeco.2015.02.008.

59. Helen F. Ladd and Lucy C. Sorensen, "Returns to Teacher Experience: Student Achievement and Motivation in Middle School," *Education Finance and Policy* 12, no. 2 (2017): 241–79.

60. Gregory Gilpin and Michael Kaganovich, "The Quantity and Quality of Teachers: Dynamics of the Trade-Off," *Journal of Public Economics* 96, nos. 3–4 (2012): 417–29; Jesse Rothstein, "Teacher Quality Policy When Supply Matters," *American Economic Review* 105, no. 1 (2014): 100–130, doi:10.1257/aer.20121242.

61. Gilpin and Kaganovich, "The Quantity and Quality of Teachers."

62. Rothstein, "Teacher Quality Policy."

63. Matthew M. Chingos, "The False Promise of Class-Size Reduction" (report, Center for American Progress, Washington, DC, April 1, 2011.

64. See, for example, Dominic J. Brewer, Cathy Krop, Brian P. Gill, and Robert Reichardt, "Estimating the Cost of National Class Size Reductions Under Different Policy Alternatives," *Educational Evaluation and Policy Analysis* 21, no. 2 (1999): 179–92. While this article provides insights into the cumulative costs of adding large numbers of teachers, it makes no comparisons to other strategies that might be employed for the same dollar. It acknowledges the research on positive effects of class size and then estimates large-scale implementation costs, seemingly implying either that achieving these positive effects is simply too expensive or that there might be more cost-effective uses of the same dollar.

65. See "Identifying and Implementing Educational Practices Supported by Rigorous Evidence: A User Friendly Guide"(white paper, Institute for Education Sciences, National Center for Education Evaluation and Regional Assistance, Washington, DC, 2003), http://www2.ed.gov/rschstat/research/pubs/rigorousevid/rigorousevid .pdf; Jeremy D. Finn and Charles M. Achilles, "Tennessee's Class Size Study: Findings, Implications, Misconceptions," *Educational Evaluation and Policy Analysis* 21, no. 2 (1999): 97–109; Jeremy D. Finn, Susan B. Gerber, Charles M. Achilles, and Jayne Boyd-Zaharias, "The Enduring Effects of Small Classes," *Teachers College Record* 103, no. 2 (2001): 145–83; Alan B. Krueger and Diane M. Whitmore, "Would Smaller Classes Help Close the Black-White Achievement Gap?" (paper, vol. 451, Industrial Relations Section, Princeton University, 2001), doi:www.irs.princeton .edu/pubs/pdfs/451.pdf; Henry M. Levin, Clive Belfield, Peter Muennig, and Cecilia Rouse, "The Public Returns to Public Educational Investments in African-American Males," *Economics of Education Review* 26, no. 6 (2007): 699–708, doi:10.1016/j.econedurev.2007.09.004; Spyros Konstantopoulos and Vicki Chung, "What Are the Long-Term Effects of Small Classes on the Achievement Gap? Evidence from the Lasting Benefits Study," *American Journal of Education* 116, no. 1 (2009): 125–54, doi:10.1086/605103.

66. Alan B. Krueger, "Experimental Estimates of Education Production Functions," *Quarterly Journal of Economics* 114, no. 2 (1999): 497–532. Project STAR (Student Teacher Achievement Ratio) was a large-scale, state-supported research study designed to determine the influence of providing smaller classes to students in Tennessee. The study randomly assigned teachers and students to three groups, "small" (13–17 students) classes, "regular" (22–25) classes with a paid aide, and "regular" (22–25) classes with no aide. In total some 6,500 students in about 330 classrooms

at approximately 80 schools participated. See Frederick Mosteller, "The Tennessee Study of Class Size in the Early School Grades," *The Future of Children* (1995): 113–27.

67. Spyros Konstantopoulos and Vicki Chung, "What Are the Long-Term Effects of Small Classes on the Achievement Gap? Evidence from the Lasting Benefits Study," *American Journal of Education* 116, no. 1 (2009): 125–54, doi:10.1086/605103.

68. Susan Dynarski, Joshua Hyman, and Diane Whitmore Schanzenbach, "Experimental Evidence on the Effect of Childhood Investments on Postsecondary Attainment and Degree Completion," *Journal of Policy Analysis and Management* 32, no. 4 (2013): 692–717.

69. Another relevant study showing positive effects of pupil-to-teacher ratio reduction (different from class size) is Alex Molnar, Philip Smith, John Zahorik, Amanda Palmer, Anke Halbach, and Karen Ehrle, "Evaluating the SAGE Program: A Pilot Program in Targeted Pupil-Teacher Reduction in Wisconsin," *Educational Evaluation and Policy Analysis* 21, no. 2 (1999): 165–77. Unlike STAR, which was a true randomized experiment in Tennessee, SAGE in Wisconsin was designed as "a 5-year K–3 pilot project that began in the 1996–97 school year. The program required that participating schools implement 4 interventions including reducing the pupil-teacher ratio within classrooms to 15 students per teacher" (ibid., 165). Molnar and colleagues found that "results of the 1996–97 and 1997–98 first grade data reveal findings consistent with the Tennessee STAR class size experiment" (165). For an example of a study based on natural variation, finding no positive effects of smaller class size, see Caroline M. Hoxby, "The Effects of Class Size on Student Achievement: New Evidence from Population Variation," *Quarterly Journal of Economics* 115, no. 4 (2000): 1239–85. Hoxby uses grade-level, not student-level, data on 649 elementary schools in Connecticut, concluding that "class size does not have a statistically significant effect on student achievement" (1239).

70. Matthew M. Chingos, "The False Promise of Class-Size Reduction" (report, Center for American Progress, Washington, DC, April 1, 2011).

71. Matthew M. Chingos, "Class Size and Student Outcomes: Research and Policy Implications," *Journal of Policy Analysis and Management* 32, no. 2 (2013): 411–38.

72. Estimates provided by Alan B. Krueger, "Experimental Estimates of Education Production Functions," *Quarterly Journal of Economics* 114, no. 2 (1999): 497–532. See also Hyunkuk Cho, Paul Glewwe, and Melissa Whitler, "Do Reductions in Class Size Raise Students' Test Scores? Evidence from Population Variation in Minnesota's Elementary Schools," *Economics of Education Review* 31, no. 3 (2012): 77–95, doi:10.1016/j.econedurev.2012.01.004.

73. Dynarski et al., "Experimental Evidence."

74. This includes recent work linking participation in smaller class sizes with postsecondary degree attainment.

75. For other relatively recent studies on class size reduction, see Raj Chetty, John N. Friedman, Nathaniel Hilger, Emmanuel Saez, Diane Whitmore Schanzenbach, and Danny Yagan, "How Does Your Kindergarten Classroom Affect Your Earnings? Evidence from Project STAR," *Quarterly Journal of Economics* 126, no. 4 (2011): 1593–660, doi:10.1093/qje/qjr041; Peter Blatchford, Paul Bassett, and Penelope Brown, "Teachers' and Pupils' Behavior in Large and Small Classes: A Systematic Observation Study of Pupils Aged 10 and 11 Years," *Journal of Educational Psychology* 97, no. 3

(2005): 454; Phillip Babcock and Julian R. Betts, "Reduced-Class Distinctions: Effort, Ability, and the Education Production Function," *Journal of Urban Economics* 65, no. 3 (2009): 314–22, doi:10.1016/j.jue.2009.02.001; Sarah Theule Lubienski, Christopher Lubienski, and Corinna Crawford Crane, "Achievement Differences and School Type: The Role of School Climate, Teacher Certification, and Instruction," *American Journal of Education* 115, no. 1 (2008): 97–138, doi:10.1086/590677.

76. Christopher Jepsen and Steven Rivkin, "What Is the Tradeoff Between Smaller Classes and Teacher Quality?" (report no. w9205, National Bureau of Economic Research, Cambridge, MA. 2002): "The results show that, all else being equal, smaller classes raise third-grade mathematics and reading achievement, particularly for lower-income students. However, the expansion of the teaching force required to staff the additional classrooms appears to have led to a deterioration in average teacher quality in schools serving a predominantly black student body. This deterioration partially or, in some cases, fully offset the benefits of smaller classes, demonstrating the importance of considering all implications of any policy change" (1). For further discussion of the complexities of evaluating class size reduction in a dynamic policy context, see David P. Sims, "A Strategic Response to Class Size Reduction: Combination Classes and Student Achievement in California," *Journal of Policy Analysis and Management* 27, no. 3 (2008): 457–78, doi:10.1002/pam.20353; David P. Sims, "Crowding Peter to Educate Paul: Lessons from a Class Size Reduction Externality," *Economics of Education Review* 28, no. 4 (2009): 465–73, doi:10.1016/j.econedurev .2008.06.005; Matthew M. Chingos, "The Impact of a Universal Class-Size Reduction Policy: Evidence from Florida's Statewide Mandate," *Economics of Education Review* 31, no. 5 (2012): 543–62, doi:10.1016/j.econedurev.2012.03.002.

77. Ronald G. Ehrenberg, Dominic J. Brewer, Adam Gamoran, and J. Douglas Willms, "Class Size and Student Achievement," *Psychological Science in the Public Interest* 2, no. 1 (2001): 1–30.

CHAPTER 6

This chapter draws on collaboration with Jesse Levin of the American Institutes for Research.

1. Paul R. Mort and Walter Christian Reusser, *Public School Finance: Its Background, Structure, and Operation* (New York: McGraw-Hill, 1951), 371.

2. Ibid., 373.

3. George Drayton Strayer and Robert Murray Haig, *The Financing of Education in the State of New York*, Educational Finance Inquiry Commission (New York: Macmillan, 1923).

4. Matthew M. Chingos and Kristin Blagg, *Do Poor Kids Get Their Fair Share of School Funding?* (Washington, DC: Urban Institute, 2017).

5. *Fiscal Equity v. State of NY*, 801 N.E.2d 326, 100 N.Y.2d 893, 769 N.Y.S.2d 106 (2003); *Campaign for Fiscal Equity, Inc. v. State*, 2006 N.Y. Slip Op 8630 (2006).

6. "A 28-Member Commission Studying the Problem of School Funding Inequities Will Hold a Meeting in San Jose March 4," *San Jose Mercury News*, February 24, 2011, http://www.mercurynews.com/2011/02/24/a-28-member-commission -studying-the-problem-of-school-funding-inequities-will-hold-a-meeting-in-san -jose-march-4/.

7. Bruce D. Baker, *Does Money Matter in Education?* (Washington DC: Albert Shanker Institute, 2016).

8. To a large extent, education operates as a positional good, whereby the advantages obtained by some necessarily translate to disadvantages for others. See Bruce D. Baker and Preston C. Green III, "Conceptions of Equity and Adequacy in School Finance," in *Handbook of Research in Education Finance and Policy*, ed. Helen F. Ladd and Edward Fiske (New York: Routledge, 2008), 203–21; William S. Koski and Rob Reich, "When Adequate Isn't: The Retreat from Equity in Educational Law and Policy and Why It Matters," *Emory Law Journal* 56 (2006): 545.

9. William Duncombe and John Yinger, "How Much More Does a Disadvantaged Student Cost?" *Economics of Education Review* 24, no. 5 (2005): 513–32, doi:10.1016/j.econedurev.2004.07.015.

10. Andrew Smarick, *The Urban School System of the Future: Applying the Principles and Lessons of Chartering* (New York: R & L Education, 2012). The premise of Smarick's book is that urban school systems have failed despite receiving massive resources, an idea largely borrowed from Paul Hill, Lawrence C. Pierce, and James W. Guthrie, *Reinventing Public Education: How Contracting Can Transform America's Schools* (Chicago: University of Chicago Press, 2009). See also Natalie Wexler, "Should We Give Up on Urban Public School Districts and Replace Them with Something Completely Different?" *Greater Greater Washington*, May 7, 2014, https://ggwash.org/view/34640/should-we-give-up-on-urban-public-school-districts-and-replace-them-with-something-completely-different. Smarick was appointed president of the Maryland State Board of Education in 2016.

11. See Bruce D. Baker, "Stop School Funding Ignorance Now: A Philadelphia Story," *School Finance 101*, June 20, 2013, https://schoolfinance101.wordpress.com/2013/06/20/stop-school-funding-ignorance-now-a-philadelphia-story/. Andy Smarick mentions Baltimore, Boston, Detroit, Milwaukee, and New York in an exchange found in Jack Schneider, "Does Money Matter? Is School Funding Fair?" *Flypaper* (blog), Thomas Fordham Institute, December 15, 2014, https://edexcellence.net/articles/does-money-matter-is-school-funding-fair.

12. Bruce D. Baker, "America's Most Screwed City Schools," *School Finance 101*, June 2, 2012, https://schoolfinance101.wordpress.com/2012/06/02/americas-most-screwed-city-schools-where-are-the-least-fairly-funded-city-districts/.

13. Joy Resmovitz, "Reading, Pennsylvania: Poorest U.S. City Loses Pre-Kindergarten, 170 Teachers," *Huffington Post*, June 15, 2012, http://www.huffingtonpost.com/2012/06/14/reading-pennsylvania-schools_n_1598398.html.

14. Bruce D. Baker, *America's Most Financially Disadvantaged School Districts and How They Got That Way: How State and Local Governance Causes School Funding Disparities* (Washington, DC: Center for American Progress, 2014); Bruce D. Baker, Theresa Luhm, Danielle Farrie, and David Sciarra, *America's Most Financially Disadvantaged School Districts 2016* (Newark, NJ: Education Law Center, 2016).

15. Michael Q. McShane, "Fact Checking HuffPost: It's Not About the Money," *American Enterprise Institute*, October 5, 2012, https://www.aei.org/publication/fact-checking-huffpost-its-not-about-the-money/.

16. William Duncombe and John Yinger, "Why Is It So Hard to Help Central City Schools?" *Journal of Policy Analysis and Management* 16, no. 1 (1997): 85–113;

William Duncombe and John Yinger, "How Much More Does a Disadvantaged Student Cost?" *Economics of Education Review* 24, no. 5 (2005): 513–32, doi:10.1016 /j.econedurev.2004.07.015.

17. Bruce D. Baker and Preston C. Green III, "Tricks of the Trade: State Legislative Actions in School Finance Policy That Perpetuate Racial Disparities in the Post-*Brown* Era," *American Journal of Education* 111, no. 3 (2005): 372–413, doi:10.1086/428886; Tony Ortega, "Funny Math," *Kansas City Pitch*, April 14, 2005, http://www.pitch .com/kansascity/funny-math/Content?oid=2177356.

18. Bruce D. Baker, "What Will It Take to Make Kansas School Funding Cost Based?" *Kansas Policy Review* 27, no. 2 (2005): 21–30, http://www.ipsr.ku.edu/publicat/kpr /kprV27N2/kprv27n2.pdf.

19. Kevin Fox Gotham, "Urban Space, Restrictive Covenants and the Origins of Racial Residential Segregation in a US City, 1900–50," *International Journal of Urban and Regional Research* 24, no. 3 (2000): 616–33.

20. Bruce D. Baker, "Arizona's State School Finance Formula Fails to Guarantee Equal Educational Opportunity" (report, Arizona Center for Law in the Public Interest, Phoenix, 2007).

21. Bruce D. Baker and Sean P. Corcoran, *The Stealth Inequities of School Funding: How State and Local School Finance Systems Perpetuate Inequitable Student Spending* (Washington, DC: Center for American Progress, 2012).

22. Tae Ho Eom and Ross Rubenstein, "Do State-Funded Property Tax Exemptions Increase Local Government Inefficiency? An Analysis of New York State's STAR Program," *Public Budgeting and Finance* 26, no. 1 (2006): 66–87, doi:10.1111/j.1540 -5850.2006.00839.x.

23. Jonah Rockoff, "Local Response to Fiscal Incentives in Heterogeneous Communities," *Journal of Urban Economics* 68, no. 2 (2010): 27, doi:10.1016/j.jue.2010.03.010.

24. Goodwin Liu, "Improving Title I Funding Equity Across State, Districts, and Schools," *Iowa Law Review* 93 (2007): 973.

25. Bruce D. Baker, Lori Taylor, Jesse Levin, Jay Chambers, and Charles Blankenship, "Adjusted Poverty Measures and the Distribution of Title I Aid: Does Title I Really Make the Rich States Richer?" *Education Finance and Policy* 8, no. 3 (2013): 394–417, doi:10.1162/EDFP_a_00103.

CHAPTER 7

1. Bruce D. Baker, *Exploring the Consequences of Charter School Expansion in US Cities* (Washington, DC: Economic Policy Institute, November 30, 2016), https://www. epi.org/publication/exploring-the-consequences-of-charter-school-expansion -in-u-s-cities/.

2. Bruce D. Baker, "Evaluating the Recession's Impact on State School Finance Systems," *Education Policy Analysis Archives* 22 (2014).

3. *Lake View School District No. 25 v. Huckabee*, 91 S.W.3d 472, 351 Ark. 31, 351 A.R. 31 (2002).

4. *Montoy v. State*, 279 Kan. 817, 112 P.3d 923 (2005).

5. Richard E. Levy, "Gunfight at the K–12 Corral: Legislative vs. Judicial Power in the Kansas School Finance Litigation," *University of Kansas Law Review* 54 (2005): 1021.

6. *Abbott by Abbott v. Burke*, 710 A.2d 450, 153 N.J. 480 (1998).
7. Andrew Wagman, "Plan to Eliminate Property Taxes Gives Lehigh Valley School Officials Nightmares," *Morning Call*, February 6, 2017, http://www.mcall.com /news/local/watchdog/mc-lehigh-valley-schools-property-tax-elimination-impact -20170204-story.html.
8. Robert Tannenwald, "Are State and Local Revenue Systems Becoming Obsolete?" *National Tax Journal* 55, no. 3 (2002): 467.
9. Daria Hall and Natasha Ushomirsky, *Close the Hidden Funding Gaps in Our Schools: K–12 Policy* (Washington, DC: Education Trust, 2010); Ary Spatig-Amerikaner, *Unequal Education: Federal Loophole Enables Lower Spending on Students of Color* (Washington, DC: Center for American Progress, 2012).
10. Bruce D. Baker and Kevin G. Welner, "Premature Celebrations: The Persistence of Inter-District Funding Disparities," *Education Policy Analysis Archives* 18 (2010).
11. Lindsey Luebchow, *Equitable Resources in Low Income Schools: Teacher Equity and the Federal Title I Comparability Requirement* (Washington, DC: New America Foundation, 2009); Mark Dynarski, and Kirsten Kainz, *Requiring School Districts to Spend Comparable Amounts on Title I Schools Is Pushing on a String*, Evidence Speaks Reports (Washington, DC: Center on Children and Families at Brookings, 2016).
12. Baker and Welner, "Premature Celebrations." See also Dynarski, and Kainz, *Requiring School Districts*.
13. Bruce D. Baker and Mark Weber, "State School Finance Inequities and the Limits of Pursuing Teacher Equity Through Departmental Regulation," *Education Policy Analysis Archives* 24 (2016): 47.
14. Matthew J. Carr, Nathan L. Gray, and Marc J. Holley, "Shortchanging Disadvantaged Students: An Analysis of Intra-District Spending Patterns in Ohio," *Journal of Educational Research & Policy Studies* 7, no. 1 (2007): 36–53.
15. Bruce Baker, "Review of *Fund the Child: Bringing Equity, Autonomy, and Portability to Ohio School Finance*," Education and the Public Interest Center & Education Policy Research Unit, 2008, http://epicpolicy.org/thinktank/review-fund-child.
16. "Press Release: The Cost of Failure," Families for Excellent Schools, February 2, 2015, http://www.familiesforexcellentschools.org/news/press-release-cost-failure.
17. For a recent application and discussion of related studies, see Drew Atchison, Jesse Levin, Bruce Baker, Iliana Brodziak, Andrew Boyle, Adam Hall, and Jason Becker, "Study of Funding Provided to Public Schools and Public Charter Schools in Maryland" (report, Maryland Department of Education, Baltimore, 2017), http:// marylandpublicschools.org/stateboard/Documents/01242017/TabG-Charter PublicSchoolFundingStudy.pdf.
18. Bruce D. Baker, Ken Libby, and Kathryn Wiley, "Charter School Expansion and Within-District Equity: Confluence or Conflict?" *Education Finance and Policy* 10, no. 3 (2015): 423–65, doi:10.1162/EDFP_a_00169.
19. Mark Weber and Bruce Baker, "Do For-Profit Managers Spend Less on Schools and Instruction? A National Analysis of Charter School Staffing Expenditures," *Educational Policy* (2017).
20. Robert Bifulco and Randall Reback, "Fiscal Impacts of Charter Schools: Lessons from New York," *Education Finance and Policy* 9, no. 1 (2014): 86–107.

CHAPTER 8

This chapter draws on a series of collaborations with Kevin Welner.

1. Robert Berne, *Study on Cost-Effectiveness in Education* (Albany: State University of New York and State Education Department, 1996).

2. *Supporting Cost-Effective School Reform: New York State Board of Regents 1996–97 Detailed Proposal on School Aid* (Albany: State University of New York & State Education Department, 1996); William Duncombe and Jerry Miner, "Productive Efficiency and Cost-Effectiveness: Different Approaches to Measuring School Performance," *Study on Cost-Effectiveness in Education: Final Report*, ed. R. Berne (Albany: State Education Department & New York State Board of Regents, 1996), 141–56.

3. Archived materials from the Texas School Finance Project available at http://bush.tamu.edu/research/faculty/TXSchoolFinance/.

4. Celeste D. Alexander, Timothy Gronberg, Dennis W. Jansen, Harrison Keller, Lori L. Taylor, and Philip Uri Treisman, *A Study of Uncontrollable Variations in the Costs of Texas Public Education: A Summary Report Prepared for the 77th Texas Legislature* (Austin: Charles A. Dana Center, University of Texas, 2000), http://www.utdanacenter.org/research/reports/ceireport.pdf; Lori L. Taylor., Celeste D. Alexander, Timothy J. Gronberg, Dennis W. Jansen, and Harrison Keller, "Updating the Texas Cost of Education Index," *Journal of Education Finance* 28, no. 2 (2002): 261–84; Lori L. Taylor and Harrison Keller, "Competing Perspectives on the Cost of Education," in *Developments in School Finance 2001–2002*, ed. William Fowler (Washington, DC: US Department of Education, 2003), 111–26; Bruce D. Baker, Lori Taylor, and Arnold Vedlitz, "Measuring Educational Adequacy in Public Schools" (report, Texas Legislature Joint Committee on Public School Finance, the Texas School Finance Project, Austin, 2006).

5. Jay G. Chambers, "Public School Teacher Cost Differences Across the United States: Introduction to a Teacher Cost Index (TCI)," in *Developments in School Finance*, ed. William J. Fowler (Washington, DC: NCES, 1995), 19–32; Andrew Reschovsky and Jennifer Imazeki, "The Development of School Finance Formulas to Guarantee the Provision of Adequate Education to Low-Income Students," in *Developments in School Finance*, ed. William J. Fowler (Washington, DC: NCES, 1997): 121–48; Robert Bifulco and William Duncombe, "Evaluating School Performance: Are We Ready for Prime Time?" in *Developments in School Finance, 1999–2000*, ed. William J. Fowler (Washington, DC: NCES, 2002), 9; Ross Rubenstein, Leanna Stiefel, Amy Ellen Schwartz, and Hella Bel Hadj Amor, "Distinguishing Good Schools from Bad in Principle and Practice: A Comparison of Four Methods," in *Developments in School Finance: 2003*, ed. William J. Fowler (Washington, DC: NCES, 2004), 53; Leanna Stiefel, Hella Bel Hadj Amor, and Amy Ellen Schwartz, "Best Schools, Worst Schools, and School Efficiency: A Reconciliation and Assessment of Alternative Classification Systems," in *Developments in School Finance: 2004*, ed. William J. Fowler (Washington, DC: NCES, 2005), 81–101.

6. Michael J. Petrilli and Marguerite Roza, "Stretching the School Dollar: A Brief for State Policymakers" (policy brief, Thomas B. Fordham Institute, Washington, DC, 2011), http://edex.s3-us-west-2.amazonaws.com/publication/pdfs/20110106_STSD_PolicyBrief_8.pdf.

7. Henry M. Levin and Patrick J. McEwan, *Cost-Effectiveness Analysis: Methods and Applications*, vol. 4 (Thousand Oaks, CA: Sage, 2001).

8. Geoffrey D. Borman and Gina M. Hewes, "The Long-Term Effects and Cost-Effectiveness of Success for All," *Educational Evaluation and Policy Analysis* 24, no. 4 (2002): 243–66.

9. Henry M. Levin, Gene V. Glass, and Gail R. Meister, "Cost-Effectiveness of Computer-Assisted Instruction," *Evaluation Review* 11, no. 1 (1987): 50–72.

10. Jennifer King Rice and L. Jane Hall, "National Board Certification for Teachers: What Does It Cost and How Does It Compare?" *Education Finance and Policy* 3, no. 3 (2008): 339–73.

11. W. Steven Barnett and Leonard N. Masse, "Comparative Benefit–Cost Analysis of the Abecedarian Program and Its Policy Implications," *Economics of Education Review* 26, no. 1 (2007): 113–25, doi:10.1016/j.econedurev.2005.10.007.

12. Brian A. Jacob and Jonah E. Rockoff, "Organizing Schools to Improve Student Achievement: Start Times, Grade Configurations, and Teacher Assignments," *Education Digest* 77, no. 8 (2012): 28. While the study does not offer full-blown cost-effectiveness or cost-benefit analyses, it does provide guidance on how pilot studies might be conducted. See also Patrick McEwan, "Review of "Organizing Schools to Improve Student Achievement" (report, National Education Policy Center, Boulder, CO, 2011), http://nepc.colorado.edu/thinktank/review-organizing-schools.

13. See, for example, Petrilli and Roza, "Stretching the School Dollar."

14. Eric A. Hanushek, "The Economic Value of Higher Teacher Quality," *Economics of Education Review* 30, no. 3 (2011): 466–79, doi:10.1016/j.econedurev.2010.12.006.

15. Bruce D. Baker, "A Few Comments on the Gates/Kane Value-Added Study," *School Finance 101*, December 13, 2012, http://schoolfinance101.wordpress.com/2010/12/13/a-few-comments-on-the-gateskane-value-added-study/; Steven Cantrell and Thomas J. Kane, "Ensuring Fair and Reliable Measures of Effective Teaching: Culminating Findings from the MET Project's Three-Year Study" (MET Project Research Paper, Bill & Melinda Gates Foundation, New York, 2013), http://k12education.gatesfoundation.org/resource/ensuring-fair-and-reliable-measures-of-effective-teaching-culminating-findings-from-the-met-projects-three-year-study/; Jason Song and Jason Felch, "LA Unified Releases School Ratings Using 'Value Added' Method," *Los Angeles Times*, June 21, 2011, 2012; Jason Felch, Jason, Song, & D. Smith, D., "Who's Teaching L.A.'s Kids?" *Los Angeles Times*, August 14, 2010, http://www.latimes.com/news/local/la-me-teachers-value-20100815,0,258862,full.story.

16. Peter Z. Schochet, and Hanley S. Chiang, "Error Rates in Measuring Teacher and School Performance Based on Student Test Score Gains" (Report No. 2010-4004, National Center for Education Evaluation and Regional Assistance, Washington, DC, 2010).

17. John P. Papay and Matthew A. Kraft, "Productivity Returns to Experience in the Teacher Labor Market: Methodological Challenges and New Evidence on Long-Term Career Improvement," *Journal of Public Economics* 130 (2015): 105–19, doi:10.1016/j.jpubeco.2015.02.008; Helen F. Ladd and Lucy C. Sorensen, "Returns to Teacher Experience: Student Achievement and Motivation in Middle School," *Education Finance and Policy* 12, no. 2 (2017): 241–79.

18. Ladd and Sorensen, "Returns to Teacher Experience."

19. Preston C. Green III, Bruce D. Baker, and Joseph Oluwole, "The Legal and Policy Implications of Value-Added Teacher Assessment Policies," *BYU Education & Law Journal* 1 (2012): 1–29; Bruce D. Baker, Joseph Oluwole, and Preston C. Green, "The Legal Consequences of Mandating High-Stakes Decisions Based on Low-Quality Information: Teacher Evaluation in the Race-to-the-Top Era," *Education Policy Analysis Archives* 21, no. 5 (2013).

20. Katharine O. Strunk, Dan Goldhaber, David S. Knight, and Nate Brown, "Are There Hidden Costs Associated with Conducting Layoffs? The Impact of RIFs and Layoffs on Teacher Effectiveness" (CALDER Working Paper 140, Calder Center, Fordham University, Armonk, NY, 2015), http://www.caldercenter.org/sites/default /files/Working% 20 Paper% 20140_0. pdf, 2015.

21. Numerous authors have addressed the conceptual basis and empirical methods for evaluating technical efficiency of production and cost efficiency in education or government services more generally. See, for example, Authella Bessent and E. Wailand Bessent, "Determining the Comparative Efficiency of Schools Through Data Envelopment Analysis," *Educational Administration Quarterly* 16, no. 2 (1980): 57–75; William Duncombe, Jerry Miner, and John Ruggiero, "Empirical Evaluation of Bureaucratic Models of Inefficiency," *Public Choice* 93, no. 1 (1997): 1–18; Bifulco and Duncombe, "Evaluating School Performance"; Shawna Grosskopf, Kathy J. Hayes, Lori L. Taylor, and William L. Weber, "On the Determinants of School District Efficiency: Competition and Monitoring," *Journal of Urban Economics* 49, no. 3 (2001): 453–78.

22. William Duncombe and John Yinger, "Does School District Consolidation Cut Costs?" *Education Finance and Policy* 2, no. 4 (2007): 341–75.

23. Tae Ho Eom and Ross Rubenstein, "Do State-Funded Property Tax Exemptions Increase Local Government Inefficiency? An Analysis of New York State's STAR Program," *Public Budgeting & Finance* 26, no. 1 (2006): 66–87, doi:10.1111/j.1540-5850.2006.00839.x.

24. Lori L. Taylor, Shawna Grosskopf, and K. Hayes, *Is Low Instructional Share an Indicator of School Inefficiency? Exploring the 65 Percent Solution* (College Station: Bush School of Public Policy, Texas A&M University, 2007).

25. Shawna Grosskopf and Chad Moutray, "Evaluating Performance in Chicago Public High Schools in the Wake of Decentralization," *Economics of Education Review* 20, no. 1 (2001): 1–14, doi:10.1016/S0272-7757(99)00065-5.

26. See, for example, Bifulco and Duncombe, "Evaluating School Performance."

27. Shawna Grosskopf, Kathy J. Hayes, and Lori L. Taylor, "Efficiency in Education: Research and Implications," *Applied Economic Perspectives and Policy* 36, no. 2 (2014): 175–210.

28. Matthew Andrews, William Duncombe, and John Yinger, "Revisiting Economies of Size in American Education: Are We Any Closer to a Consensus?" *Economics of Education Review* 21, no. 3 (2002): 245–62, doi:10.1016/S0272-7757(01)00006-1.

29. Bruce D. Baker, "Exploring the Sensitivity of Education Costs to Racial Composition of Schools and Race-Neutral Alternative Measures: A Cost Function Application to Missouri," *Peabody Journal of Education* 86, no. 1 (2011): 58–83.

30. Lars-Erik Borge, Torberg Falch, and Per Tovmo, "Public Sector Efficiency: The Roles of Political and Budgetary Institutions, Fiscal Capacity, and Democratic

Participation," *Public Choice* 136, no. 3 (2008): 475–95, doi:10.1007/s11127-008 -9309-7; Grosskopf et al., "On the Determinants of School District Efficiency."

31. Duncombe and Yinger explain that the cost model perspective is more useful for sorting out cost versus inefficiency because it permits (more logically than the production model) the inclusion of measures of fiscal capacity and public monitoring to more precisely isolate "cost." William Duncombe and John Yinger, "A Comment on School District Level Production Functions Estimated Using Spending Data" (report, Maxwell School of Public Affairs, Syracuse University, Syracuse, NY, 2007). Baker and Levin explain, much of this seemingly inefficient spending involves jurisdictions with resources providing "extras" that matter to their constituents, even if they don't affect testing outcomes. Statistically, this spending might be characterized as "inefficient," but that does not mean it is unimportant, or considered so by the constituents who support the spending. Bruce D. Baker and Jesse Levin, "Educational Equity, Adequacy, and Equal Opportunity in the Commonwealth: An Evaluation of Pennsylvania's School Finance System" (report, American Institutes for Research, Washington, DC, 2014), https://files.eric.ed.gov/fulltext/ED553400.pdf.

32. Alternatively, we could focus on levels of student outcomes to the extent that they sufficiently capture student background characteristics predictive of students' initial performance.

33. Robert Bifulco and Stuart Bretschneider, "Estimating School Efficiency: A Comparison of Methods Using Simulated Data," *Economics of Education Review* 20, no. 5 (2001): 417–29, doi:10.1016/S0272-7757(00)00025-X.

34. Timothy J. Gronberg, Dennis W. Jansen, and Lori L. Taylor, "The Relative Efficiency of Charter Schools: A Cost Frontier Approach," *Economics of Education Review* 31, no. 2 (2012): 302, doi:10.1016/j.econedurev.2011.07.001.

35. Lori L. Taylor, Beverly L. Alford, Kayla B. Rollins, Danielle B. Brown, Jacqueline R. Stillisano, and Hersh C. Waxman, *Evaluation of Texas Charter Schools* (College Station: Bush School of Public Policy, Texas A&M University, 2011).

36. Robin Lake, Brianna Dusseault, Melissa Bowen, Allison Demeritt, and Paul Hill, *The National Study of Charter Management Organization (CMO) Effectiveness: Report on Interim Findings* (Seattle: Center on Reinventing Public Education, 2010); Will Dobbie and Roland G. Fryer Jr., "Getting Beneath the Veil of Effective Schools: Evidence from New York City," *American Economic Journal: Applied Economics* 5, no. 4 (2013): 28–60; Bruce D. Baker, Ken Libby, and Kathryn Wiley, "Charter School Expansion and Within-District Equity: Confluence or Conflict?" *Education Finance and Policy* 10, no. 3 (2015): 423–65., doi:10.1162/EDFP_a_00169; Bruce D. Baker, Ken Libby, and Kathryn Wiley, *Spending by the Major Charter Management Organizations: Comparing Charter School and Local Public District Financial Resources in New York, Ohio, and Texas* (Boulder, CO: National Education Policy Center, 2012); Gronberg et al., "The Relative Efficiency of Charter Schools."

37. Baker et al., "Charter School Expansion and Within-District Equity"; Courtney Preston, Ellen Goldring, Mark Berends, and Marisa Cannata, "School Innovation in District Context: Comparing Traditional Public Schools and Charter Schools," *Economics of Education Review* 31, no. 2 (2012): 318–30, doi:10.1016/j.econedurev .2011.07.016.

38. Baker et al., *Spending by the Major Charter Management Organizations.*

39. Meagan Batdorff, Larry Maloney, Jay F. May, Sheree Speakman, Patrick Wolf, and Albert Cheng, "Charter Funding: Inequity Expands" (report, Fayetteville: University of Arkansas, Department of Education Reform, University of Arkansas, Fayetteville, 2014); Patrick J. Wolf, Albert Cheng, Meagan Batdorff, Larry Maloney, Jay May, and Sheree Speakman, "The Productivity of Public Charter Schools" (report, Department of Education Reform, University of Arkansas, Fayetteville, 2014); Gene V. Glass, "Review of *The Productivity of Public Charter Schools*" (report, National Education Policy Center, Boulder, CO, 2014), http://nepc.colorado.edu/thinktank /review-productivity-public-charter.

40. Bruce D. Baker, "Review of *Charter Funding: Inequity Expands*" (report, National Education Policy Center, Boulder, CO, 2014), http://nepc.colorado.edu/files /ttruarkcharterfunding.pdf.

41. Wolf et al., *The Productivity of Public Charter Schools*.

42. Glass, "Review."

43. Douglas N. Harris and Matthew F. Larsen, "The Effects of the New Orleans Post-Katrina School Reforms on Student Academic Outcomes" (technical report, Education Research Alliance for New Orleans, New Orleans, 2016), https://education researchalliancenola.org/files/publications/The-Effects-of-the-New-Orleans-Post -Katrina-School-Reforms-on-Student-Academic-Outcomes.pdf.

44. Dennis Epple, Richard Romano, and Ron Zimmer, "Charter Schools: A Survey of Research on Their Characteristics and Effectiveness," in *Handbook of the Economics of Education*, vol. 5 (Amsterdam: Elsevier, 2016), 139–208.

45. Christian Buerger and Douglas N. Harris, *How Did the New Orleans School Reforms Influence School Spending?* (technical report, Education Research Alliance for New Orleans, New Orleans, 2017), https://educationresearchalliancenola.org/publications /does-school-reform-spending-reform-the-effect-of-the-new-orleans-school-reforms -on-the-use-and-level-of-school-expenditures.

46. Bruce D. Baker, "The Efficiency Smokescreen, Cuts Cause No Harm Argument and the 3 Kansas Judges Who Saw Right Through It," *School Finance 101*, January 12, 2013, http://schoolfinance101.wordpress.com/2013/01/12/the-efficiency-smokescreen -cuts-cause-no-harm-argument-the-3-kansas-judges-who-saw-right-through-it/.

47. Bruce D. Baker, *Does Money Matter in Education?* (Washington, DC: Albert Shanker Institute, 2016).

48. Bruce D. Baker and Kevin G. Welner, "Evidence and Rigor: Scrutinizing the Rhetorical Embrace of Evidence-Based Decision Making," *Educational Researcher* 41, no. 3 (2012): 101.

CHAPTER 9

This chapter draws on collaboration with Jesse Levin of the American Institutes for Research.

1. Eric A. Hanushek, "The Alchemy of 'Costing Out' an Adequate Education" (Education Working Paper Archive, September 14, 2006); Eric A. Hanushek "The Alchemy of Costing Out an Adequate Education," in *School Money Trials: The Legal Pursuit of Educational Adequacy*, ed. Martin R. West and Paul E. Peterson (Washington, DC: Brookings Institution Press, 2007), 77; Eric A. Hanushek, "Science Violated: Spending Projections and the 'Costing Out' of an Adequate Education," *Courting Failure: How School Finance Lawsuits Exploit Judges' Good Intentions and Harm Our*

Children, (Palo Alto: Education Next Books, 2006), 257–311; Eric A. Hanushek, "The Confidence Men: Selling Adequacy, Making Millions," *Education Next 7*, no. 3 (2007): 73–78, http://hanushek.stanford.edu/sites/default/files/publications /Hanushek%202007%20Ednext%207%283%29.pdf.

2. Bruce D. Baker, Lori L. Taylor, and Arnold Vedlitz, *Adequacy Estimates and the Implications of Common Standards for the Cost of Instruction* (Washington, DC: National Research Council, 2008).

3. William Duncombe and John Yinger, "Performance Standards and Educational Cost Indexes: You Can't Have One Without the Other," in *Equity and Adequacy in Education Finance: Issues and Perspectives*, ed. Helen Ladd, Rosemary Chalk, and Janet Hansen (Washington, DC: National Academies Press, 1999), 261.

4. Henry M. Levin, *Cost-Effectiveness: A Primer*, vol. 4 (Thousand Oaks, CA: Sage, 1983); Jay G. Chambers, *Measuring Resources in Education: From Accounting to the Resource Cost Model Approach* (Washington, DC: National Center for Education Statistics, 1999).

5. Jay G. Chambers and Thomas B. Parrish, *The Development of a Resource Cost Model Funding Base for Education in Illinois* (Springfield: Illinois State Board of Education, (1983); Jay G. Chambers and Thomas B. Parrish, *The Development of a Program Cost Model and Cost-of-Education Model for the State of Alaska* (report for the Alaska Department of Education, Associates for Education Finance and Planning, Stanford University, Palo Alto, CA 1984); James Guthrie, James Guthrie, Gerald Hayward, James Smith, Richard Rothstein, Ronald Bennett, Julia Koppich, Ellis Bowman, Lynn DeLapp, Barbara Brandes, and Sandra Clark, *A Proposed Cost-Based Block Grant Model for Wyoming School Finance* (Davis, CA: Management Analysis and Planning Associates, 1997).

6. Baker et al., *Adequacy Estimates.*

7. In "The Confidence Men" Hanushek provides a critique of the Odden/Picus Evidence-Based model, highlighting the problems with aggregating effect sizes across interventions (studied with different outcome measures), which is a quite reasonable argument. Allen Odden & Sarah Archibald make similar suspect claims, regarding the statistically improbable idea of "doubling student performance." See Allan R. Odden and Sarah J. Archibald, *Doubling Student Performance . . . and Finding the Resources to Do It* (Thousand Oaks, CA: Corwin Press, 2009), doi:10 .4135/9781452219400.

8. Walter I. Garms and Mark C. Smith, "Educational Need and Its Application to State School Finance," *Journal of Human Resources 5*, no. 3 (1970): 304–17; Thomas A. Downes and Thomas F. Pogue, "Adjusting School Aid Formulas for the Higher Cost of Educating Disadvantaged Students," *National Tax Journal 47*, no. 1 (1994): 89–110; William Duncombe and John Yinger, "Why Is It So Hard to Help Central City Schools?" *Journal of Policy Analysis and Management* 16, no. 1 (1997): 85–113; Andrew Reschovsky and Jennifer Imazeki, "The Development of School Finance Formulas to Guarantee the Provision of Edequate Education to Low-Income Students," in *Developments in School Finance*, ed. William J. Fowler (Washington, DC: NCES, 1997), 121–48.

9. Lori L. Taylor, Bruce D. Baker, and Arnold Vedlitz, *Measuring Educational Adequacy in Public Schools* (College Station: Bush School of Government and Public Service, Texas A&M University, 2005).

10. Critiquing New York State's approach to excluding the upper-half spending districts in their Successful Schools analysis, John Yinger and William Duncombe explain in their amicus brief: *"Using only the lowest spending schools is equivalent to assuming that the lowest-spending schools are the most efficient and that other schools would be just as efficient if they were better managed. Both parts of this assumption are highly questionable. The Successful Schools approach on which these figures are based makes no attempt to determine why some schools spend less per pupil than others; the low spending in the selected schools could be due to low wage costs and a low concentration of disadvantaged students, not to efficiency. Moreover, even if some schools get higher performance for a given spending level than others, controlling for wages and student disadvantage, there is no evidence that the methods they use would be successful at other schools"* (*Campaign for Fiscal Equity v. New York. State Supreme Court of New York*, 2004, http://cpr.maxwell.syr.edu/efap/about_efap/Amicus_brief.pdf).

11. Sylvia Allegretto, Sean Corcoran, and Lawrence Mishel, *The Teaching Penalty: Teacher Pay Losing Ground* (Washington, DC: Economic Policy Institute, 2008). See also chapter 1 in this volume for a discussion of teacher wages.

12. William Duncombe, Anna Lukemeyer, and John Yinger, "The No Child Left Behind Act: Have Federal Funds Been Left Behind?" *Public Finance Review* 36, no. 4 (2008): 381–407, doi:10.1177/1091142107305220; William Duncombe and John Yinger, "Financing Higher Student Performance Standards: The Case of New York State," *Economics of Education Review* 19, no. 4 (2000): 363–86, doi:10.1016/S0272-7757(00)00004-2; William Duncombe and John Yinger, "School Finance Reform: Aid Formulas and Equity Objectives," *National Tax Journal* 51, no. 2 (1998): 239–62; Duncombe and Yinger, "Why Is It So Hard to Help Central City Schools?"; Downes and Pogue, "Adjusting School Aid Formulas"; Reschovsky and Imazeki, "The Development of School Finance Formulas."

13. School Funding Reform Act of 2008, New Jersey Department of Education, http://nj.gov/education/sff/; "A Formula for Success: All Children, All Communities" (report, New Jersey Department of Education, Trenton, January 3, 2008), http://nj.gov/education/sff/reports/AllChildrenAllCommunities.pdf.

14. See court syllabus at http://www.edlawcenter.org/assets/files/pdfs/abott-v-burke/Abbott_XX.pdf.

15. *Gannon v. State*, 368 P.3d 1024, 303 Kan. 682 (2016).

16. Lori Taylor, Jason Willis, Alex Berg Jacobson, Karina Jaquet, Ruthie Caparas, "Estimating the Costs Associated with Reaching Student Achievement Expectations for Kansas Public Education Students: A Cost Function Approach" (report, Kansas State Legislature, Topeka, 2018), http://kslegislature.org/li/documents/kansas_adequacy_study_corrected_cost_function_approach_20180315_final.pdf.

17. Details on the Pennsylvania costing out study can be found at http://www.paschoolfunding.org/get-the-facts/pa-costing-out-study/.

18. Initial proposals by the legislature for the follow-up study requested that the Legislative Division of Post Audit look only at the bare bones, required inputs to schooling (based on historical spending of a subset of districts) to determine the cost of their constitutional mandates. Kansas, unlike other states, has a four-branch government, with an independently elected state board of education that has independent constitutional authority for "general supervision of public schools." While the legislature sets the budget, the state board sets outcome standards. During oral

arguments in the spring of 2005, board attorney Dan Biles argued that the updated cost study must include consideration of outcomes mandated by the state board or the system would remain in constitutional conflict (that meeting the legislatures goals without regard for the state board's constitutional authority was insufficient). The Kansas high court agreed with Biles's argument, and the outcome-based cost function analysis was added. As explained in the court's June 3, 2005, decision, *Montoy v. State*, 279 Kan. 817, 112 P.3d 923 (2005): "It also appears that the study contemplated by H.B. 2247 is deficient because it will examine only what it costs for education 'inputs'—the cost of delivering kindergarten through grade 12 curriculum, related services, and other programs 'mandated by state statute in accredited schools.' It does not appear to demand consideration of the costs of 'outputs'—achievement of measurable standards of student proficiency. As the Board pointed out in its brief, nowhere in H.B. 2247 is there specific reference to K.S.A. 72-6439(a) or (c), which provided the criteria used by this court in our January 2005 opinion to evaluate whether the school financing formula provided a constitutionally adequate education" (31). See http://www.robblaw.com/PDFs/Z998 MONTOYCOMBINEDDECISIONS1-5.pdf.

19. The high court did not accept this reasoning: "Counsel for the State could not substantiate, when asked at oral arguments, its rationale that those seventeen districts pay higher salaries or would pay higher salaries to teachers or that higher education costs are linked to housing prices. Further, as the plaintiffs noted, the evidence at trial demonstrated that [***37] it is the districts with high-poverty, high at-risk student populations that need additional help in attracting and retaining good teachers" (ibid., 28). The Court ultimately declared the formula constitutional as a whole, indicating that overturning this (and other) specific piece would require additional trial court fact finding.

CHAPTER 10

1. Bruce Baker, Mark Weber, and Ajay Srikanth, *School Funding Fairness Data System*, (New Brunswick, NJ: Rutgers Graduate School of Education; Newark, NJ: Education Law Center, 2017), http://www.schoolfundingfairness.org/data-download.

2. Bruce D. Baker, Lori Taylor, Jesse Levin, Jay Chambers, and Charles Blankenship, "Adjusted Poverty Measures and the Distribution of Title I Aid: Does Title I Really Make the Rich States Richer?" *Education Finance and Policy* 8, no. 3 (2013): 394–417.

3. Education Comparable Wage Index, 2018, http://bush.tamu.edu/research/faculty /taylor_CWI/.

4. For details of cost model estimation, see Bruce D. Baker, Bob Kim, Mark Weber, Ajay Srikanth, and Michael Atzbi, *The Real Shame of the Nation: The Causes and Consequences of Interstate Inequity in Public School Investments* (Newark, NJ: Education Law Center; New Brunswick, NJ: Rutgers Graduate School of Education, 2018).

5. Bruce D. Baker and Kevin Welner, "School Finance and Courts: Does Reform Matter, and How Can We Tell," *Teachers College Record* 113, no. 11 (2011): 2374–414.

6. Baker et al., "Adjusted Poverty Measures and the Distribution of Title I Aid."

7. Bruce Baker, David G. Sciarra, and Danielle Farrie, "Is School Funding Fair? A National Report Card" (report, Education Law Center, Newark, NJ, 2014).

8. Jared Walczak, Scott Drenkard, Joseph Bishop-Henchman, Tax Foundation. State Business Tax Climate Index, 2018, https://taxfoundation.org/publications/state -business-tax-climate-index/.

9. Robert Tannenwald, Jon Shure, and Nicholas Johnson, *Tax Flight Is a Myth* (Washington, DC: Center on Budget and Policy Priorities, 2011). For more on this, see chapter 2 in this volume.

10. Henryk Sadura, "Building State Rainy Day Funds" (report, Pew Charitable Trusts, New York, 2014), http://www.pewtrusts.org/~/media/assets/2014/07/sfh_rainy-day -fund-deposit-rules-report_artready_v9.pdf.

11. Robert Tannenwald, "Are State and Local Revenue Systems Becoming Obsolete?" *New England Economic Review* 4 (2001): 27.

12. Helen F. Ladd, "State-Wide Taxation of Commercial and Industrial Property for Education," *National Tax Journal* 29, no. 2 (1976): 143–53; Brian O. Brent, "An Analysis of the Influence of Regional Nonresidential Expanded Tax Base Approaches to School Finance on Measures of Student and Taxpayer Equity," *Journal of Education Finance* 24, no. 3 (1999): 353–78.

13. Baker et al., *School Funding Fairness Data System.*

14. Baker et al., "Is School Funding Fair?"

15. Bruce D. Baker, "Exploring the Consequences of Charter School Expansion in US Cities" (report, Economic Policy Institute, Washington, DC, November 30, 2016), https://www.epi.org/publication/exploring-the-consequences-of-charter-school -expansion-in-u-s-cities/.

16. Paul E. Barton and Richard J. Coley, "The Black-White Achievement Gap: When Progress Stopped" (Policy Information Report, Educational Testing Service, Princeton, NJ, 2010), https://www.ets.org/Media/Research/pdf/PICBWGAP.pdf.

ACKNOWLEDGMENTS

This book would not have been possible without the assistance of numerous collaborators, editors, coauthors, and funders with whom I've worked over the years on various projects that provide most of the substantive content in this book. Organizations that have supported this work include Rutgers University Graduate School of Education, which granted me a sabbatical, as well as the Education Law Center of New Jersey, the National Education Policy Center at the University of Colorado at Boulder, the Albert Shanker Institute, the Learning Policy Institute, Educational Testing Services, and the Center for American Progress. The William T. Grant Foundation provided funding for the development of the *School Funding Fairness Data System* database.

Coauthors and project editors who have provided valuable support along the way include Preston Green, University of Connecticut; Kevin Welner, University of Colorado; Gary Miron, Western Michigan University; Jesse Levin, American Institutes for Research; Matt Di Carlo, Shanker Institute; Lori Taylor, Texas A&M; and my stellar doctoral students, Mark Weber and Ajay Srikanth.

ABOUT THE AUTHOR

BRUCE D. BAKER is a professor in the Department of Educational Theory, Policy and Administration at Rutgers Graduate School of Education in New Brunswick, New Jersey. He previously served on the faculty at the University of Kansas from 1997 through 2008. In addition to publishing numerous articles, chapters, and a textbook on school finance, he has testified on school funding inequities and inadequacies in state and federal courts. He has also worked with state legislatures and boards of education in Kansas, Texas, Missouri, and Maryland to inform and reform various aspects of state school finance systems. He blogs at Schoolfinance101.wordpress.com and can be found on Twitter @schlfinance101.

INDEX